# The San Diego Padres 1969—2002

## A Complete History

(Includes 200 Padres trivia questions)

## Nelson Papucci

Big League Press
San Diego, California

## The San Diego Padres, 1969–2002: A Complete History

For information or orders, contact:

Big League Press
7280 Calle Cristobal, Suite 63
San Diego, California  92126
www.padrebook.com
bigleaguepress@aol.com
800-431-1579

ISBN 0-9719466-0-4

*For Mom, Bob, and Betsy*
*And my father*


*Special thanks to the*
*San Diego Hall of Champions,*
*who provided so many*
*photographs from their archives*

*Bill Swank, author of*
Echoes From Lane Field

*Coach John Kentera and*
*Randy Jones*

The Union-Tribune, North County Times,
*Topps, Fleer, Donruss, and Upper Deck*
*for their generous permissions*

*And to my friends, students, and*
*fellow Padres fans, who provided*
*support and encouragement throughout.*

# Contents

# Trivia

BEFORE YOU BEGIN reading, play this ten-inning Padre trivia game. The answers are provided in the back.

The game is divided into ten innings, with a home team and a visiting team. Each inning contains twenty questions—ten for the home team, ten for the visitor. There are 200 questions in all. Good luck!

**Inning one**

*Visiting team*

1. Name the five one-time Padres elected to the Baseball Hall of Fame.

2. Which three members of the Padres stole 50 or more bases in 1980?

3. Which three Padres have won the Cy Young award?

4. Who was the manager of the Padres during their inaugural season of 1969?

5. Who was the Padres' first choice in the 1968 expansion draft?

6. Which pitcher holds the Padres' all-time record for wins?

7. Which pitcher has the *second*-most wins as a Padre?

8. Which pitcher has the *third*-most wins as a Padre?

9. Who was the Padres' starting pitcher in their first major league game in 1969?

10. Among players who have had at least 1,000 at bats, who has the highest career slugging percentage as a Padre?

*Home team*

11. Who collected 5 HRs and 13 RBIs in a doubleheader (setting a major league record) in 1972?

12. Re: Question # 11: Against which team did he accomplish this feat?

13. On January 25, 1974, Ray Kroc purchased the San Diego Padres. What famous business did Kroc found?

14. Name all 20-game winners in the history of the Padres.

15. After the 1986 season, in a swap of Kevins, the Padres traded Kevin McReynolds to the Mets for which native San Diegan?

16. Tony Gwynn holds the record for most games played as a Padre. Who is *second* in team history in games played?

17. Who is second in team history (again, behind Gwynn) in runs scored?

18. Broadcaster Jerry Coleman became manager of the Padres for the 1980 season. Whom did he replace as field manager?

19. When Coleman returned to the broadcasting booth after the 1980 season, who replaced him as manager?

20. After the 1991 season, the Padres traded Bip Roberts to the Cincinnati Reds for which relief pitcher?

| Inning two | Visiting team | Home team |
|---|---|---|

**Visiting team**

21. Against what team did Tony Gwynn make his major league debut?

22. Against what team did Gwynn make his final major league appearance?

23. Which two teams did Sterling Hitchcock play for, prior to coming to the Padres?

24. Which batter holds the Padres' single-season record for bases on balls?

25. Who recorded the Padres' first-ever home run, run, and RBI?

26. Against what team did the Padres clinch their first divisional title in 1984?

27. In 1996, the Padres and Tigers swapped shortstops and catchers. The Tigers received shortstop Andujar Cedeno and catcher Brad Ausmus. The Padres received catcher John Flaherty and *what shortstop*?

28. Who holds the Padres' single-season record for stolen bases?

29. Name the four Padres who stole 30 or more bases in 1999.

30. Which pitcher holds the team's all-time record for appearances?

**Home team**

31. Against what team did Tony Gwynn get his 3,000th base hit?

32. Against what pitcher did Gwynn get that 3,000th hit?

33. Whom did the Padres trade to acquire Phil Nevin?

34. What team dealt Nevin to the Padres in 1999?

35. Nevin was acquired because which player became injured in spring training?

36. Who won the Padres' only victory in the 1984 World Series?

37. Who holds the Padres' single-season home run record?

38. Name the 1998 N.L. Championship Series MVP.

39. Who did the Padres defeat in the first round of the playoffs in 1998 (the N.L. Divisional Series)?

40. Name one of the two pitchers who led the Padres in wins during the team's first season, 1969.

**Inning three**

| Visiting team | Home team |
|---|---|
| 41. Against what team did the Padres clinch the N.L. West in 1996? | 51. Against what team did the Padres clinch the N.L. West in 1998? |
| 42. Which member of the original '69 Padres remained with the team longest? {*Hint—his son is a star player with the Pittsburgh Pirates.*} | 52. Who is the only Padre to win the league MVP award? |
| 43. Which pitcher holds the Padres' single-season strikeout record? | 53. Who did the Padres play in the 1996 Divisional Series? |
| 44. Tony Gwynn holds 8 batting titles, to tie the N.L. record. Whose record did he tie? | 54. How many games did the Padres win in the '96 post-season? |
| 45. Trevor Hoffman is the Padres' all-time save leader. Who is *second* in saves in team history? | 55. Who is the only Padre to win the Manager of the Year award? |
| 46. In 1997, the Padres played three home games in another state. Where was that? | 56. In 1996, the Padres were the first team to play home games outside the United States or Canada. In what city and nation were they held? |
| 47. Against what team did the Padres play those three games? | 57. The Padres traded pitcher Dennis Rasmussen to the Yankees on March 30, 1984, for which infielder? |
| 48. Who has the most career innings pitched as a Padre? | 58. Who is the only Padre to homer in the All-Star game? |
| 49. What was Rich Gossage's nickname? | 59. Which pitcher issued more walks in a single season than any other Padre in history? |
| 50. Which pitcher has the most career strikeouts as a Padre? | 60. Who holds the mark for most walks allowed in a career as a Padre? |

**Inning four**

*Visiting team*

61. Who finished second in the National League in batting with runners in scoring position in 1998?

62. Who was named MVP of the 1998 World Series between the Padres and Yankees?

63. On June 1, 1970, which Padre pitcher had a no hitter in the eighth inning, yet was pulled for a pinch hitter because his team was trailing, 1-0?

64. On January 25, 1978, the Padres sent Dave Tomlin and cash to the Rangers for which starting pitcher?

65. Who holds the team's *second*-longest consecutive-game hitting streak (27)?

66. Kevin Towers became general manager of the Padres in late 1995. Whose place did he take?

67. Which Padres have hit for the "cycle"?

68. What other major league team did Randy Jones play for besides the Padres?

69. When Bruce Bochy was named manager, whom did he replace?

70. Leon Joseph Roberts III is better known as who?

*Home team*

71. Who holds the Padres' single-season record for RBI's?

72. In 1994, Tony Gwynn hit .394. What stopped his possible run at .400?

73. Who was the last major leaguer to have a higher batting average than Gwynn's .394?

74. Which starting pitcher (162 or more innings pitched) had the lowest *single-season* ERA in Padres history?

75. What Cubs pitcher hit a home run against the Padres in game one of the 1984 N.L. Championship season?

76. Who was the oldest person ever to play for the Padres?

77. Who is the only Padre to win the N.L. home run title?

78. Who is the only Padre other than Tony Gwynn to win a batting title?

79. There have been six no hitters thrown against the Padres. Name *four* of the opposing pitchers.

80. During the 1988 season, whom did Jack McKeon replace as the Padres manager?

**Inning five**

| *Visiting team* | *Home team* |
|---|---|

81. Who are the two Padres to win the Rookie of the Year award (one was a tie)?

91, Who has played more games at first base than any other Padre?

82. Who was the Padres' opening-day starter in 1999, the year following their World Series appearance?

92. In what year did the Padres have their first winning season?

83. What was the Padres' total win-loss record in the 1984 post-season?

93. Re: Question #91: Who managed the Padres to that first winning season?

84. Among Padres hitters with at least 1,500 at bats, who has the *lowest* career batting average?

94. What is the Padres' *total* win-loss record in the World Series?

85. Who once coached his two sons on the Padres?

95. Who represented the Padres in the 1978 All-Star game—the first All-Star game played in San Diego?

86. Who is the only Padre to win an All-Star MVP Award?

96. The Padres traded two players to acquire Reggie Sanders and Damian Jackson following the '98 campaign. Name at least one of them.

87. What country music star was invited to spring training in 1999?

97. Who was the Padres' DH in the '84 World Series?

88. Name the first owner of the Padres.

98. Who gave up Pete Rose's record-breaking 4,192nd career hit?

89. Who did the Padres trade to acquire shortstop Garry Templeton?

99, Which former Padre, who was later a member of the Giants, suffered a career-ending and life-threatening tumor in his pitching arm?

90. Who was drafted by the NBA's Clippers the same day he was drafted by the Padres?

100. Who pitched ten shutout innings for the Padres in the 1984 post-season?

| Inning six | *Visiting team* | *Home team* |
|---|---|---|

101. In 1978, Bob Horner of the Braves won the N.L. Rookie of the Year award. Which Padre came in second place in the voting?

102. Who was drafted by the Padres, the NBA's Atlanta Hawks, the ABA's Utah Stars, and the NFL's Minnesota Vikings?

103. Which future Padre was the first pick in the amateur draft in 1992?

104. Who was traded for outfielder Bubba Trammell in the spring of 2001?

105. Who had the game-winning RBI in the final game of the 1984 NLCS?

106. Who led N.L. outfielders in assists in 1984 and 1985?

107. What Padre threw a one-hitter in his major league debut in 1986?

108. After the 1990 season, the Padres sent Joe Carter and Roberto Alomar to the Blue Jays. Name at least one of the players they got in return.

109. Who has the lowest career ERA among Padres with at least 500 innings pitched?

110. On September 29, 1996, who belted a pinch-hit double in the 11th inning to give the Padres a 2-0 win over the Dodgers, clinching the N.L. West title?

111. In 1986, which Padres pitcher was traded to the Tigers for pitcher Dave LaPoint?

112. During the '84 season, what did the 'RAK' on the Padres jerseys refer to?

113. Who managed the Padres to their first post-season appearance?

114. Which team did Trevor Hoffman briefly play for before coming to the Padres in the trade involving Gary Sheffield?

115. Who has the *best* career winning percentage as a Padre, with at least 500 innings?

116. Who has the *worst* career winning percentage as a Padre, with at least 500 innings?

117. Who co-broadcasts Padres games with Jerry Coleman on KOGO, AM 600?

118. Who has played more games at catcher than any other Padre?

119. After the 1984 season, which shortstop, who would win Rookie of the Year honors the following season, was traded by the Padres?

120. In 1984, which Padres pitcher blasted a three-run homer en route to a 5-4 division-clinching victory over the Giants?

**Inning seven**     *Visiting team*     *Home team*

121. Prior to the 1974 season, the Padres traded pitcher Mike Caldwell to the San Francisco Giants for which slugger?

122. Who is the Padres' all-time home run leader?

123. Which Padres pitcher led the league in starts in 1995, and had the league's third-best ERA that year?

124. After the 1999 season, the Padres traded Wally Joyner, Quilvio Veras, and Reggie Sanders to the Braves, in exchange for two players *[Name one of them]:*

125. Which Padre tied Johnny Bench's record for doubles (40) in a season by a catcher?

126. Who was the only Padre named to the 2000 All-Star team?

127. Who became the first major leaguer to belt home runs in three different countries?

128. Which Padre batted .800 (4-for-5) in the 1998 World Series?

129. Who led the National League in RBIs in 1979?

130. Who played for four different teams, including the Padres, in 1977?

131. Who holds the Padres consecutive-game hitting streak (34)?

132. On July 4, 1997, Greg Vaughn was traded to the Yankees but failed his physical, thus voiding the trade. Which pitcher were the Padres to have gotten in return?

133. Which Padre was the first major leaguer to have at least 100 RBIs while playing in *both* leagues during the season?

134. What longtime Dodgers executive was the first president of the Padres?

135. Which pitcher was obtained from Kansas City for pitcher Brian Meadows in 2000?

136. After the '99 season, the Padres obtained pitcher Brian Meadows from the Florida Marlins for what middle reliever?

137. Who purchased the team from Joan Kroc in 1990?

138. Which Padre was named Comeback Player of the Year in 1975?

139. Fiore Gino Tenaci was better known as which former Padre?

140. After the 1995 season, Bip Roberts was traded (for the second time) by the Padres to Kansas City for which infielder?

**Inning eight**

| Visiting team | Home team |
|---|---|

Visiting team

141. Which former Padre is a cousin of Mariners DH Edgar Martinez?

142. What does Tony Gwynn mean when he refers to the "5.5 hole"?

143. Gwynn went 3-for-4 on the last day of the 1989 season to win the N.L. batting title. Which Giants player did he edge out?

144. After the 1998 season, the Padres received Woody Williams, Carlos Almanzar, and Pete Tucci from the Toronto Blue Jays in exchange for which pitcher?

145. Who was expected to replace Ken Caminiti at third base after he signed as a free agent with Houston after the 1998 season?

146. Which Padre got the save in the 1984 All-Star game?

147. What city did the Padres almost move to in 1974, only to have the club purchased by Ray Kroc at the last minute, thereby preserving baseball in San Diego?

148. Who holds the Padres' single-season record for runs scored?

149. What was the Padres' total win-loss record in the 1998 post-season?

150. Who is the first player to wear a Padres cap on his plaque in the Baseball Hall of Fame?

Home team

151. Which television star did an embarrassing rendition of the National Anthem before a game between the Padres and Reds in 1990?

152. The Padres traded Scott Sanders to the Mariners after the 1996 season in exchange for which starting pitcher?

153. Gregory Scott Williams is better know to Padres fans as who?

154. Who is the winningest manager in Padres history?

155. Who surrendered a grand slam to Tino Martinez in the 1998 World Series?

156. Who was the MVP of the 1984 N.L. League Championship Series?

157. Six Padres have won a Gold Glove award. Name *five* of them.

158. Which batter holds the Padres' career record for strikeouts?

159. Who was the only member of the 1993 Padres with 100 RBIs?

160. Four Padres have played in every game of the regular season. Name *two* of them.

| Inning nine | Visiting team | Home team |
|---|---|---|
| | 161. Who had more at-bats in a single season than any other Padre? | 171. What rookie led the team in wins (12), innings (214), and strikeouts (146) in 1977? |
| | 162. Name the Padres pitchers who have thrown a no-hitter. | 172. Which former outfielder was quoted as saying, "I only have trouble with fly balls?" |
| | 163. Which catcher was named Padres team MVP in 1973? | 173. On December 28, 1994, the Padres obtained Ken Caminiti, Steve Finley, Andujar Cedeno, and minor leaguers in the biggest deal in baseball since 1957. With which team was the trade completed? |
| | 164. Who holds the Padres record for consecutive wins as a starter (11)? | 174. Who made the last out in the 1998 World Series? |
| | 165. Which member of the original 1969 Padres lost 20 games, the league high? | 175. What two Yankees were obtained by the Padres after the 1983 season, making an enormous contribution to the Padres' '84 pennant drive? |
| | 166. Who has played more games at *third base* than any other Padre? | 176. On June 23, 2000, which Padres second baseman slammed three home runs against the Cincinnati Reds, his former team? |
| | 167. Who was the first Padres pitcher ever to record a stolen base? | 177. Kevin McReynolds played for the Padres from 1983-86. Which team did he play for after leaving the Padres? |
| | 168. Name *four* of the five Padres named to the 1998 All-Star team. | 178. After the 1999 season, the Padres traded outfielder John Vander Wal to the Pirates for which outfielder? |
| | 169. Name one of the two teams, other than the Padres, that Bruce Bochy played for in his major league career? | 179. Who led the Padres in wins in 1996, the year they won the N.L. West? |
| | 170. On July 18th, 1972, which Padre had a no-hitter with two out in the ninth inning, before allowing a single to Philadelphia's Denny Doyle? | 180. Who were the three catchers on the Padres' 1998 World Series roster? |

**Inning ten**

| Visiting team | Home team |
|---|---|
| 181. What pitcher appeared in more games in a season than any other Padre? | 191. Which sportswriter fought to bring major league baseball to San Diego, and campaigned for years for the city to build a new stadium? |
| 182. Randy Jones and one other pitcher each hold the franchise record for shutouts in a single season (6). Who is the other? | 192. On February 15, 1980, the Padres traded pitcher Gaylord Perry and a pair of minor leaguers to the Texas Rangers for what first baseman? |
| 183. Who was the first player chosen in the nation in the 1974 draft, signing with the Padres for $100,000? | 193. In 1989, which Padre (and future All-Star) was the youngest player on any N.L. opening-day roster? |
| 184. Who broke Babe Ruth's all-time record for walks? | 194. Which former manager and general manager had the nickname "Trader Jack"? |
| 185. Who was the Padres' first All-Star in 1969? | 195. Name six of the seven Padres on the 1985 N.L. All-Star team. |
| 186. The Padres traded outfield prospect Gary Matthews Jr. to the Cubs for what middle reliever? | 196. In 1977, who set a major league record for stolen bases by a rookie (a mark which was later broken)? |
| 187. With what other three teams did the Padres enter the major leagues in 1969? | 197. Who was the Padres' pitching coach in 1998, their N.L. championship season? |
| 188. On February 28, 1978, Mike Ivie was traded to the Giants for what utility infielder? | 198. In 1991, the Padres traded Garry Templeton to the Mets for which infielder? |
| 189. Who hit the game-winning home run against the Cubs in the 1984 N.L.C.S? | 199. Who was the Padres' team MVP in their pennant-winning season of 1998? |
| 190. Re: Question # 189: Against what Cubs pitcher did he hit that dramatic homer? | 200. Although they finished in last place, 39 games out, the 1970 Padres finished third in the league in home runs. Name two of their top three HR producers. |

# Foreword

THE ANTICIPATION WAS killing me.

I was eleven years old when that magical April night finally arrived. It still seems like yesterday…My brother and his wife picked me up from school, and we stopped off for a brown-bag dinner at Balboa Park. They wanted to walk around the park to enjoy another beautiful evening in paradise, but I was growing more impatient by the minute. After enough nagging on my part, we finally arrived at our final destination, the one I'd been looking forward to all winter—*San Diego Stadium*!

I thought I'd died and gone to heaven.

It was April 1969, and the Padres were playing their very first major league ballgame. *And I was there!* Night games in those days started at 8, and we arrived at least two hours early. It's a memory I will always treasure, but just the first of many that the Padres have provided my family and me through the years. Those hallowed grounds of Mission Valley became my second home that summer, and for 33 years since.

I also had the privilege of attending the first home game of the 1974 season—the inaugural game of the "Kroc era". The Padres were within an eyelash of moving to Washington the previous winter when Mr. Kroc purchased the team, keeping them in San Diego.

I sat with my mom and dad near the Padres' bullpen for that game. The Padres weren't playing very well, and around the eighth inning, Kroc spoke into the public address system, which was very unusual at the time. He complained about the "stupid ballplaying" he was seeing.…The crowd was stunned, but at that very moment, a streaker ran onto the field, which distracted everyone's attention. He ran out to second base, did a pirouette, pointed at the ump, then took off for right field. Kroc was in the middle of his remarks and immediately shouted, "Throw him in jail!"

We actually wondered if the whole event was staged, to generate publicity and get more people to the ballpark…The crowd buzzed the rest of the evening, and we didn't know if it was because of Kroc's remarks or the streaker. Kroc was really fired up, having just bought the ballclub, and he may have had some unrealistic expectations.

A decade later, I took my fiancé, Kelly, to a weekday evening game during the 1982 season. We sat in the Plaza level, and unbeknownst to me, there was a rookie in the lineup making his major league debut for the Padres. His name was Tony Gwynn. I knew him well as a college phenom, and I stood up and cheered. "Kelly!" I shouted, "That's the kid from San Diego State!"

I'm really proud of being at that game—maybe even more than being at the Padres' first game back in '69. It was really an honor to see Tony's first big league appearance. When you see a guy break into the big leagues, it's memorable. He's a man who truly respects the game of baseball. I missed his final appearance as a Padre—I had to do a talk show that afternoon, and left the inning before his last at bat—but standing in for me was Kelly and my daughter, Ashley. I did have the good fortune of sitting with Tony for 45 minutes before that last game, listening to his recollections of twenty seasons in a Padre uniform. That was quite an emotional day.

I also had the opportunity to witness Dave Winfield's first game. He made a sensational throw from right field to third base, and I remember thinking what a great arm he had. At that moment, I knew he'd be a star.

Another of my good friends is Randy Jones. When Randy walked from the first base dugout to the bullpen to warm up, the fans would stand up *by section* and applaud. That was quite a sight! A couple years later, I saw Randy win his twentieth game of the season, and when the final out was recorded, the media poured onto the field. I've never seen so many cameras come flying out like that! Randy was our first legitimate player, and he really gave the Padres something to hang their hat on nationally.

Yes, the Padres have really given me, and scores of other fans, our share of memories.

For the first time, someone has chronicled the ballclub's complete history, from the expansion draft in '68 to Tony's final at bat. Nelson has put a "face" on the history of our Padres, bringing it alive and preserving it for posterity. The pages ahead will take you on a nostalgic journey through 33 seasons of baseball in Mission Valley. So without further ado…

"And here come the Padres!"

Coach John Kentera
Xtra Sports 690

# Introduction

TO MY FELLOW Padres fans, I ask: *What was the greatest single moment in the history of the San Diego Padres?*

The Padres have a 33-year history (1969-2002)—one which may seem inconsequential by the standards of the Yankees and Dodgers of the world—but one that's brought its share of memories to America's Finest City.

When I first embarked on this project, I couldn't believe that I'd find such a wealth of material; the words 'Padres' and 'tradition' fit together as well as 'San Diego' and 'snowfall'. No, we can't boast of Ruth's called shot, Gehrig's farewell address, Robinson breaking the color barrier, or Bobby Thompson's "shot heard 'round the world"—in fact not a single world championship, for that matter. But as I researched, I became amazed at what a fascinating history the San Diego Padres have, just waiting to be told to the world. In this book I've tried to bring to life those names, faces, and events long forgotten.

So in these last 33 years, is there one unique, defining moment that we Padres fans can hang our floppy hats on? Something we can call the most memorable moment in the history of our beloved Friars?

Many would immediately point to the "Steve Garvey home run". When talking to any longtime Padres fan, to elicit a nostalgic smile you need only mention the words *"Steve Garvey home run"*. No further elaboration is necessary—the event speaks for itself in the annals of Padres history.

Still, there are other moments that also stand out as classics…Who can forget the moment that the Padres clinched their first N.L. West title in 1984? Or when we came back on the last weekend of the season in 1996 to beat our rival Dodgers to win the division, after a 12-year post-season drought? Or the moment we clinched the West again in 1998—against those same Dodgers—with a full house chanting "Beat LA!"?

How about the win at home over Randy Johnson and the Astros in the '98 National League Divisional Series, defying all odds to launch the underdog Padres into the next round of the playoffs? And don't forget the final victory of the '98 championship series in Atlanta, when Sterling Hitchcock pitched us past the heavily favored Braves into the World Series.

If these moments bring a glisten to your eye and a nostalgic lump to your throat, join the club of die-hard Padres fans.

Certainly any of these memorable events could be considered the all-time, *numero uno*, greatest single moment in the history of the San Diego Padres. But there is one moment which my good friend and fellow lifelong fan, Chris Clark, shared with me…

It was the fourth and final game of the 1998 World Series between the Padres and the Yankees (who, to lifelong Padres fans, might be the *second*-most hated team on the planet). George Steinbrenner, owner of the Bronx Bombers, was on national television criticizing the field at the 'Q', which was badly chewed up by the Chargers and Aztecs football games. Steinbrenner was criticizing the conditions of our beloved park—the hallowed grounds on which Tony Gwynn, Steve Garvey, Dave Winfield, Nate Colbert, and other Padres legends once roamed.

Well, even if what Steinbrenner said was true (and technically, it was—by October, football had once again made a war-zone out of the playing surface at Qualcomm, one of many reasons the Padres need a baseball-only park), we took offense…As with a family member, *we* can criticize Qualcomm Stadium, but we'll be darned if some fat-cat east-coast outsider does.

Every San Diego fan knew it would be tough to beat the Yankees, considered by many the greatest team in history. But the Padres wanted to give them a run for their money, just as we had the "favored" teams (Houston, Atlanta) throughout the playoffs so far.

As it turned out, the Yankees swept the series in four straight…We were competitive in three of the games, losing heartbreakers that still hurt today.

If only Richie Garcia had called Mark Langston's pitch to Tino Martinez a strike in game one, Martinez would have struck out instead of clouting a game-winning grand slam on the next pitch…Ashby reportedly had the flu in game two, when the Yanks gave him a pounding too painful to watch…

Game three was ours until Scott Brosius broke our hearts with a game-winning home run off our ace reliever. And game four was also close, but by then the end seemed inevitable. As we watched a broken-down Caminiti collapse at the plate, we knew the clock was ticking on many of our old favorites.

So getting back to my point—what *was* the single greatest moment in Padres history? We've had 33 years to think about it, and I believe I've come to an answer.

When game four of the '98 World Series ended, something amazing happened: *No one left the stadium*. The Padres faithful stayed and applauded for what seemed like an eternity, expressing in unison their appreciation for such an incredible and memorable season. After enough tears and cheers, the players themselves came back onto the field to show *their* appreciation to the fans. We'd all endured a nail-biting, heart-breaking World Series sweep, but we took the occasion to salute one another, and it became one of those moments for which simple words could never do justice.

But even though this was San Diego, not everyone in the crowd was a Padres fan…

My friend Chris was one of those in attendance, standing and applauding as the Padres made their emotional curtain call. During the ceremony two obnoxious (and no doubt inebriated) Yankee fans walked by with a banner, gloating and taunting the home fans. They settled in front of Chris and his friend Isaac, blocking their view.

At this point Chris asked them, simply and politely, in his uniquely California way: "Dudes…Have some respect." With that, the Yankee fans showed a moment of class appropriate for the occasion: they looked at each other, took down their banner, and quietly walked away, allowing Padres fans to continue their tribute without further distraction.

*That*, says Chris, was the single greatest moment in San Diego Padres history. Who can argue with a life-long fan?

# The Beginning

THE YEAR WAS 1935. William "Hardrock" Lane, a rugged miner from the old west, faced a dilemma. His professional baseball team, the Hollywood Stars, finished last in the Pacific Coast League, and at the height of the Depression, fans weren't coming to the park. Worse, his rent at Wrigley Field in Los Angeles was to be doubled for the following year. The team needed a new home.

In January 1936, Lane staked a claim in San Diego, a growing community centered around a thriving seaport two hours south of Los Angeles.

Civic leaders welcomed the team with open arms. With help from the New Deal, tiny Sports Field was hastily converted into a baseball-only stadium that met PCL standards. Named for the team's owner, *Lane Field* could seat 8,000 fans. Its present-day location would be at the corner of Broadway and Harbor Drive.

Lane held a contest to allow fans to determine a name more appropriate for the team's new surroundings. Among the names submitted were the Balboas, Vaqueros, Skippers, Aviators, and Don Juans. Inspired by the Roman Catholic Mission *San Diego de Alcala*, the winning applicant submitted 'Padres', the Spanish word for 'priests'.

In baseball's early days, the Pacific Coast League (PCL) represented the highest level of minor league ball. A number of future major league stars came through San Diego during the Padres' two decades at Lane Field. Hometown fans were treated to the heroics of a local boy, Ted Williams, who led the Padres to the PCL title in 1937, their second year in San Diego. Though the team wasn't winning much over the next years, they established a devoted following among local fans.

Recollections of the old PCL Padres are captured in Bill Swank's nostalgic book, *Echoes From Lane Field*.

By 1957, the small wooden structure was weakened by termites and was deemed too cramped to accommodate a professional baseball team. After just two decades but a lifetime of memories, Lane Field was torn down. Today, all that remains of this historic site is an empty parking lot, with no signs or markers to commemorate the first home of the Padres.

Mirroring the population flow, the Padres fled downtown in 1958. Their new home, Westgate Park, was built on inexpensive grazing land northeast of downtown. (Fashion Valley mall now inhabits that former site.) The Padres won three more PCL titles during the 1960s, but as the decade wound down they were ready for the big time.

Born February 29, 1860, "Hardrock Bill" Lane died at the age of 78, two years after giving San Diego its first taste of professional baseball.

"The city still has a debt to Bill Lane," said Padres catcher Bill Starr. "He was the first man to risk his money on San Diego as a sports town. He did it during a depression when most everyone doubted his reasoning."[1]

**Jack Murphy** It was primarily for the efforts of Jack Murphy, a sportswriter and editor for the San Diego *Union* from 1953-1980, that Major League Baseball awarded an expansion franchise to San Diego. As one of the city's most prominent media personalities, he helped recruit the NFL's Chargers almost a decade earlier.

With Major League Baseball poised to add additional expansion teams in the late-1960s, Murphy was determined to secure one of those franchises for San Diego. A state-of-the-art sports facility was an important first step toward attracting a team, so he focused his efforts on generating community support for a new stadium. Murphy tirelessly lobbied, campaigned, and persuaded city leaders and baseball officials to approve a stadium and an expansion team for San Diego. Others, including *Union* writer Phil Collier, contributed mightily to the effort as well.

In 1965, San Diego voters overwhelmingly approved a referendum to raise $27.75 million for construction of a multi-purpose stadium. Murphy described that as the happiest night he ever enjoyed, knowing that would make everything that followed possible.

City planners selected the area reflecting San Diego's natural growth pattern: east of Hotel Circle, along Interstate 8, between Interstates 15 and 805. The facility was built to host a wide range of events—baseball, football, concerts, off-road events, etc. It lies

San Diego Stadium was originally open in the outfield, allowing panoramic views of the hills of Mission Valley. (Courtesy, Hall of Champions)

almost within shouting distance of the famous Mission, just off aptly named Friars Road.

*San Diego Stadium*, as it was then known, was constructed in the heart of Mission Valley where land was plentiful and cheap. Several cities were competing for a limited number of expansion franchises, and the new facility made San Diego an odds-on favorite.

**Arnholt Smith and Buzzie Bavasi** C. Arnholt Smith originally purchased the PCL Padres in 1955. Smith was one of the most powerful and influential businessmen in San Diego and was well connected politically, counting Richard Nixon as a close friend. But it was the involvement of E. J. "Buzzie" Bavasi, long-time Dodgers general manager, which put the effort to secure an expansion team over the top.

Bavasi had a distinguished career in the front office of all three southern California teams, serving as general manager of the Dodgers (1951-68), president of the Padres (1968-77), and general manager of the Angels (1978-84). Smith offered a partnership to Bavasi, believing that the longtime Dodger executive's involvement would resolve concerns over the viability of major league baseball in San Diego.

Bavasi initially declined, citing his allegiance to the Dodgers. But he was encouraged to accept the offer from an unlikely corner: Dodgers owner Walter O'Malley. Though O'Malley expressed his personal opposition to further expansion (which might cut into the Dodgers' fan base) he realized that it was inevitable. As such, he told Bavasi that knowledgeable, upstanding men, who'd given their lives to the game, should run the new teams.

With his boss's consent and encouragement, Bavasi accepted the San Diego offer.

Still, it was no guarantee of success. Smith and Bavasi anticipated that the National League would assess an expansion fee in the neighborhood of $6 million. The actual amount turned out to be $10 million.

This was over thirty years ago. Imagine what that figure would be today! Nonetheless, the Smith/Bavasi team held firm. Had they not, the franchise would likely have been awarded to Buffalo, Dallas, or a number of cities that were vying for an expansion team.

"This is ridiculous," said Bavasi of the expansion fee. "I don't want to mortgage the future of my children."

"I was disturbed when we heard the price," said Smith, who even wavered himself. "Buzzie was in a state of shock. He wanted to abandon the whole project. Finally, he agreed to stay in there and pitch.

"All of Southern California is really beginning to get up and go. The day is coming when the continental shelf will tip everything to the west.

"I thought the franchise would be a fine thing for the community. San Diego deserves big league baseball. It's part of the development and maturity of the city. I've been impressed by what the Chargers have done for San Diego's image; perhaps baseball can make an equally important contribution."[2]

**Four new teams** On May 27, 1968, major league owners formally approved the addition of four expansion teams, one of which was awarded to San Diego. The PCL Padres played out their final season in 1968 (playing that year at the new San Diego Stadium) before making the jump to major league status in 1969. It was decided that the team would retain the name 'Padres', which had long since become a household name in San Diego.

When expansion added four new teams, creating a total of 24 in all, Major League Baseball determined that it was necessary to subdivide the leagues along geographic lines. Prior to 1969, there were no divisions or League Championship Series. From 1901-68, the best team in the N.L. faced the best team in the A.L. in the World Series, with no playoff beforehand. The format changed the year the Padres entered the National League.

Each league was split into two divisions, with six teams in each: the N.L. East, N.L. West, A.L. East, and A.L. West. The Padres found a home in the N.L. West, while their counterparts, the Montreal Expos, were a continent away in the N.L. East. This marked the beginning of international baseball, with players having to clear customs on trips to Montreal.

Over in the A.L., the Kansas City Royals and Seattle Pilots were placed in the western division. After just one year, the Pilots moved to Milwaukee and were thereafter known as the Brewers.

These four teams—the Padres, Expos, Royals, and Pilots/Brewers—made up the expansion class of 1969. They all enjoyed limited success but share a common theme: post-season heartbreak.

The Royals have been the most successful of the class. They lost several tough playoffs to the Yankees in the late 70s, but with a win over St. Louis in the 1985 World Series, they became the only member of the class to capture a world championship.

The Brewers made the postseason twice, losing a tough seven-game World Series to the Cardinals in '82. The Expos saw play-off action only once, falling to the Dodgers in the 1981 NLCS.

We all know the Padres' record in the postseason—still more heartbreak for the class of '69. But more on that to come.

**Expansion woes**  In the 1960's, expansion teams were restricted to selecting players from clubs in their own league. Instead of simply picking unprotected players, they also had to buy them from their previous teams. Naturally, this put the 1969 expansion teams at a significant disadvantage, unlike their counterparts in future expansion seasons, who enjoyed the luxury of free agency.

This helps to explain why the Padres, Royals, Brewers, and Expos usually finished poorly in the early 70s. At the time, it was extremely difficult for an expansion team to compete during its first seasons. (By comparison, the Arizona Diamondbacks won the N.L. West in 1999, their second year of existence, and the World Series in 2001, thanks to free agency and an owner with very deep pockets.) In major league baseball, thirty years have brought a lifetime of changes.

**Expansion Draft**  In the expansion draft, held October 14, 1968, the Padres selected the following players:

| Round | Player | Position | Club |
|-------|--------|----------|------|
| 1 | Ollie Brown | OF | SF |
| 2 | Dave Guisti | P | StL |
| 3 | Al Santorini | P | Atl |
| 4 | Dick Selma | P | NY |
| 5 | Jose Arcia | IF | Chi |
| 6 | Clay Kirby | P | StL |

| 7  | Fred Kendall    | C    | Cin |
|----|-----------------|------|-----|
| 8  | Jose Morales    | OF   | NY  |
| 9  | Nate Colbert    | 1B   | Hou |
| 10 | Zoilo Versalles | IF   | LA  |
| 11 | Frank Reberger  | P    | Chi |
| 12 | Jerry DaVannon  | IF   | StL |
| 13 | Larry Stahl     | OF   | NY  |
| 14 | Dick Kelley     | P    | Atl |
| 15 | Al Ferrara      | OF   | LA  |
| 16 | Mike Corkins    | P    | SF  |
| 17 | Tom Dukes       | P    | Hou |
| 18 | Dick James      | P    | Chi |
| 19 | Tony Gonzalez   | OF   | Phi |
| 20 | Dave Roberts    | P    | Pit |
| 21 | Ivan Murrell    | OF   | Hou |
| 22 | Jim Williams    | OF   | LA  |
| 23 | Billy McCool    | P    | Cin |
| 24 | Roberto Pena    | IF   | Phi |
| 25 | Al McBean       | P    | Pit |
| 26 | Steve Arlin     | P    | Phi |
| 27 | Rafael Robles   | IF   | SF  |
| 28 | Fred Katawczik  | P    | Cin |
| 29 | Ron Slocum      | C/IF | Pit |
| 30 | Cito Gaston     | OF   | Atl |

**The first Padre** The distinction of being the first Padre belongs to outfielder Ollie Brown. Chosen first by the Padres in the expansion draft, Brown earned the nickname "Downtown" in the minor leagues but never really lived up to it in the majors. His best two seasons came with the Padres in 1969 and 1970, in which he hit 20 and 23 HRs respectively, but his career dropped off from there.

After leaving San Diego, Brown played with Oakland, Milwaukee, Houston, and Philadelphia. He retired in 1977 with 102 HRs and a .265 career average—not quite the numbers you'd expect from someone so nicknamed.

Still, "Downtown" Ollie Brown deserves a place of honor as the first member of the San Diego Padres. Now there's a trivia question to stump your friends!

**Brown and gold** The Padres' original colors were brown and gold, a departure from the traditional reds and blues of most team uniforms. Most people think the brown reflected the robes of the friars at the old missions. Actually, according to Jim Mulvaney, former president of the PCL Padres, it was because the owner's favorite color was brown:

"I recall that Arnholt Smith liked everything brown. He painted his bank buildings, his shipyards, his tuna cannery, and other buildings brown. He wore brown suits all the time and his letterhead was on brown tinted paper."[3]

The first home jerseys were white. Across the front "PADRES" was written in brown letters with gold edges. Uniform numbers were in brown outlined in gold. Socks were brown with three gold stripes. The original caps were brown with the interlocking "SD" in gold. Road uniforms were a unique shade of beige with the brown-and-gold "San Diego" across the front. Some spectators said the beige looked almost pink from a distance.

The early uniforms were much more conservative than in later years, when the team explored wild yellow, brown, and orange schemes, some of which were unsightly even by 1970s fashion standards.

The team's logo was a baby-faced friar known as "The Little Swinger". He resembled our modern mascot, "The Swinging Friar", only 40 pounds lighter.

**Dodger connections** Among the Padres' first coaches were future Hall of Famers Duke Snider and Sparky Anderson. Snider, the former Dodgers centerfielder, served as scout, spring training hitting instructor, and color broadcaster for the early Padres. Anderson, who later managed the Reds and Tigers to world championships, coached third base.

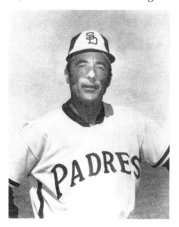

Cuban-born Preston Gomez was considered the only choice as manager of the young Padres. The 46-year old Gomez played just eight major league games in his career, then managed several years in the minors. He was the Dodgers' third base coach from 1965-68 while Bavasi was their general manager. Gomez became the first major league skipper born in Latin America.

The first manager of the Padres was Cuban-born Preston Gomez. His managerial record was 180 wins, 316 losses in just over three seasons. (Courtesy, Hall of Champions)

With Bavasi assuming the position of team president, Gomez as manager, Al

Ferrara in the outfield, Snider as coach, and Johnny Podres on the mound, the Padres had a strong connection with the old Dodgers.

"Preston is perfect for the job for several reasons," said Bavasi. "He believes in fundamentals, he knows how to teach young players, he knows the National League, and he'll work harder than anyone we could hire."

"It'll take us from five to ten years to build a strong team," said Gomez during the Padres' first spring training.[4]

Not wishing to raise expectations, Gomez openly hoped that the Padres would win 60 games in 1969. Even that turned out to be optimistic: the young Padres won just 52, losing 110.

# The Young Padres

1969 MARKED THE 200th birthday of the city of San Diego and the 100th anniversary of major league baseball. On April 8 at San Diego Stadium, the Padres played their inaugural game. The opening-day lineup was:

*Rafael Robles   ss*
*Roberto Pena   2b*
*Tony Gonzalez   cf*
*Ollie Brown   rf*
*Bill Davis   1b (replaced late in the game by Nate Colbert)*
*Larry Stahl   lf*
*Ed Spiezio   3b*
*Chris Cannizzaro   c*
*Dick Selma   p*

The Padres defeated the Astros, 2-1 before a crowd of 23,370. It's surprising that the Padres drew so poorly for their inaugural game; today, they routinely draw at least that for weekday-afternoon games. Selma was brilliant, tossing a complete-game five-hitter with twelve strikeouts. There was something of a World Series atmosphere to the Padres' debut; after the final out, players and fans celebrated wildly.

Shortstop Rafael Robles, who played just six games in 1969, was the first-ever Padre to step to the plate. With a homer in the fifth, third baseman Ed Spiezio, father of future Angels infielder Scott, lay claim to the Padres' first run, RBI, and home run.

**Johnny Podres and Dick Selma**  Johnny Podres joked that the young Friars looked more like the Dodgers of old. Podres, a star on the Brooklyn and Los Angeles teams of the 50s and 60s, was scheduled to start the second game of the season.

Years later, Selma recalled an odd event which occurred at the Baseball Writers' dinner the night before the opener. Houston starter Don Wilson approached him and boasted that the upstart Padres would lose tomorrow's game. Selma admitted that the unsportsmanlike comment annoyed him and gave him added motivation.

Selma kept one of the game balls which was autographed by the entire starting lineup. The ball had a place of honor in his living room for over twenty years until it was stolen during a party.

Alas, neither Podres nor Selma stayed around long. Podres went 5-6 for San Diego in just 17 games, which marked the end of his distinguished major league career. Selma pitched in only four games for the Padres before he was traded to the Cubs to bolster their staff for the pennant drive. In return, the Cubs sent pitchers Joe Niekro and Gary Ross.

Thirty-two years later, Selma was diagnosed with terminal liver cancer.

"This cancer thing is pretty frustrating. The hardest thing is being healthy and never being sick a day in my life, and bam...I just hope some people in San Diego remember me as much as I remember what we did that first night."[5]

Dick Selma, the first man to throw a pitch in a San Diego uniform, died on August 29, 2001.

**Early stars** Astute fans are probably familiar with knuckleballer Joe Niekro. Joe later combined with his Hall of Fame brother Phil to set the major league record for victories by siblings, breaking the mark held by Jim and Gaylord Perry. Acquired in the Selma deal, Joe Niekro finished his only season in San Diego with a 8-17 mark, enough to tie for the team lead in wins with Al Santorini.

Santorini, drafted third overall by the Padres, had a record of 8-14 in 1969, then went a disappointing 1-10 over the next two seasons.

The Padres' three main outfielders in 1969 were Brown, Cito Gaston, and Al Ferrara. Ferrara, a member of the '66 champion Dodgers, played piano at Carnegie Hall in his youth. "I wanted to be a big-league baseball player so I could see my picture on a bubble gum card," he said. Ferrara spent two seasons in San Diego, averaging .268 with 14 homers a year in slightly less than full-time play. He retired in 1971.

Catcher Fred Kendall remained with the club longer than any original Padre. Kendall, father of future Pirates star Jason, played with the Padres from 1969-76 and was the team's regular catcher from 1973-76.

Kendall was traded to Cleveland in '76 and was reacquired by San Diego three years later. He retired after the 1980 campaign. Only Kendall and Tony Gwynn have played for the Padres in three different decades.

**Chris Cannizaro**  Chris Cannizzaro, the team's regular catcher from 1969-70, was the Padres' first All-Star. Cannizzaro was really selected for the All-Star game by default: he hit just .220 in 1969, but every team had to have at least one representative on the All-Star team.

Cannizzaro was one of Casey Stengal's original 1962 Mets. The Old Professor frequently mispronounced his name, calling him 'Canzeroni'.

He played with the Cubs and Dodgers from 1971-73 and returned to San Diego for his final season, 1974. Cannizzaro retired with a .235 average over 13 major league seasons. Today, he serves as assistant baseball coach at the University of San Diego.

**Pitching**  Clay Kirby led the '69 Padres in innings and game starts. With little offensive support, the twenty-one year old won seven games against 20 losses, leading the league in defeats. Kirby was the first of three Padres to achieve the dubious distinction of losing 20 games. Thirty years ago, it wasn't that uncommon for pitchers to lose twenty or more games in a season, when starters went deeper into games and logged more starts and innings than today.

The Padres' first closer by default was Billy McCool, who led the team with seven saves. Of course, times have changed in this regard too; thirty years ago, the role of a closer was much different. Today, saves are one of baseball's most prominent statistics, alongside wins and ERA, and a new statistic—holds—has even been added for middle relievers.

Obtained in the Selma trade, Gary Ross (3-12 in 1969) threw long relief for the Padres for six seasons. He joined the Angels in 1974. By the time he left San Diego, Ross had logged more games than any other Padre hurler to that point. Tommie Sisk (2-13), Jack Baldschun (7-2), and Frank Reberger (1-2) rounded out the bullpen.

One of the Padres' first highlights occurred on July 14 when the Niekro brothers, Joe and Phil, faced one another.

"We'll have dinner together tonight," said Joe. "Then we'll call home. Our parents are probably a nervous wreck."[6]

The Padres actually asked Joe to wait an extra day in the rotation so the brothers could face each other, hoping that the event might attract more fans. But it didn't seem to have helped. Despite the team's best marketing efforts, only 6,456 fans showed up, a figure that was common in the early days.

Though the Padres finished 41 games behind the Braves in the N.L. West, they prevailed on this occasion: Joe edged out his older brother, 1-0.

**Dave "Soup" Campbell**

After the 1969 season Niekro was traded to Detroit for pitcher Pat Dobson and infielder Dave Campbell.

Campbell became a regular for San Diego in 1970, leading N.L. second basemen in errors, but also pacing the league in assists and putouts. He hit .219 with 12 HRs and 18 steals that season, then averaged .230 during the next two injury-plagued years. Campbell missed most of the 1972 season with a torn Achilles' tendon.

It was while recovering from those injuries that he first tried his hand at broadcasting. "After I got hurt, I called Buzzie (Bavasi) and volunteered to do color commentary. I told him I'd do it for free if he'd pick up my hotel and meal money. He agreed, so I did 10 or 11 games that season."[7]

Campbell apparently made an impression. He was dealt to St. Louis in 1973 and retired the following season, but he was hired as a broadcaster after his playing days were over. "Soup" called Padres games from 1978-88, and today fans recognize him as a respected baseball analyst for ESPN.

**The "acid" test**

During their first seasons the Padres did very little to be noticed around major league baseball. They routinely finished last in the National League West, while powerhouses like Cincinnati, Atlanta, and Los Angeles reigned as perennial division champs.

The Padres have been the victims of six no-hitters throughout their history. The first was thrown by Pittsburgh's Dock Ellis on June 12, 1970 at San Diego Stadium. Ellis later admitted that he threw the no-hitter while under the influence of LSD.

**The big boppers**

The 1970 Padres went 63-99, finishing 39 games behind the division-winning Reds. On the bright side, the Padres made an 11-game improvement over their inaugural season. They also showed impressive muscle, clubbing 172 home runs, third best in the league. Their offensive output was not bad for a second-year ballclub, relying solely on the expansion draft. That total is even more impressive considering that in 1970, the fences at San Diego Stadium were higher and deeper than today.

The original home run fence was the 18' permanent structure, which sits *behind* today's shorter, closer outfield fence. Palm trees now occupy the space between the two. Next time you visit the stadium, notice the difference between the two fences, and you realize how much more difficult it was to hit a home run in the Padres' early days.

First baseman Nate Colbert led the way in 1970 with 38 round-trippers. Ollie Brown belted 23 homers, batted .292, and was second on the team with 89 RBIs. Spiezio chipped in with 12 HRs and a .285 average.

Outfielder Clarence "Cito" Gaston had the finest all-around year in '70, his second full major league season. He was second on the team with 29 home runs and paced the club with a .318 average and 93 RBIs. Chosen from the Braves in the 30th round of the expansion draft, Gaston remained in San Diego until 1974, when he returned to Atlanta. He represented the Padres on the All-Star team in 1970, his only selection to the mid-summer classic.

Gaston retired after the 1978 season, never living up to the potential he'd shown during his outstanding 1970 campaign. He ultimately earned his greatest acclaim as a major league manager. In 1989, Gaston was named skipper of the Toronto Blue Jays. He led the Jays to four first-place finishes, including two world championships. In so doing, he became the first African-American manager to lead a team to the postseason.

**Clay Kirby's disappointment** On July 21, 1970 at San Diego Stadium, Clay Kirby fell victim to one of history's most infamous managerial decisions.

Kirby had a no-hitter through eight innings against the world champion New York Mets. He was just three outs away from achieving baseball immortality and securing his name in the record books forever. However, going into the bottom of the eighth, the Padres were *losing* the ballgame, 1-0.

Kirby gave up walks to Tommie Agee and Ken Singleton in the first inning. They executed a double steal, then Art Shamsky grounded out, scoring Agee. That one run, without the benefit of a base hit, made all the difference.

After the first inning, Kirby matched goose eggs with Mets starter Jim McAndrew and the score remained 1-0. Only 10,372 were on hand, but they were well aware of Kirby's no-hit bid and cheered his every pitch.

In the top of the eighth Colbert made a spectacular play to nail a runner at the plate. "That play got me up…It really started my adrenaline flowing," said Kirby. When the inning ended, the star of the moment charged off the mound to the roar of the crowd. Padres fans didn't have much to cheer about in the team's early days, but this time they were witnessing something historic.

On July 21, 1970, Clay Kirby had a no-hitter through eight innings, but was removed for a pinch hitter because the Padres were losing the game, 1-0. (Courtesy, Hall of Champions)

Unfortunately, Kirby's spot in the order was due up in the bottom of the eighth. Gomez faced a dilemma: his starter had a no-hitter, but the team was actually *losing* the game. The Padre manager made his fateful decision, lifting Kirby for a pinch hitter.

The move shocked the crowd and players alike. As the pinch hitter was announced, one fan jumped from the stands and made his way toward the dugout, screaming for Gomez. He was removed by security.

Gaston, the pinch hitter, went down on strikes.

Jack Baldschun took the mound in the top of the ninth, entering to a chorus of boos. Any chance of a combined no-hitter was lost when the Padres reliever promptly allowed the Mets' first base hit, and a total of three hits in all. The Mets plated two more runs that inning to add to their lead. The final score was 3-0.

The controversy lived on. Most other managers agreed with Gomez's decision to remove Kirby. However, the question raged: Was it reasonable to ruin a young pitcher's no-hit bid in a meaningless game? After the last out, fans stood near the railing shouting, "Gomez must go! Gomez must go!" Angry callers jammed the stadium's switchboards. For once, the young Padres made national headlines.

"I think Gomez had visions of catching Cincinnati," cracked New York's Shamsky. The Padres were already 30 games out in July.

"Our bench just gasped in disbelief," said Tom Seaver. "I personally would have let him hit. Maybe not if the pennant race were involved, but definitely in this situation."

"Sure, I was mad," said Kirby. "It was my first chance at a no-hitter. A no-hitter would have been something special, but I would rather have won the game than to have pitched one.

"He's the manager and it's his decision. I know he would have kept me in there if he thought he could have."

Gomez said he was simply trying to win the ball game: "I don't blame the fans. I hated to take the kid out, but we had to score some runs. I'm here to try to win games."[8]

Bavasi tepidly backed his manager, but he sensed a brewing public relations nightmare. The Dodgers rewarded Bill Singer with a $500 bonus for throwing a no-hitter earlier. Bavasi announced that Kirby would be given a bonus of $250 for his efforts, not an insignificant sum for a ballplayer in those days.

Kirby flirted with a no-hitter again a year later, September 18, 1971. He actually had a perfect game in the eighth inning before surrendering a home run to San Francisco's Willie McCovey. That was the Giants' only hit as Kirby prevailed, 2-1.

On November 9, 1973, Kirby was traded to the Cincinnati Reds for outfielder Bobby Tolan. By then, Gomez was managing the Houston Astros.

That sequence of events set up the ultimate irony. In 1974, Kirby was in the Cincinnati dugout while Don Wilson of the Astros—then managed by Gomez—was losing a no-hitter after eight innings. Wilson's spot in the order was due up. A teammate asked Kirby if he thought Gomez would pinch-hit for Wilson. Kirby replied, "I guarantee he will."

He was right—Wilson was pulled for a pinch hitter, robbing him of a chance for a no-hitter. It was the second time Gomez made the same call.

Kirby pitched in San Diego from 1969 to 1973 and was the Padres' winningest pitcher over their first five years of existence. Kirby's 231 strikeouts in 1971 stood as a team record for 27 years. Arm injuries ended his career in 1976.

Clay Kirby, who pitched in such tough luck throughout his career, died of a heart attack in 1991. He was 43.

**Trading for the future, part I**
Acquired in the Niekro deal, Pat Dobson became the ace of the Padres' staff in 1970, posting a 14-15 mark. It was believed that if he could win 14 games with a last-place club, he'd be of significant value to a contender.

The Padres swung the biggest deal of their short history on December 1, 1970, sending Dobson to the Baltimore Orioles for pitchers Tom Phoebus, Fred Beene, and Al Severinsen and heralded shortstop prospect Enzo Hernandez.

Eddie Leishman, general manager of the Padres, sought to improve the team's pitching. But the key player in the deal was Hernandez, whom the Padres coveted as their everyday shortstop. Hernandez's abilities were even compared to the great Luis Aparicio.

Though San Diego appeared to get the better of the deal at the time, hindsight shows otherwise. Dobson went 20-8 with the Orioles in 1971, leading them to the American League championship. He averaged sixteen wins over each of the next six seasons.

The new hurlers obtained in the trade were all busts for the Padres. Beene never pitched a single game for San Diego, and Severinsen won just two games in two years. Phoebus went 3-12 and was out of baseball in two years.

Light-hitting Enzo Hernandez was San Diego's regular shortstop for six seasons (1971-76). (Courtesy, Hall of Champions)

Thus, the trade essentially boiled down to Dobson-for-Hernandez. Enzo Hernandez became the Padres' regular shortstop from 1971-76. In his first season, he led N.L. shortstops with 33 errors and hit .222. Amazingly, Hernandez drove in just 12 runs, setting the record for fewest RBIs by a player with over 500 at bats in a season. Over time he improved his glovework, but he never hit for average or power.

It should be noted the shortstop position was regarded quite differently thirty years ago. Today, shortstops are often the cornerstone of a team's offense and are expected to hit for average and power. In the 1970s, speed and steady glovework were the hallmarks of a valuable shortstop.

Hernandez stole a total of 129 bases, which ranks seventh on the Padres' all-time list. He finished in the league's top ten in steals three times, a remarkable feat considering that he was on base so infrequently. Hernandez retired in 1978.

The early comparisons with fellow Venezuelans Aparicio and Dave Concepcion never materialized. During his six seasons in San Diego, Hernandez hit just .225, which today ranks as the lowest average by any Padre with at least 1,500 at bats. Still, for six years he solidified an important infield position and provided adequate speed and defense.

On balance, the Padres' first blockbuster trade was a disappointment. It was the first of several trades that looked good on paper but ended up haunting the young Padres.

**Trading for the future, part II**  1971 saw the Padres' losses hit the century-mark again. The offense took a giant step back, generating 76 less home runs than the previous season. Team batting also plummeted from .246 to .233, nineteen points below the league average. The signs were not encouraging, especially for a young franchise struggling to catch on with fans.

The team's strongest suit in 1971 was pitching. Aided by San Diego Stadium's then-spacious outfield, the staff's 3.22 ERA was third best in the league. Kirby (15-13, 2.83) blossomed into a top-rate starter.

Dave Roberts had an outstanding season despite a sub-.500 record (14-17). His 2.10 ERA ranked second in the league. Roberts' outstanding performance for a last-place ballclub earned him a sixth-place finish in the Cy Young voting.

As with Dobson the year before, the Padres dealt Roberts when his trade value was highest, gambling for untested, less expensive players. Roberts was sent to Houston after the '71 season for infielder Derrel Thomas and pitchers Bill Greif and Mark Schaeffer. The results eerily mirrored the Dobson trade.

Roberts had a brilliant career after leaving the Padres. He went 12-7 and 17-10 over the next two years for the Astros. He played for seven more clubs, retiring in 1981.

How did the Padres fare in the exchange? Schaeffer won a total of two games. Greif gave the Padres what his name implied: Inserted into the starting rotation in 1972, he posted a record of 5-16. Greif stayed in San Diego for over four seasons, compiling an overall mark of 29-61. That ranks as the lowest winning percentage (.322) among Padres with at least 500 innings pitched.

Thomas became a regular for the Padres from 1972-74, splitting his time between second and short. Like his double-play partner Hernandez, he had decent speed but didn't hit much for average or power.

The Padres' record in major trades was now 0 and 2.

**The future looks bleak** Another hard-luck member of the early Padres staffs was right-hander Steve Arlin.

His grandfather, Harold Arlin, did the play-by-play on the first radio broadcast of a major league baseball game in 1921.

Steve Arlin is one of three Padres pitchers to lose 20 or more games in a season. Arlin, who practiced dentistry in the off-season, nearly managed the feat twice, going 9-19 in 1971 and 10-21 the following year.

Southpaw Fred Norman joined the Padres in 1971. As the fifth starter he went 3-12. His fine 3.32 ERA and his horrible win-loss record underscore the anemia of the team's offense. The pitching was strong, but without an offense the Padres continued to languish deep in last place, with little hope for improvement in sight.

Most troublesome for the young Friars was the attendance, or lack thereof. In their inaugural season the Padres drew 521,970 fans, an average of 6,333 per game. Attendance picked up in 1970 (643,679) but dropped again in 1971 (557,513)—last in the league.

Attendance-wise, the Padres weren't only last: they were far behind even the *next*-worst team. The viability of major league baseball in San Diego was coming into serious question.

# Struggling For Survival

ELEVEN GAMES INTO the 1972 season, Bavasi realized that a change was needed. With the team's fortunes continuing to lag, manager Preston Gomez was fired on April 27.

In his 32 years in professional baseball, Bavasi had never fired anyone. He admitted that he hadn't slept the night before. It was something he didn't want to do, but he decided that it couldn't be put off any longer.

Gomez took the news in stride: "When you accept a job as manager, you know you'll be fired sooner or later."

Said Kirby of his former manager, "I learned an awful lot from him, and he stuck with me while I lost 20 games. If he had a shortcoming, maybe he didn't communicate with ballplayers as well as he wanted to."[9]

Gomez was replaced by coach Don Zimmer. The Padres hoped his old-school brand of baseball would light a fire under the young team.

The previous season, when Zimmer was coaching at Montreal, Arlin hit the Expos' Ron Hunt with a pitch. That set off a brawl between Hunt and Padres catcher Bob Barton. As Arlin ran toward the plate, Zimmer, coaching third base, grabbed Arlin and began punching him in the ribs. He and Arlin later joked about the incident.

Nicknamed "Popeye" for his strength and resemblance to the famous cartoon character, 'Zim' managed the Padres for the rest of 1972 and the entire 1973 season.

Zimmer once said of himself, "I'm just a .235 hitter with a metal plate in his head." In 1953 he was beaned in the head and was unconscious for two weeks. Zimmer underwent surgery, resulting in the famous 'plate' inserted in his head. Not baseball's most fortunate soul, three years later *another* pitch fractured his cheekbone and ended his season.

The change in managers didn't make much of a difference. The Padres finished 58-95 in 1972, deep in the cellar once more.

**Nate Colbert**  Where would the early Padres have been without first baseman Nate Colbert?

San Diego's ninth-round pick in the expansion draft, Colbert hammered 163 HRs during his six-year tenure with San Diego (1969-74). To this day, that stands as the team's career home run mark.

First baseman Nate Colbert carried the offense during San Diego's first seasons. His 163 home runs are a team record. (Courtesy, Hall of Champions)

Colbert places third in Padres history in slugging percentage (.469), fifth in at-bats, and sixth in games played. He could also flash the leather, leading N.L. first basemen in assists in 1972 and '73. He represented the Padres on the All-Star team from 1971-73.

Some years, Colbert seemed to carry the Padres offense single-handedly. In 1972 he drove in 22.7% of the team's runs, which stands as the major league record.

Playing in small-market San Diego, Colbert never got the recognition that would have come playing for a contending ballclub in a major media hub. But on August 1, 1972, the nation got a glimpse of the Padres' talented first baseman, who turned in one of the greatest individual performances of all time. Facing the Braves in Atlanta, Colbert belted *five* home runs and collected 13 RBIs in a doubleheader.

In the first game, Colbert hit two round-trippers and knocked in five runs as the Padres cruised to a 9-0 rout. But that was just the opening act. In game two he blasted a grand slam and a pair of two-run homers for eight more RBIs, leading the Padres to a 11-7 win.

Colbert almost didn't get his final home run. With two outs in the ninth inning Larry Stahl singled, giving Colbert one last at-bat. He promptly banged Cecil Upshaw's first pitch out of the park for home run number five. Colbert received a standing ovation from the small Atlanta crowd for his incredible afternoon.

In one of those ironies that prove truth is stranger than fiction, an 8-year old Nate Colbert was in attendance at Sportsman's Park in St. Louis on May 2, 1954. That day, young Colbert bore witness as Stan Musial hit five home runs in a twinbill—the very record he would tie eighteen years later.

The 5 home runs tied Musial's mark, and the 13 RBIs for a doubleheader set an all-time record (the Cardinals' Mark Whiten tied it in 1993). Colbert's 22 total bases in a doubleheader is a record which stands to this day.

Colbert actually hurt his knee the week before, prompting Zimmer to ask if he wanted to sit out the games. But the Padres first baseman, in the midst of a white-hot streak, insisted on playing. Including the doubleheader, Colbert hit 15 home runs over a span of 28 games.

"When I hit the fourth (home run), I remembered seeing Musial hitting five that time in St. Louis," said Colbert. "He was my first baseball idol."

Of his lack of national exposure, Colbert said, "I'm not all that crazy about attention, but it isn't because I don't like people. I've never wanted to be fussed over."[10]

After a poor 1974 campaign, Colbert spent parts of two seasons with Detroit, Montreal, and Oakland. Suffering back problems, his promising career ended in 1976 at age 30. For the Padres' first five years he was the backbone of the offense, and for one incredible day, the greatest player in the game.

**Arlin's heartbreaker** Third baseman Ed Spiezio, the man who recorded San Diego's first home run, RBI, and run, retired in 1972. Spiezio was never an everyday player, posting a high of 355 at bats in 1969. His lifetime average over nine years was .238. Spiezio was a member of the Cardinals' 1967-68 world championship teams, coming to the plate once in each World Series.

Dave Roberts—not to be confused with the pitcher who was previously traded by the Padres—took Spiezio's spot at third base. The number-one pick by the Padres in the '72 draft, Roberts went straight to the majors from the University of Oregon. He manned the hot corner in San Diego from 1972-74.

Neither Roberts nor Arlin will forget the events of July 18, 1972. Facing the Philadelphia Phillies, Arlin was but *one strike* away from a no-hitter.

Denny Doyle came to bat with two out in the ninth inning. Roberts was playing shallow at third to guard against a possible bunt. After Arlin got two strikes on Doyle, Roberts wanted to move back into position, but Zimmer told him to stay in close.

Doyle chopped the next pitch just over Roberts' head for a single, breaking up the no-hitter. Had the third baseman been playing in his usual position, he would have gloved it for the third out. For his part, Doyle couldn't believe Roberts was in so shallow.

Zimmer took full responsibility: "I (bleeped) it up."

"It's like a big bubble burst," said Arlin, who settled for a two-hit complete game and a 5-1 win.

"I'm just sick," moaned Roberts afterwards. "If I'm playing back, it would have been a routine play."[11]

**Pappas'**
**masterpiece** First Kirby lost two near no-hitters, and now Arlin joined the hard-luck club. To this day, no Padres pitcher has accomplished the feat.

As if to rub salt in the wound, the Friars found themselves on the wrong end of a no-hitter just two months later. It was September 2, 1972 at Wrigley Field. The Cubs' Milt Pappas mowed down 26 straight Padres and was one out away from not only a no-hitter, but a *perfect game*—a true baseball rarity. To that point, only five pitchers had accomplished the feat in the entire century.

Pinch-hitter Larry Stahl was the Padres' final batter. Stahl worked the count full, leaving Pappas just one strike away from a perfect game. Pappas' next pitch appeared to catch the corner...but was called ball four. To a chorus of boos from the angry Chicago crowd, Stahl took first base, thus ending the perfect game.

Pappas was furious, but he hung on to retire the next batter, settling for the no-hitter. "They were so close, I don't know how he (Stahl) could take them," he said of the pitches that spoiled the perfect game.

It was the second time the Padres had been no-hit. At least this time, the opposing pitcher wasn't stoned.

**The Madres** The San Diego Madres, an organization of about 500 members, was formed in 1972. The Madres sponsored five youth baseball teams during their inaugural season. Three decades later, that figure had grown to 134. They also assist with various causes at both home and road events. For their longstanding efforts, the Madres have been rewarded with a banner which flies proudly over the stadium. They always welcome donations and are seeking volunteers as they continue their work throughout the community.

**Fred Norman** By the team's fifth season, the Padres had finished in last place each and every year. In 1973, they lost an embarrassing 102 games, 39 games behind Cincinnati. Five years, five last-place finishes. Other than San Diego's gorgeous weather, nothing seemed to be going right. An appropriate modern-day equivalent might be the Tampa Bay Devil Rays.

Their struggles were best illustrated on August 5 when the Padres were no-hit by Atlanta's Phil Niekro. The 9-0 whitewashing was the third no-hitter thrown against the Padres, with Ellis and Pappas having previously accomplished the feat.

On June 12, 1973, Fred Norman was traded to the pitching-starved Reds for outfielder Gene Locklear, minor leaguer Mike Johnson, and cash.

The move was a shot in the arm for Norman, who became a key figure in the Big Red Machine's rotation. After starting just 1-7 with the Padres, he went 12-6 for the remainder of the year, placing sixth in the Cy Young voting.

Norman posted double-figures victories to Cincinnati for seven straight years, never recording an ERA above four, contributing to Cincinnati's two world championships.

The new Padres made almost no impact: Locklear was a reserve outfielder for three seasons, and Johnson pitched just 18 games in the major leagues.

It was another trade that didn't work out. Because of lagging gate receipts and other hardships facing Smith's once-indomitable financial empire, Padres management was forced to pinch pennies and cut corners. Throughout the 1973 season, the team was dogged by on-again, off-again rumors that the beleaguered Smith might have to sell the team to out-of-town buyers.

After the 1973 season, management made several highly publicized moves to strengthen the lineup. Critics contended that the moves were made solely to increase the ballclub's value to prospective buyers.

**Matty Alou and Willie McCovey** In the first of those moves, the Padres purchased veteran outfielder Matty Alou from the St. Louis Cardinals. Alou, 35, was a lifetime .309 hitter over 14 big league seasons, and San Diego hoped he could bring that consistency and leadership to their young team.

It was one more move that looked great at the time, but once again the Padres were burned. Carrying a .198 average with only three extra base hits, Alou was released in July 1974, thus ending his long, creditable big league career.

Just two days after the Alou signing, the Padres raised eyebrows around the league again, trading left-handed pitcher Mike Caldwell to the Giants for future Hall of Famer Willie McCovey.

In two-plus seasons with San Diego, Caldwell split his time between the starting rotation and the bullpen. He compiled a record of 13-25 with 12 saves.

McCovey became the Padres' first $100,000-a-year player. The 35-year-old first baseman walloped 29 homers the previous season with the Giants, with a total of 413 for his career.

The trade of McCovey, who'd manned first base in Frisco since 1959, shocked Giants' fans. The former Rookie of the Year and MVP was enormously popular in the Bay Area and was one of the game's most respected hitters. But the Giants were desperate for pitching help, and McCovey, with his advanced age and high salary, was deemed expendable. He had also undergone surgery on both knees, making it painful to play the field.

McCovey made it clear that he wanted to stay on the west coast for the remainder of his career. As a veteran, having heard rumors of the Padres' move to Washington, he could have vetoed the trade. However, at the time of the deal McCovey was given assurances that the Padres were to remain in San Diego indefinitely.

Caldwell went on to have a stellar season (14-5, 2.95) with San Francisco after the trade. He enjoyed a prosperous career, finishing second in the Cy Young voting with Milwaukee in 1978.

McCovey had two fairly productive seasons with San Diego, initially sharing first base with Colbert. "Stretch" averaged 23 homers and 66 RBIs in mostly part-time play with the Padres from 1974-75.

McCovey brought his experience and star power to San Diego, which lent prestige to the franchise at a critical juncture. But by giving up a promising young left-handed pitcher, the Padres paid a steep price for his services.

**Glenn Beckert** Still seeking to make the ballclub more attractive for a potential buyer, San Diego pulled off another big trade after the 1973 season. The Padres acquired veteran second baseman Glenn Beckert from the Cubs in exchange for outfielder Jerry Morales.

Beckert was an All-Star four straight years (1969-72) and a former gold glover. Morales was a semi-regular outfielder for the Padres for two seasons. He hit .281 in his final year in San Diego.

Although Beckert fought heel and ankle ailments the previous two seasons, the deal initially looked like a steal for San Diego. The Padres were giving up a part-time outfielder for a proven (albeit injured) All-Star middle infielder.

But for the umpteenth time, the deal didn't work out. Slowed by his various injuries, Beckert was relegated to pinch-hitting and part-time duties after joining San Diego. He retired after stepping to the plate just 188 times as a Padre.

Meanwhile, Morales played ten more years after the trade. He averaged .276 with nearly 80 RBIs a year over the next four seasons.

**Needing a miracle**  After the '73 season, the long-term prospects of major league baseball in San Diego looked bleak. It would take a miracle to save baseball in America's Finest City. The Padres needed a Hall of Fame-caliber player whose heroics on the field would bring respectability to the team and put fans in the seats. And even more urgently, they needed a new owner with the will and the way to keep the Padres in San Diego.

# A Team Nearly Lost

THE FINANCIAL EMPIRE of Padres owner C. Arnholt Smith, which included a bank and a number of other industries, began to collapse in
the early-70s. Once one of the most politically connected and influential figures in San Diego, Smith faced a desperate situation.

Bavasi was repeatedly frustrated during the ballclub's early years.
"If Mr. Smith had not got into trouble, we would have been all right,"
said Bavasi. "But we had to sell the good players to make payroll. We
did that again and again. It was disheartening. I just wish we could
have kept the players we gave up."[12]

Federal regulators declared Smith's bank insolvent in 1973, which
was the biggest bank failure in U.S. history at the time. He was indicted
for bank fraud, tax evasion, and making illegal campaign contributions. The man once known as "Mr. San Diego" had no choice but to
sell off his assets, the Padres included.

In 1973, a Washington-based group led by food chain magnate
Jerry Danzansky signed a letter of intent to buy the Padres for $12 mil-
lion. The Danzansky group planned to relocate the ballclub to Washington D.C. for the 1974 season. The nation's capital had been
without major league baseball since 1971, when the Washington Senators became the Texas Rangers.

**Moving to
Washington?** When the season ended, Bavasi stated that he would not remain with
the team if they moved to the east coast. Bavasi and community lead-
ers scrambled to find a buyer agreeable to keeping the team in San
Diego, but the Padres' poor attendance and concerns over the fran-
chise's long-term viability scared off potential investors. Finally, a Los
Angeles-based group headed by Marjorie Everett emerged. Mrs.
Everett, owner of the Hollywood Park Race Track and a friend of
Bavasi, pledged to keep the team in San Diego. However, any vote by

league owners on the Everett group's proposal would come after a vote on Danzansky's offer.

Like most San Diegans, Smith did not want to see the Padres relocate. In October 1973 he gave the city brief cause for optimism when he announced that he was not relinquishing ownership after all. Smith believed that he could obtain the necessary financing to retain the ballclub, keeping them in San Diego for the foreseeable future. (It was during this time that McCovey and others were assured the team would not be moved.)

**Reprieve?**    But the soap opera continued: In December, the night before National League owners were scheduled to meet, Smith's attorney John Holt convinced him to change his mind one more time, and to proceed with the sale after all.

"You're fighting for your very existence," Holt reminded his embattled client. "You can't possibly run the club in a decent manner, and I tell you in your own interest to just knock it off."[14]

With no choice but to heed his attorney's advice, Smith asked the league to proceed with the vote on the Danzansky proposal.

The Padres were so close to moving to Washington in 1974 that the ballclub designed new uniforms. Dave Freisleben models the uniforms which, fortunately, were never worn in a major league game. (Courtesy, Larry Littlefield)

The city of San Diego threatened legal action if the team was moved. But congressional leaders, anxious to bring baseball back to the nation's capital, assured the league that they would protect against indemnification (financial compensation that might be ordered by the courts to the city of San Diego). Thus emboldened, league owners voted unanimously to accept the Danzansky bid on December 6, 1973. Baseball commissioner Bowie Kuhn and National League president Chub Feeney also favored the move to D.C., convinced that San Diego was not a viable major league venue.

With that, the Padres were to relocate to Washington for the 1974 season. Bavasi emerged from the meeting in tears. "Last night we were assured we had the club for San Diego, and we woke up this morning and found out that Mr. Smith had changed his mind. He changed his mind and a lot of peoples' lives."[13]

Though it looked like a done deal, the move to Washington wasn't entirely guaranteed. Still facing the city's lawsuits, the league obligated Danzansky to ante five million dollars in potential damages. He was given a deadline of December 21 to meet that condition.

With 15 years remaining on the Padres' original stadium lease, city attorney John Witt filed a breach of contract suit. He also filed an anti-trust suit, which sought $72 million in damages from the league. Witt alleged that losing the Padres would cost the city an estimated $24 million in revenue and asked the court to triple the damages, bringing the amount to $72 million.

The Padres' move was so expected that Topps replaced 'San Diego' with 'Washington' on its 1974 baseball card set. They quickly corrected the error, and the 'Washington' cards are rare today. (Courtesy, Topps)

For their part, the league received repeated assurances from Vice President Ford (who was sworn in two days earlier), House Speaker Carl Albert, and others in positions of influence that Congress and the city of Washington would help defray any court-ordered damages.

In effect, U.S. taxpayers (including those in San Diego) were funding the move of the Padres to RFK Stadium. Mayor Pete Wilson was furious: "It's a modern version of the public be damned. The city will wage war against the league on both the legal and political fronts to keep our baseball team in San Diego," he declared.[14]

The Padres' move to Washington was so expected that the team packed everything and even designed new uniforms. The Topps baseball card company actually changed the team name on its 1974 set to the eerily generic "Washington Nat'l. Lea.", before correcting the error.

Topps took a gamble by printing its cards *before* the move was official. If you come across a '74 set, check the cards closely. The "Washington" cards are relatively scarce and carry substantial value.

**Disappointed players** McCovey, traded to the Padres just six weeks earlier, was crestfallen by the events. A five-and-ten player who could block any trades, McCovey said he would not have approved the deal had he known of the move. He even explored the option of voiding the trade after the fact, questioning its legality.

Other players were also disappointed. "I thought the city of San Diego put out a real good effort to keep the team here," said Kendall. "I still say if the team were to stay here, we could get 100 percent support…Right now I can't even react to the move."

"It's just like being traded," said outfielder Leron Lee. "There's nothing the individual player can do or say about it. It's too bad we had to go through this to get the support now…I wonder where they (fans) all were when we were playing."

"Weather-wise, I'd have taken San Diego," added new acquisition Beckert. "But either way, I'm just glad to see it settled. The players had been in limbo."

"I had more or less resigned myself that I might have to go to Washington," said Colbert. "I never felt we'd go to Seattle or Toronto (two other cities that were eyeing a major league team). If we left, I always felt it would be Washington."

"It's bad to leave a place as pretty as San Diego," added Johnny Grubb. "I liked San Diego, but all those empty seats were discouraging."[15]

**Nothing is firm** It looked like a done deal, but the wild roller coaster was far from over.

The original deal called for Danzansky to pay Smith $9 million up front and the remainder in annual payments. But Danzansky, increasingly nervous over the damages sought by the city, attempted to renegotiate the deal. He wanted to reduce the up-front money and spread the payments out over more years. Smith, in need of immediate cash, refused.

The Danzansky group opted not to guarantee its $5 million against indemnities as required by the December 21 deadline. As such, the sale was voided. "We just want a club that is free and unencumbered," said Danzansky. "We are not prepared to take an inordinate risk more than our $12 million that we are paying for the club."[15]

Though it was no guarantee that the team would remain in San Diego, the turn of events did buy time. "The National League knew it would lose in our lawsuit, so did Danzansky," said Mayor Wilson.

"We're back where we were," said Feeney. "Smith is the owner of the franchise, the team is in San Diego."

But the league president cautioned: "Nothing is firm. We have a serious problem, because of Smith's problems."[16]

**Another nail in the coffin** Feeney's point was valid, as Smith was still in urgent need of a buyer. Was there anyone who could keep the Padres in San Diego?

The answer was yes: the Los Angeles-based group headed by Mrs. Everett. The league never had a chance to vote on the Everett group's offer earlier in the month, having approved the Danzansky proposal first.

One week after the Washington deal was voided, Smith agreed to the sale to the Everett group. It looked like the perfect solution: up-front cash to settle some of Smith's financial problems, and assurances that the team would remain in San Diego. All that awaited was approval by the league owners.

That was the catch.

Kuhn and some owners expressed concerns over Mrs. Everett's involvement in gambling operations. In particular, they cited her alleged involvement in a racetrack scandal, which resulted in the conviction of an Illinois judge. The city of San Diego authorized a thorough investigation of Mrs. Everett's business dealings. She was found to be of the highest character, without a hint of impropriety. City attorney Witt was even prepared to appear as a character witness for her before the owners.

It mattered not. On January 9, 1974, the National League owners voted 9-3 against the sale of the Padres to the Everett group. Only the Cubs and Giants voted to approve the sale. Mrs. Everett was gracious in defeat, but many took exception to the innuendoes and rumors.

Everett's attorney felt that the owners used the allegations against his client as an excuse. Their real reason for rejecting the sale, he contended, was that the league didn't see San Diego as a viable major league market and were unwilling to give the city a second chance. Well-heeled investors in Washington, New Orleans, Toronto, and Seattle were lobbying for a major league franchise, and the Padres seemed ripe for the taking.

After rejecting the Everett group, the league had two options. Knowing Smith's desperate situation, they could handpick buyers in another city, which still meant relocation. The other alternative was for the league itself to assume control of the Padres. The latter option was just as unpleasant; the league probably wouldn't run the team for more than a year or so before selling to an out-of-town buyer.

The final payment of $750,000 on Smith's initial investment on the ballclub was due in January 1974. It was no secret that he didn't have the funds available. Mrs. Everett had written a check to the league to cover the payment, but when the sale of the team was rejected, her check was returned.

The clock was ticking. If Smith defaulted, the league would assume control of the ballclub. Unless a buyer could be found quickly, major league baseball in San Diego was on its last breath.

**Cheeseburger in paradise** Brothers Richard and Maurice McDonald operated a small hamburger stand in San Bernadino, California, about an hour inland from Los Angeles. Little did they realize that, thanks to a 52-year old milkshake machine salesman from Chicago, their name would become synonymous with fast food throughout the world.

That salesman was *Ray Kroc*.

At 15, Kroc dropped out of school and lied about his age to join the Red Cross ambulance corps during World War I. His first job was musical director for a radio station in Chicago. There, he hired a team that later became famous as Amos 'n Andy.

By his early-50s, Kroc peddled a milkshake machine that could make five shakes simultaneously. He regularly traveled throughout the country, and one day in 1954, he happened upon the McDonald brothers' fast-food stand.

"This had to be the most amazing merchandising operation I'd ever seen," Kroc later wrote. He marveled at the efficiency with which the McDonald brothers operated their small establishment, delivering a limited menu of burgers, fries, and shakes in a minute or less, at affordable prices.

It hit like a brainstorm: Kroc realized that the concept could work on a much larger scale. He persuaded the McDonald brothers to open more units similar to the one in San Bernadino. Reluctant at first, the brothers finally agreed. The deal called for Kroc to sell additional franchises, keeping 1.4 percent of all sales. The new stores would carry the arches and bear the McDonald's name ("What are you going to do with a name like Kroc?", he quipped).

The McDonald's Corporation was officially launched April 15, 1955, in Des Plaines, Illinois, near Kroc's Chicago home. Hamburgers sold for 15 cents, french fries for a dime, and milkshakes for 20 cents. Kroc bought out the McDonald brothers in 1961 for $2.7 million. The rest is history.

By 1963, the billionth hamburger was sold and the five hundredth McDonald's restaurant was opened. "We take the hamburger business more seriously than anyone else," he wrote.[17]

By 1970, the golden arches were seen in every state in the nation, and McDonald's was ready to go global. Kroc's imagination, perseverance, and ingenuity made him one of the wealthiest and most respected men in the country.

**Kroc to the rescue!** In addition to his astute business sense, Kroc was an avid baseball fan, and particularly a fan of the Chicago Cubs. He grew up as one of the original 'bleacher bums' and joked that he was the most sunburned man in Chicago. He tried unsuccessfully to buy the Cubs several times.

It was January 1974 and Kroc, as much a fan as ever, read that the league rejected the Everett offer.

Kroc later recalled: "I turned to my wife and said, 'Honey, what would you think if I bought the Padres?'"

"I would think," replied his wife Joan, "that you are nuts."[18]

Kroc answered the Padres' prayers in the nick of time. Shortly before the league was poised to assume control of the team, he submitted a proposal to purchase the ballclub. This time, it was impossible for the league to turn down a man of such stature and integrity. The sale was easily approved, and the Padres still had a home in San Diego.

Ray A. Kroc, founder of McDonald's, used his enormous wealth to purchase the Padres in January 1974, saving major league baseball in San Diego. (Courtesy, Hall of Champions)

"I am totally inclined to keep the team in San Diego. Mr. Smith is very emphatic about keeping the club in San Diego and I'm 100 percent cooperative," said Kroc.

"I wouldn't buy the franchise because of monetary considerations. I think San Diego can be a great sport town. The attendance of the Gulls right now is proving that. I think we can make it a proud sports city.

"I won't be an absentee owner. I'll be involved. I want our athletes to be proud men. I don't feel I ever worked a day in my life—working is doing what you hate to do. I want ballplayers who enjoy baseball. One thing I've learned is that anything is possible if you have both talent and money. But talent is first. If you have talent, there are ways to find money."[18]

"I can't believe our luck," said Mayor Wilson. "It's too good to be true."

"It will be fun to start at the bottom," said Kroc, referring to the Padres' perennial last-place status. "Anticipation is greater than realization."

"He's a fan, and that's something that has been lacking in major league ownership," said Bavasi. "Now we will be in a position, financially, to compete with other clubs."

"I think I'll have 10,000 times more involvement with the ballclub than most of the National League owners do," he said. "We're going to have to get some salesmen out to reach the public. I hope we can develop a team so strong that the fans will demand that the out-of-town games be televised."

"I'm relieved...I haven't slept for weeks," said an exhausted Bavasi, who had the front seat on the emotional roller coaster. "Now we can unpack."[19]

C. Arnholt Smith's legal battles continued for another five years. The Padres' original owner was finally convicted in 1979 of embezzling $9 million from his holdings. He served eight months in a county honor camp.

Smith passed away in a Del Mar nursing home at the age of 97. That night, June 8, 1996, in a game against the Pittsburgh Pirates, a crowd of 41,000 held a moment of silence in his memory.

# Kroc Makes His Mark

RAY KROC BECAME actively involved in charitable activities throughout the community, contributing to research into diabetes, arthritis, multiple sclerosis, and other causes.

Kroc said the team needed to spend an additional $1.5 million right away. He also set about to improve conditions at the stadium, upgrading the quality of concessions, playing more day games, running buses to the park, and strengthening relationships with local businesses. One of his goals was to bring more women and families to the games.

The new owner made a splash in the team's home opener on April 9. The Padres were trailing the Houston Astros 9-2, on the verge of losing their fourth straight game. In the eighth inning, Kroc grabbed the public address microphone and announced to the crowd:

"I have some good news and some bad news. The good news is that we've outdrawn the Dodgers. They had 31,000 for their opener and we had 39,000 for ours…The bad news is that I've never seen such *stupid* ball playing in my life. Ladies and gentleman, I suffer with you."

While he was speaking, a streaker ran across the field. Without missing a beat Kroc shouted into the mike, "Throw him in jail!"

The crowd roared, and it was immediately apparent that life with Ray Kroc was going to be very, very different. But Commissioner Bowie Kuhn didn't find the event so humorous: He ordered Kroc to apologize for his remarks.

**Dave Winfield** Even with the ambitious Kroc at the helm, the Padres had a long way to go before achieving contender status. Fortunately, they had a budding superstar around whom to build.

David Mark Winfield was born October 3, 1951. An exceptionally gifted athlete, Winfield starred in basketball and baseball at the University of Minnesota. He was drafted by the NBA's Atlanta Hawks and the

ABA's Utah Stars. He was also drafted by the NFL's Minnesota Viking—despite having never played football in high school or college.

But Winfield's love was baseball. "I never had any real doubt which offer I would take. Football was out of the question, not my game. I contemplated pro basketball, but from the time I was a little boy and people asked me what I wanted to be, I always said a professional baseball player."[20]

Dave Winfield made the leap directly from the University of Minnesota to the Padres, becoming one of the few players to bypass the minor leagues. (Courtesy, Hall of Champions)

Standing 6'6", Winfield was named MVP of the 1973 College World Series, pitching and playing outfield for the Golden Gophers. He is one of the few players to have never played in the minor leagues, going directly to the Padres in 1973. The 21-year old appeared in 56 games that year, hitting .277.

Winfield stayed with the Padres for nearly eight full seasons (1973-80), becoming the team's first bona fide superstar. He was consistently among the league leaders in power numbers and possessed above average speed. Winfield also owned one of the strongest arms in the game. He represented the Padres on the N.L. All-Star squad four straight years (1977-80) and won a Gold Glove in 1979 and '80.

Today, Winfield ranks high on every career offensive statistic for the Padres. He is second in HRs (154) and RBIs (626), and places in the top three in games, at-bats, runs, hits, doubles, triples, and walks.

Summarizing his approach to hitting, Winfield said, "Good hitters don't just go up and swing. They always have a plan. Call it an educated deduction. You visualize. You're like a good negotiator. You know what you have, you know what he has, then you try to work it out.

After the 1980 season, Winfield signed a huge ten-year contract with the New York Yankees. The deal stipulated that Yankee owner Steinbrenner had to donate $3 million to Winfield's charity for troubled youth. Winfield played with the Yankees from 1981-90, missing the '89 season due to back surgery. He joined the Angels in 1990, then spent 1992 with Toronto (where he won his only world championship), 1993-94 with Minnesota (where he got his 3,000[th] career hit), and finally, the 1995 season with Cleveland.

"Tom Cruise only makes one or two film appearances a year. A baseball player can be the hero or the goat one hundred and sixty-two times a year.

"These days, baseball is different. You come to spring training, you get your legs ready, you arms loose, your agent ready, your lawyer lined up."[21]

Winfield ended his career with 3,110 base hits, 465 home runs, and 1,833 RBIs. He shares the record for hitting safely in seven straight All-Star games. One of the game's most articulate spokesmen, Winfield appeared in a total of twelve All-Star games and won seven gold gloves. In 1999, *The Sporting News* ranked him 94th on its list of baseball's 100 Greatest Players.

The Padres retired his number 31 in 2001. Fans in attendance that night were given vintage Winfield-replica jerseys. A banner flies over Qualcomm Stadium in his honor.

Winfield was elected to the Baseball Hall of Fame in 2001 along with Kirby Puckett, Bill Mazeroski, and Negro League player Hilton Smith.

On the day of Winfield's induction, Padres management wanted players to wear 70s-style 'retro' caps. The players refused; one described the hats as 'stupid'. The comment was directed at the old brown-and-gold that adorned Padres uniforms during Winfield's playing days.

The Hall of Fame gave Winfield the choice of wearing a Yankee or Padre cap on his plaque. Despite an effort by Steinbrenner to persuade him to go in as a Yankee, Winfield chose the team he broke into professional baseball with. "I went with the team that gave me my very first opportunity," he said in a statement released by the Hall of Fame. "All of my 'firsts' happened in San Diego and that is where I developed as a player."

**The Chicken**   A central figure in Padres history was a man with an unfamiliar name: Ted Giannoulas. You know him better as…*The Chicken*!

As a college student in 1974, Giannoulas agreed to appear in a rented chicken suit and pass out Easter candy at the San Diego Zoo as a promotion for radio station KGB. None of the station's regular employees would consent to the stunt, so they searched the San Diego State campus for a student in need of a job. Giannoulas, who originally wanted to be a sportswriter, agreed. He was paid just $2 an hour, but a legend was born.

Giannoulas did the gimmick for a week, then approached the Padres about appearing as the chicken at the stadium ("I figured I could see some games for free", he recalled). The team loved what they saw.

At the time, Giannoulas' act was unprecedented in professional sports. The Hoover High alumnus described the first costume as "a simple red, rag-tag outfit" made out of papier-mâché.

With that, the Chicken became a fixture during Padres home games, mingling, flirting, dancing in the aisles and entertaining the crowd. A chicken may have nothing to do with the Padres, but the fans loved him anyway. All the while, he was an employee of the radio station, not the baseball team, which became an important distinction later.

The Chicken, who was the first mascot in professional sports, gained national attention and sparked dozens of copycats. His high jinks gave people another reason to come to the ballpark—something very important for the Padres of the 70s, who weren't exactly packing them in.

The late Jack Murphy wrote, "The Chicken has the soul of a poet. He is an embryonic Charles Chaplin in chicken feathers."

"More than anything, baseball should learn to peddle the real nostalgia—Jackie Robinson breaking the color barrier, Lou Gehrig's farewell speech, the first appearance of the San Diego Chicken," wrote *Time* magazine.

The Chicken helped jump-start attendance in San Diego at a time when the team needed it most. (Courtesy, Donruss)

*The Sporting News* would name him one of the Top 100 Most Powerful People in Sports for the twentieth century, and the Baseball Hall of Fame requested one of his costumes to head a display honoring mascots.

Giannoulas eventually took his act on the road—appearing, among numerous other venues, at Elvis Presley concerts and at the White House. All the publicity led to the inevitable clash with KGB over rights to the character. At one point in 1979, Giannoulas was fired for violation of his contract. A lawsuit was filed, and Giannoulas was banned from appearing in the chicken costume.

After the firing, the Chicken re-emerged on June 29, 1979 with a stunt that ranks among the greatest in professional sports.

The California Highway Patrol entered San Diego Stadium on motorcycles, leading an armored truck with a giant egg perched on top. A sell-out crowd of 47,000 watched as "Also Sprach Zarathustra" blared from the speakers. Even the players got into the gag, helping lower the giant egg off the truck. The egg sat a few seconds then slowly rolled toward second base. Finally, the Chicken burst out: the mascot was 'reborn'!

The classic stunt became known as "The Grand Hatching". A ten-minute ovation ensued. The event made national news. After several minutes of antics on the field, the Chicken was carried away triumphantly on the shoulders of Kurt Bevacqua and John D'Acquisto. Cigars were distributed to the media, reading: "It's a Bird." Even the radio station's attorney couldn't help laughing when asked about the stunt.

"I was so excited I got chills up and down my spine," said Giannoulas. "I was really crying, it was one of the greatest thrills of my life."

Because of the lawsuit, the costume was different. "It's a compilation bird with a little from everything, and the colors are completely different," he said.[22]

The suit eventually made its way to the California Supreme Court, which ruled that Giannoulas had essentially created the character himself. From then on he could appear anywhere in a chicken costume—provided it did not bear the call letters KGB.

The station and Giannoulas later mended fences, and he was even allowed to use his old KGB costume at the five-year anniversary of his 'rebirth'.

Alas, all good things must come to an end, and the Chicken finally took his show to the national stage, moving beyond the relative limitations of Padres games.

**Slow change** John McNamara became the Padres' third manager, replacing Zimmer for the 1974 season. McNamara skippered the Friars from 1974-76 and part of 1977.

Zimmer continued to enjoy a distinguished career long after departing San Diego. He managed the Red Sox from 1976-80, losing a heartbreaking one-game playoff to the Yankees in '78. He later managed the Rangers and Cubs. Today, "Popeye" is a coach with the Yankees, basking in the team's phenomenal successes of the late-90s.

With Kroc stirring up the front office and Winfield leading the charge on the field, the young Padres began to show promise. But change wouldn't come overnight; despite Kroc's infusion of money and spirit, the '74 club finished just 60-102, a mark identical to the year before. It was the Padres' sixth consecutive last-place finish, a full 42 games behind the Dodgers.

San Diego was last in the league in hitting and pitching in 1974. Yet fan support improved dramatically in the first year of the Kroc era. Attendance topped the one million mark—a better than *75 percent* increase over the season before!

The Padres' representative on the 1974 All-Star team was Johnny Grubb (.286, 8 HRs). Grubb was with the Padres from 1973-76, hitting an impressive .311 in his rookie campaign. Among Padres with at least 1,500 at bats, Grubb's .286 average ranks sixth. He retired in 1987, his fifteenth and final season in the major leagues.

Despite a somewhat nondescript performance, outfielder Bobby Tolan was the Padres MVP for the 1974 season. Acquired from Cincinnati in the Clay Kirby trade, Tolan hit .266 with 8 home runs in 1974. He had another solid but unspectacular season in '75 before moving to Philadelphia. He spent 1978 in Japan and returned to San Diego for a cameo in 1979. Tolan later coached for the Padres.

Pitcher Dave Freisleben, at the tender age of 20, made his debut in 1974. Despite concerns that he was being rushed to the big leagues, Freisleben was inserted into the rotation and finished second on the team with 211 innings in '74. He tied for the club lead with nine wins, and his 3.66 ERA was best on the staff. His innings dropped every year after that, and he was soon splitting time in the bullpen. Freisleben pitched three more seasons for the Padres, compiling an overall mark of 31-53.

**Randy Jones** One beacon for the Padres in the mid-70s was pitcher Randall Leo "Randy" Jones. Jones broke into the big leagues in 1973 alongside Winfield.

**RANDY JONES** PITCHER

Randy Jones won the Cy Young award in 1976, leading the league in wins, complete games, starts, and innings. (Courtesy, Donruss)

The young left-hander produced a 7-6 record with a 3.16 ERA in his rookie year. He dropped to 8-22 in 1974, becoming the third Padre (after Kirby and Arlin) to lose 20 games in a season. Jones was frequently victimized by lack of run support, but he'd quickly turn his fortunes—and the Padres'—around.

Born January 12, 1950, Jones became the Padres' first true ace in 1975, posting a 20-12 mark with 6 shutouts and a league-best 2.24 ERA. He was the Padres' representative on the '75 N.L. All-Star team and threw the final inning.

Jones finished second to the Mets' Tom Seaver in the Cy Young voting. This amazing performance earned him the 1975 Comeback Player of the Year award; rarely in baseball history has a pitcher immediately turned a 20-loss season into a 20-win season. Jones won a staggering 28% of the Padres' victories that year. But the best was still ahead.

In 1976, Jones turned in the greatest season ever (22-14, 2.74) by a Padre pitcher, leading the league in victories, complete games, starts, and innings pitched. He threw 25 complete games, 5 shutouts, and an amazing 315 innings—figures unheard of today. Helping himself in the field as well, Jones set a record for pitchers by handling 112 chances without committing an error.

On July 22, Jones tied Christy Mathewson's N.L. record of 68 consecutive innings without allowing a walk.

"I didn't even know about there being a record until we're in St. Louis one night and (pitching coach) Roger Craig told me I was at 54 innings and the record was 68," he said. "That's when I got nervous. I had a lot of three-ball counts before I got to 68."[23]

Jones tied the record by striking out the Giants' Darrell Evans to end the seventh inning. The first batter in the top of the eighth was Marc Hill, who worked Jones to a full count and then fouled off two pitches. Jones missed with his next delivery, settling for a tie with the great Matthewson.

The record stood for twenty-five years before it was broken by the Braves' Greg Maddux.

How dominating was Jones in his 1976 campaign? He set a modern National League record with 16 wins at the All-Star break. *Sports Illustrated* featured Jones on its cover in July under the heading, "Threat to Win 30". Indeed, he was on pace to become baseball's first 30-game winner in eight years, a feat not accomplished since. He was the consensus choice to start the '76 All-Star game and recorded the victory over the American League.

Unfortunately, his quest for 30 wins fell victim to low run support, especially in the second half. Jones lost seven games by one run, two by 1-0 scores.

After finishing a close second the year before, Jones easily won the Cy Young Award in 1976. His 22 victories that season remain a team record.

In contrast to many young pitchers today, Jones worked quickly, which helped keep his defense on their toes. Jones also jump-started attendance in San Diego, pitching before large, enthusiastic crowds throughout his two amazing seasons. His heroics were principally responsible for establishing a permanent fan base in San Diego.

In his final start of 1976, Jones felt a tear in his left forearm. The stress of so many innings had taken its toll, and a nerve attached to his biceps tendon was severed. His career was never the same.

Jones remained with the Padres through the 1980 season, never coming close to Cy Young consideration again. These are the years he called "futility and frustration". He fell to 6-12 the following season, and 13-14 with a respectable 2.88 ERA in 1978.

On May 13, 1979, Jones became the first Padres pitcher to ever steal a base. 1980 was his final season in San Diego. He spent two injury-filled years with the Mets and retired in 1982.

Today, Padres statistics are dominated by the name Randy Jones. He ranks second on the team in wins (93), and first in starts, complete games (more than twice any other Padre), innings, and shutouts. His number 35 was retired by the Padres, and a banner in his honor flies proudly over the stadium.

Today, Randy Jones is still very much a part of the Padres family. Fans hear his analyses on pre-game and post-game radio broadcasts. He also has his famous barbecue stand at the stadium, where fans line up for the "Cy Young Special" and other mouth-watering dishes served up by the one-time ace. Jones is frequently seen mingling with fans near his barbecue stand, sharing stories and signing autographs.

"Life is good…I love what I do. I love the interaction," he says. "I sign for the kids, and then I have to convince them that I was a major leaguer at one time."[24]

**Baby steps** In 1975, for the first time in their seven-year existence, the Padres escaped the cellar of the National League West. San Diego won 71 games against 91 losses, an 11-game improvement over the year before. Despite avoiding last place, the Padres were still 37 behind Pete Rose, Joe Morgan, and the rest of the world champion Big Red Machine.

Prior to the season, the Padres swung a trade that worked better than their previous deals. On December 8, 1974, infielder Derrel Thomas was sent to the San Francisco Giants for second baseman Tito Fuentes and pitcher Butch Metzger.

"We got the best of the trade," said the Cuban-born Fuentes, who was thrilled to be coming to San Diego. "The Giants have traded away their most popular players—Mays, McCovey, Bonds, now me."[25]

Considered a bit of a hot dog, Fuentes was the Padres' regular second baseman for two seasons (1975-76). The switch-hitter led the Padres in hitting (.280) his first season with the club, though he possessed little power or speed.

The Padres' offensive leaders in 1975 included Fuentes, Grubb (.269), Winfield (.267, 15 HR—yet to hit his stride as a perennial All-Star), and McCovey (a team-leading 23 HRs).

Remember, it is impossible to compare these with today's statistics, especially with the higher, deeper fences at San Diego Stadium in the 1970s. For several reasons, baseball is a much more offense-oriented sport today than twenty or thirty years ago, when pitching, speed, and defense were at the heart of the game.

On May 30, McCovey belted his 16th lifetime grand slam, tying Hank Aaron's N.L. record, a mark he'd later break. It was the third pinch-hit grand-slam of his career, tying the major league record.

Jones came close to pitching the Padres' first no-hitter on May 19, 1975. The game went ten innings, and the only hit he allowed was a seventh-inning single up the middle to the Cardinals' Luis Melendez.

Jones joined Kirby and Arlin on the list of Padres who came so close to a no-hitter.

**Rookie of the Year** San Diego continued to inch forward in 1976, ending the season with 73 wins and 89 losses—two games better than the previous season and again avoiding last place (Atlanta now perennially occupied the cellar). But there was still a high mountain to climb; the Padres found themselves 29 games behind the Reds, who repeated as world champions.

Most encouraging was the increase in attendance: The Padres drew nearly 1.5 million in 1976, fifth-best in the league. Just three years earlier, attendance at San Diego Stadium was *one-third* of that total. The credit for this revival can be attributed to Jones' phenomenal performance.

Unfortunately, the offense was still abysmal. The Padres were near the bottom in batting, home runs, slugging, and runs scored. Jones truly may have won 30 in 1976 if he'd had any reasonable support. Winfield hit .283 with 13 HRs and 26 stolen bases, despite missing the last month with a leg injury.

Long-time Dodger Willie Davis, who manned centerfield in L.A. for thirteen seasons, joined the Padres in 1976. In his only season with the Padres he hit .268 with 14 steals. He played in Japan the next two years before appearing briefly with the Angels in 1979, his final season.

McCovey's production tailed off sharply in 1976. He was hitting just .203 and his power numbers were down significantly. It looked as though his long career had finally hit the wall. The Padres sold "Big Mac" to Oakland, where he played in only 11 games.

McCovey returned to the Giants in 1977, where he briefly revived his career. He retired in 1980 with a total of 521 home runs, a sure ticket for Cooperstown. Willie McCovey is one of five Hall of Famers to have once played for the San Diego Padres.

The National League Rookie of the Year voting in 1976 resulted in a tie between the Padres' Butch Metzger and the Mets' Pat Zachary. Metzger was acquired from the Giants in the Thomas/Fuentes deal.

Used strictly in relief, Metzger went 11-4 with 16 saves for the Padres during his outstanding rookie campaign. He actually won the first 12 games of his big league career, tying the record set in 1904. Metzger's 77 games that year set a rookie record. But like so many other bright young stars, he wouldn't be around San Diego for very long.

**$30 control tower**  After McCovey's departure in 1976, Mike Ivie became the Padres' full-time first baseman. His story is a peculiar one.

The club's number-one pick in the 1970 amateur draft, Ivie began his career as a catcher, but in the minor leagues he began to experience difficulty throwing the ball back to the pitcher. He even developed a phobia of this very basic task. From then on Ivie grew to hate the position, and he once refused to report to the team because they wanted him to play catcher.

The Padres tried him at third base, but he hated that position as well. After the 1977, season he finally wore out his welcome in San Diego and was traded to the Giants for Derrel Thomas. It was Thomas' second tour of duty with the Padres.

Ivie played six more seasons after leaving San Diego, spending his time as a first baseman, pinch-hitter, and DH. He actually had a clause written into his contract stipulating that he would never have to play catcher. Padres broadcaster Rick Monday once described him as "a forty-million-dollar airport with a $30 control tower."

# Respectability

THE PADRES WERE entitled to the first pick in the June 1974 draft. Their choice that year was Bill Almon of Brown University, who was named College Player of the Year. San Diego actually selected him three years earlier out of high school, but he opted to attend college instead.

Almon was an enormous disappointment, never living up to his much-hyped potential. He became the Friars' full-time shortstop in 1977, hitting .261, but by the following year rookie sensation Ozzie Smith had taken over the position. Almon stayed on as a utility infielder for the Padres through 1979.

The '77 Padres featured several new faces, but the results were essentially the same. The team placed next-to-last in the west, 29 games behind the Dodgers.

John McNamara had managed the Padres every year since Kroc purchased the club. But on May 28, 1977, he was replaced by Alvin Dark (Bob Skinner actually managed one game in the interim). McNamara later managed the Red Sox, where he'd be forever second-guessed for leaving Bill Buckner at first base in the famous sixth game of the 1986 World Series against the Mets.

Whereas McNamara had never played in the major leagues, Dark was an established star during baseball's golden era. He was the National League Rookie of the Year in 1948 and became a three-time All-Star shortstop. In the 1951 N.L. playoff, he singled and scored on Bobby Thompson's famous "shot heard round the world". Dark retired in 1960 with over 2,000 hits and a lifetime average of .289.

As a manager, Dark skippered the Giants, A's, and Indians, winning a world championship with Oakland in '74. He managed the Padres for the remainder of the 1977 campaign, winning 48 games against 65 losses. San Diego represented the last stop in his distinguished managerial career.

Kroc's
investments

Kroc continued to open his wallet, authorizing several expensive but significant acquisitions for 1977. The Padres signed free agent catcher Fiore Gino Tennaci—better known as Gene Tenace—after the 1976 season. The Italian backstop had been a postseason hero for the Oakland A's, whose three-time championship team was being dismantled by owner Charles O. Finley. The Padres were a happy beneficiary.

Tenace spent four seasons (1977-80) in San Diego, hitting .237 with occasional power. Despite the low average, Tenace had an excellent walk-to-strikeout ratio. To this day, his .403 on-base percentage as a Padre ranks *highest* in team history among players with at least 1,500 at bats.

Another former Oakland star was lured away from the ashes of Finley' dynasty via free agency. Flaunting his trademark handlebar mustache, relief pitcher Roland Glen (Rollie) Fingers signed a five-year contract with the Padres for the 1977 season. He had an immediate impact on his new ballclub, leading the league in appearances and saves en route to capturing the Rolaids Fireman of the Year award. Fingers had the greatest impact of any player acquired via trade or free agency during the Padres' first decade.

Fingers' acquisition made the young Metzger expendable. The Padres traded  the rookie of the year to St. Louis for pitcher John D'Acquisto early in 1977. The exchange of promising young pitchers didn't work for either side: Metzger suffered arm trouble with the Cardinals and was forced to retire the following season. Likewise, D'Acquisto was a disappointment for the Padres. For the duration of 1977, he won just one game with an ERA near seven.

The Padres' third significant acquisition before the '77 season came via trade. San Diego obtained outfielder George Hendrick from the Cleveland Indians for Grubb, Kendall, and shortstop Hector Torres. Kendall was the last of the original Padres.

Hendrick had a stellar year in San Diego, batting .311 with 23 home runs. He was named MVP of the team for 1977.

Besides Hendrick, the offense was led by Winfield, who finally had a breakout year (.275, 25 HRs, 92 RBIs). Winfield represented the Padres in the All-Star game at Yankee Stadium.

The outfield was rounded out by rookie sensation Gene Richards, who hit .290 with 56 stolen bases. On July 26, Richards tied the N.L. record (which has since been broken) by banging out six base hits in an extra-inning game.

1977 saw another Padre set a record, of sorts: Dave Kingman homered with four different teams during the season (Angels, Mets, Padres, and Yankees), the only time that feat has been accomplished.

During his short stint with the Padres, Kingman clouted 11 homers on his way to 442 lifetime.

The 1977 Padres finished 69-93, four games worse than the previous season. But fans sensed that the core of a solid team was coming together.

**First winning season** Fingers produced another outstanding showing in 1978, tying the major league record of 37 saves (broken several times since) with a nifty 2.52 ERA. Despite a 6-13 record, Fingers won his second straight Fireman of the Year award.

The future Hall of Famer slumped in 1979, saving just 13 games. After that season, Fingers added a devastating forkball to his repertoire. He made a strong comeback in 1980, winning his third Fireman award in four years. It was the first time that the Padres aggressively dabbled in the free agent market, and Fingers proved to be worth every penny. His 108 saves rank second on the Padres' all-time list.

The 1977 Padres were next-to-last in the league in ERA *and* batting. By adding a couple of pieces to the puzzle, 1978 became a very nice year for the ballclub, which finally achieved that long-sought respectability.

Dark lasted less than a full season as manager. He was replaced by pitching coach Roger Craig, the team's fifth manager, during spring training. Craig can boast of managing the Friars to their first season over .500. That's right: the Padres finished *84-78* in 1978, a 15-game improvement over the previous season!

Granted, the Padres still finished in fourth place, 11 games in back of L.A. But after years of discouraging last- or near-last place finishes, winning more games than they lost was a welcome turn-about. Attendance was nearly 1.7 million in 1978, with only four teams drawing more. The Padres were on the upswing, and San Diego was increasingly becoming a baseball town.

In Winfield, Richards, and Hendrick, the Padres boasted one of the most productive outfields in the game. Nonetheless, they offered a fat free agent contract to another outfielder during the winter, Oscar Gamble. Gamble was coming off a career year with the White Sox in which he clubbed 31 home runs, but there was no room for him in the Padres' crowded outfield. Gamble split time in leftfield with Hendrick in 1978, and neither was happy with the arrangement.

The Padres decided to make a move for another starting pitcher. Less than two months into the season, Hendrick was traded to St. Louis for Eric Rasmussen. Hendrick continued to enjoy a prosperous career after the trade. He hit around .300 for several more years and helped the Redbirds to the world championship in 1982.

Hendrick's departure meant more playing time for Gamble, who manned leftfield the rest of the season. Richards took over full time in center, with Winfield in right. But Gamble was a disappointment. He suffered minor injuries during the season and ended the year with just seven home runs. Had Gamble turned in the type of season he'd had the year before, the Padres might truly have contended for the division title. He was shipped to the Rangers after the season.

The Padres were high on the young Rasmussen, despite his 17 losses the year before. Rasmussen, who changed his name from 'Harry' to 'Eric' earlier in his career, showed that their confidence might be well placed, posting a respectable 12-10 mark after joining the Padres in 1978. But that was to be his only quality year in San Diego. By the following season he was splitting time in the bullpen, and he won just ten of thirty decisions over the next two years. The Hendrick-Rasmussen trade was another move the team was left to regret.

**Gaylord Perry** Another important addition to the Padres in 1978 came in the person of 40-year old Gaylord Perry. The Padres obtained Perry from the Texas Rangers on January 25, 1978 in exchange for middle reliever Dave Tomlin and cash.

Throughout his career Perry was repeatedly accused of throwing an illegal spitball. He made no efforts to dispel the allegations, believing he had a psychological advantage if the question was on hitters' minds. Perry even titled his autobiography *Me and the Spitter*.

The veteran right-hander had a sensational first season with the Padres. He won 21 games against just six defeats, becoming the second (and last) Padre to attain the 20-win plateau. Perry led the league in wins and winning percentage, and his 2.73 ERA was sixth in the league. His outstanding campaign earned Perry the Cy Young award in 1978, making him the second Padre in three years to capture the honor. Perry was the first pitcher to capture the award in both leagues (Pedro Martinez and Randy Johnson have since accomplished the feat).

Gaylord and his brother Jim combined to win more games than any other brothers, until the mark was broken by the Niekros. The Perrys remain the only pair of brothers to have each won a Cy Young award. In 1999, *The Sporting News* ranked Perry number 97 on its list of Baseball's 100 Greatest Players.

**Four Hall** In 1978, San Diego Stadium had the honor of hosting the 49th All-Star
**of Famers** game. Fingers and Winfield represented the Padres before the hometown faithful, leading the Nationals to a 7-3 victory. The mid-summer
classic also helped call attention to the Padres' surprisingly strong
season.

Speedy Gene Richards followed his stellar rookie campaign with a
.308 average and 37 steals in 1978. Known for choking far up on the
bat (something rarely seen today), Richards' career .291 average ranks
second in Padres history. Jerry Turner led the National League with 20
pinch hits and batted .408 as a pinch-hitter.

1978 was easily the Padres' finest season to date. San Diego
claimed the Cy Young winner (Perry) and Fireman of the Year (Fingers),
and nearly boasted a third award—Rookie of the Year. Only the
Braves' Bob Horner edged out the Padres' Ozzie Smith.

Osborne Earl Smith is almost universally regarded as the greatest defensive
shortstop of all time. Nicknamed the
"Wizard of Oz" for his defensive bril-
liance, he played just 68 games in the
minors and became the Padres' everyday shortstop in 1978. Ozzie's early offensive numbers were not strong, but he
hit a respectable .258 with 40 steals in
his rookie year to go with his sensational
defense.

Early in his rookie year, Smith made
perhaps the greatest play of his career.
Ozzie dove to his left to field a hot shot
off the bat of Atlanta's Jeff Burroughs. At

During his four seasons in San Diego (1978-81), Ozzie Smith established him-self as the premiere defensive short-stop in the game. (Courtesy, Hall of Champions)

the last second, the ball took a bad hop and bounced over his head.
While in mid-air, Ozzie instinctively stuck up his bare hand, grabbed
the ball, crashed to the ground, bounced to his feet, and threw out the
runner.

Burroughs, father of the Padres' top prospect Sean, stood at first
base, dumbfounded. The play has been shown in countless highlight
films.

The '78 Padres boasted four future Hall of Famers on their roster—Perry, Fingers, Winfield, and Smith, who was elected to the Hall in
2002.

# The Doldrums

EMBOLDENED BY THEIR strong showing in 1978, San Diego had high hopes for the 1979 season. Other than unloading the underachieving Gamble, the team was essentially intact. But rather than building on their successes and moving forward, the Padres took a giant step back, dropping 93 games and barely avoiding last place. A thorough housecleaning was to follow.

Winfield certainly could not be faulted. He led the league in RBIs, won his first gold glove, appeared in his third straight All-Star game, and finished third in the National League MVP voting. It was his finest season as a member of the Padres.

But beyond Winfield, the offense was virtually nonexistent in 1979. The Padres were last in the league in team batting. Smith's average dropped to .211, though he stole 27 bases, rarely struck out, and continued to establish himself as the best defensive shortstop in baseball.

The pitching fared much better; San Diego's team ERA was fifth-best in the league. Jones went 11-12 and Bob Shirley was 8-16. Perry dropped to 12-11, albeit with a sharp 3.08 ERA. Perry joined Winfield on the All-Star team in Seattle.

Manager Roger Craig, who guided the Padres to their first winning season just the year before, was fired immediately after the 1979 season. In selecting his replacement for the start of the new decade, the ballclub made a bold and unconventional move.

**Ohhh, Doctor!** Padres fans young and old are familiar with Jerry Coleman's trademark "Ohhh Doctor!" and his famous, "You can hang a star on that one!" Coleman, a fixture on Padres broadcasts for most of the team's existence, is enormously popular with fans in San Diego. With over 30 years behind the mike, Jerry *has* committed the occasional verbal gaffe, some of which have become legendary. Among his more famous:

*"It's a base hit on the error by Roberts."*

*"Montreal leads Atlanta by three, 5-1."*

*"That noise in my earphones knocked my nose off and I had to pick it up and find it."*

*"The first pitch to Tucker Ashford is grounded into left field. No, wait a minute. It's ball one. Low and outside."*

*"That's Hendrick's 19th home run. One more and he reaches double figures."*

*"If Pete Rose brings the Reds in first, they ought to bronze him and put him in cement."*

*"There's a deep fly ball...Winfield goes back, back...his head hits the wall...it's rolling towards second base!"*

*"Grubb slides into second with a standup double."*

*"Davis fouls out to third in fair territory."*

*"There's a shot up the alley. Oh, it's just foul."*

*"That's the fourth extra base hit for the Padres—two doubles and a triple."*

*"Last night's homer was Willie Stargell's 399th career home run, leaving him one shy of 500."*

*"The Padres, after winning the first game of the doubleheader, are ahead here in the top of the fifth, and hoping for a split."*

*"At the end of six innings of play, it's Montreal 5, Expos 3."*

*"Tony Taylor was one of the first acquisitions that the Phillies made when they reconstructed their team. They got him from Philadelphia."*

*"Hector Torres, how can you communicate with Enzo Hernandez when he speaks Spanish and you speak Mexican?"*

*"I sure hope you're staying alive for the upcoming Dodgers series."*

*"Rich Folkers is throwing up in the bullpen."*

*"The way he's swinging the bat, he won't get a hit until the twentieth century."*

*"They throw Winfield out at second, but he's safe."*[26]

**Jerry Coleman**  That's all part of Jerry's appeal, and helps to explain his popularity. Fans can *relate* to him. He makes the occasional mistake, like the rest of us, but his experience and knowledge of the game are virtually unequalled in baseball today. And the fan within is never far from the surface.

Born September 14, 1924, Coleman spent nine years with the New York Yankees, playing alongside such immortals as DiMaggio, Mantle, Berra, and Rizzuto.

Jerry broke into the majors in 1949 and formed a graceful double-play tandem with Rizzuto. That season he led second basemen in fielding percentage. In his second season, he was named to the All-Star team and was voted World Series MVP.

But in 1951, Coleman suffered an injury and he never again reached that level of stardom. He played on a part-time basis through the 1957 season, when he retired with a career average of .263. Some say that before his injury, he was one of the best defensive second basemen of all time.

In his nine major league seasons, Coleman appeared in six World Series, of which the Yankees won four (1949-51, 1956). In a losing effort against the Milwaukee Braves in 1957, Coleman went 8-for-22 (.364), best on the Yankees.

After that season, Jerry moved to the broadcast booth where he paired with his old double play partner, Phil Rizzuto. Today he can be heard as the voice of the Padres, ever enthusiastic and insightful, alongside Ted Leitner on KOGO, AM 600.

Padres fans have more than one reason to be proud: Jerry also served our country in two wars, WW II and Korea. He earned two Distinguished Flying Crosses, 13 Air Medals, and three Navy Citations.

"When the war hit, your priorities went immediately into the service...I couldn't wait to get in."

**Off to the races** The hiring of a new manager was just one of many changes the Padres made for 1980. In particular, the team sought to add punch to the offense, and they were willing to sacrifice pitching to do it.

On February 15, 1980, Perry was traded back to the Texas Rangers for first baseman Willie Montanez. San Diego also included backup infielder Tucker Ashford in the deal. During his two seasons in San Diego, Perry posted an excellent record of 33-17 with a 2.88 ERA, so the Padres knew they were taking a risk. But Perry was 41 years old, and the team was looking for a proven left-handed bat behind Winfield. They felt Montanez fit the bill.

In the end, the trade was not a significant one; Montanez took over at first base and hit .274 with just 6 home runs. He was with the Expos by the end of the season. Perry was never as effective as he'd been in San Diego, and his long Hall of Fame career was nearing the end.

The same day as the Perry/Montanez deal, another pitcher was sacrificed for offensive help. The Padres acquired outfielder Jerry Mumphrey from Cleveland in return for pitcher Bob Owchinko.

In three-plus seasons with the Padres, Owchinko's record was 25-39, usually with respectable ERAs. He would spend the next six years with five different clubs, never putting together an effective season.

Mumphrey had a brilliant season as the Padres' centerfielder in 1980, hitting .298 with 52 stolen bases. The trade worked out well, at least in the short run. It was Mumphrey's lone season with the club.

Coleman had his players running at a record clip. On September 25, when Mumphrey swiped his 50th base of the season, the Padres became the first team in history to have three players with 50 stolen bases (the others being Smith and Gene Richards). Winfield added 23 steals.

Coleman brought his old-school style to the club in 1980, emphasizing conditioning, fundamentals, and more intense workouts. He had the Padres in better physical shape, and they easily led the league in stolen bases. All the running didn't translate into much scoring, however: the Padres were second-to-last in the league in runs per game. Their lack of power was largely to blame. As a case in point, Mumphrey stole 52 bases but scored just 61 runs.

Rookie infielder Tim Flannery appeared in 95 games in 1980, mostly at second base. During his freshman season, he became the subject of an urban legend. As the story goes, when he traveled to the east coast with the team for the first time, this California boy took a bottle of wine and cheese to the beach to watch the sunset—at night. He got an impromptu geography lesson.

Today, Flannery plays guitar and has recorded several albums. Padre fans recognize him as a fixture at Qualcomm Stadium, where he coaches third base for the team he's been associated with for 23 years.

Smith batted .230 in 1980 with 57 steals, a career-best. His 621 shortstop assists that season broke the record set in 1924. Smith also won the Gold Glove, the first of thirteen he'd win during his career. Richards led the majors in outfield assists with 21. He also hit .301 and stole 61 bases, fifth in the league.

John Curtis (10-8) was the only starter to reach double-digits in wins in 1980. Curtis was flanked by Jones, Steve Mura, and Rick Wise. Bob Shirley, Fingers, and John D'Acquisto were solid out of the bullpen. The staff ERA was 3.65, seventh in the league.

Jerry Coleman tried to bring his spark to the ballclub, but even he could do little with the Padres' punchless offense. Under his tutelage, the Padres finished with a record of 73-89, good for last place. After the season Coleman returned to the broadcast booth, where he was much more at home.

**Trader Jack** He was nicknamed "Trader Jack" because he loved to wheel and deal.

The Padres' revolving door during the 1980s could be attributed to new general manager Jack McKeon. Born November 23, 1930, the cigar-smoking McKeon never played at the major league level. He managed in the minors for 15 years before getting his first taste of the big show.

He was hired as manager of the Kansas City Royals in 1973, guiding the fifth-year franchise to a second place finish in the A.L. West. But halfway through the 1975 season, even though Kansas City was in second place, McKeon was fired. The Oakland A's hired him for the 1977 season, fired him in June, then *re*-hired him in early 1978.

McKeon was named Director of Baseball Operations (often referred to as 'general manager', or GM) for the Padres on September 23, 1980. He engineered the deals that brought a seemingly endless stream of new faces to San Diego. His zest for deal making was legendary, and when teams needed to make a trade, they often called McKeon first.

Throughout his decade with the organization, McKeon's trades were subject to endless second-guessing. His worldwind deals added an air of uncertainty to the clubhouse, with players coming and going and no one knowing who'd be next. But under McKeon's guidance the Padres not only became a .500 team again, but reached the unthinkable—the World Series.

**Jack Murphy Stadium** Jack Murphy, whose efforts were so instrumental toward bringing the Padres and Chargers to San Diego, died of cancer on September 24, 1980. Murphy was a member of the United States Marine Corps in World War II. He spent nearly 30 years as sports editor and writer for the *San Diego Union*.

In his honor, San Diego Stadium was renamed *Jack Murphy Stadium*—that is, until the financial realities of a 1997 expansion project resulted in one more name change.

**Major changes** Former Senators slugger Frank Howard became the Padres' new manager for 1981. Howard was a goliath of a man, standing 6'8", weighing 275 pounds. He won rookie of the year honors in 1960 with the Dodgers and was one of the game's most feared hitters throughout the 60s. Howard retired in 1973, 382 home runs later.

Trader Jack wasted no time engineering his trademark blockbuster deals. He began with an eleven-player trade with St. Louis on

December 8, 1980. San Diego sent Fingers, Tenace, Shirley, and a minor leaguer to the Cardinals in return for seven players, of whom catcher Terry Kennedy was the key (St. Louis immediately sent Fingers to Milwaukee as part of a three-team trade). McKeon wanted to make the team younger and to add a front-line catcher, and Kennedy was considered one of the best young receivers in the game.

TERRY KENNEDY

Terry Kennedy was a three-time all-star with the Padres from 1981-86. He has caught more games than anyone in team history. (Courtesy, Topps)

The next season, Fingers turned in one of the greatest performances ever by a reliever, capturing both the A.L. MVP and the Cy Young award as a member of the Milwaukee Brewers. Fingers retired in 1985 and was elected to the Baseball Hall of Fame in 1992. *The Sporting News* ranked him 96th on its list of Baseball's 100 Greatest Players—one notch ahead of Perry, his former teammate.

The same day as the Kennedy trade, McKeon acquired speedster Alan Wiggins from the Dodgers' minor league system in the annual winter draft. Wiggins set a minor league record with 120 stolen bases at Class A.

The next week saw the biggest change of all for the Padres, and by far the most devastating. On December 15, 1980, Dave Winfield, the Padres career leader in virtually every offensive category, signed a ten-year free agent contract with the New York Yankees.

With the stroke of a pen, the Padres bade a sad farewell to their undisputed team leader. For eight years, through the force of his personality, community involvement, and heroics on the diamond, Winfield's name became synonymous with the Padres of the late-70s.

The Padres acknowledged that they couldn't afford the salary the Yankees were offering, and it was fully expected that Winfield would leave. One team official said ruefully, "we're back to being an expansion team again."

With that, the charismatic leader of the Padres was gone, taking much of the heart of the team with him.

That same day, Randy Jones, San Diego's career leader in virtually every pitching category, joined the other New York team. He was traded to the Mets in return for pitcher John Pacella and infielder Jose Moreno. The Mets knew of Jones' history of arm problems, but decided to take a chance on the veteran lefthander.

"I didn't want to leave, but I no longer figure in their plans here; it's time for a change," said Jones. "I know I've pitched some disappointing games the last four years, but I hope the fans here will remember a few of the good ones."[27]

McKeon shook things up again four months later. On April 1, Mumphrey and Pacella were traded to the Yankees for outfielders Ruppert Jones and Joe Lefebvre. In effect, the trade came down to Mumphrey for Jones.

Mumphrey enjoyed continued success after leaving San Diego, averaging around .300 for the duration of his career. Jones provided the Padres solid play for the next three seasons, but his numbers never compared to Mumphrey's.

Players were growing accustomed to McKeon's penchant for wheeling and dealing. In less than seven months on the job, Trader Jack had sent away a total of 21 players. It created an atmosphere of uncertainty in the clubhouse, one that would take some getting used to.

"It's a part of the game I hate," said Curtis. "However, I respect what McKeon is doing. He's determined to improve this team and he isn't being wishy-washy."[28]

Answering allegations that the ballclub was concerned only with saving money, McKeon countered that the 1981 payroll held steady at $3.4 million. The team's entire payroll twenty years ago was about the same as a player's average salary today.

**Strike!** Players and fans had little to cheer about in 1981, which is indelibly stamped into fans' minds as the "strike season". An ongoing dispute between players and owners, centering around the issue of free-agent compensation, resulted in a work stoppage from June 12 to July 31. In all, the strike forced the cancellation of 712 major league games.

It is difficult to envision a more depressing sight than 26 major league stadiums sitting empty through the heart of the summer. The Padres lost 52 games to the strike, almost a third of the season.

When play resumed, the Padres ended the 1981 season with a woeful record of 41 wins against 69 losses, in last place once more. Favorites like Winfield were gone, taking much of the team's passion with them. It was difficult for fans to feel much excitement anymore. On top of this was lingering resentment over the strike.

The Padres drew less than 10,000 per home game in 1981, or 22% of what the world-champion Dodgers drew. The Padres' average attendance was not only last in the league, but less than *half* the league average.

**Terry Kennedy and Luis Salazar** Among the bright spots for the Padres that season was catcher Terry Kennedy, who was acquired in the Tenace/Fingers deal. Standing 6'4", 224, he was an imposing figure behind the plate. Kennedy was the Padres' starting catcher from 1981-86. He batted .301 as a rookie, and together with Ozzie Smith represented the Padres on the '81 All-Star squad.

Luis Salazar played mostly third base and hit .302 in 1981. A native of Venezuela, Salazar spent three tours of duty with San Diego, mostly as a reserve infielder. Salazar played a total of 551 games at third base—more than anyone in Padres history (Caminiti was a close second, with 547 games played at the hot corner).

**Smith for Templeton** One of Trader Jack's most famous—or infamous—deals was executed after the 1981 season. In a straightup swap of shortstops, Smith was traded to the Cardinals for Garry Templeton. The Padres hit rock bottom in 1981, and the front office was desperate to reignite the club by whatever means necessary.

It's a deal that still makes fans wonder, *What might have been?*

McKeon saw a more potent offensive force in Templeton, who hit over .300 with good speed during his five seasons with St. Louis. As it turned out, Templeton was a solid player for San Diego throughout the 80s, but he never realized the productivity he'd enjoyed with the Cardinals.

Meanwhile, Smith remained a perennial gold-glover and All-Star, improved his offense considerably, and led the Cardinals to four postseason appearances, including the 1982 world championship.

"Ozzie was a virtuoso, an absolute genius in the field," said Curtis. "We'll miss him as a talent and as a person, but I know what Templeton can do, he's an incredible talent."

"I don't think the fans in San Diego will worry much this season about him being gone," said coach Jack Krol.[29]

At the time it looked like a fair trade, one that might even favor San Diego. With the Cardinals from 1976-81, Templeton was the game's best all-around shortstop. In 1977 he became the youngest shortstop to reach 200 hits, and he finished second in the league with a .322 average. The switch-hitter had a monster season in 1979, becoming the first player in history to record 100 hits from both sides of the plate.

At the All-Star break in 1979, Templeton was leading the league in hits, and he led N.L. shortstops in virtually every offensive category. Yet he finished fourth in the All-Star balloting, behind Larry Bowa, Dave Concepcion, and Smith. Although he was named to the All-Star squad as a backup, Templeton uttered his famous proclamation: "If I ain't starting, I ain't departing."

By 1981, Templeton had worn out his welcome in St. Louis. He made an obscene gesture to fans at Busch Stadium who booed when he failed to run out a ground ball. Templeton asked to be traded, and he soon got his wish. The Cardinals and Padres both sought to replace their respective shortstops, and the situation was tailor-made for a trade.

The Padres wanted more pop out of the position. In four seasons in San Diego, Smith batted only .231 with a total of one home run. With those numbers, Kroc was not willing to meet his salary demands for 1982. By contrast, Templeton's offensive skills were exactly what the Padres wanted from their shortstop. They were willing to take a risk on the personality clashes and off-field problems Templeton experienced in St. Louis.

Originally the teams planned a four-player deal, with Smith and pitcher Steve Mura going to the Cards for Templeton and outfielder Sixto Lezcano. The Mura-Lezcano trade was consummated December 10, 1981, but because of technicalities that had to be worked out, the Smith-Templeton deal became a separate transaction.

Lezcano turned in a respectable season (.289, 16 HRs, 84 RBIs) for San Diego in 1982, his only season with the club. Mura, who'd gone just 5-14 for the Padres in 1981, went 12-11 for the Cardinals after the trade, helping them to their '82 world championship. After the World Series, Mura won just one more game. The Lezcano-Mura deal was essentially a wash.

The same couldn't be said for the Templeton-Smith trade. Playing on the natural grass at Jack Murphy Stadium as opposed to the batter-friendly turf of Busch Stadium, Templeton's stats were never the same. In his first season with San Diego, he stole 27 bases but his average fell to .247. Templeton had his finest year as a Padre in 1985, when he hit .282, was named to the All-Star team, and was voted the team MVP. But his output declined from there.

Templeton never experienced the public-relation problems that plagued him in St. Louis. He became popular with teammates and fans, and several players praised his leadership as critical to the club's success in 1984. But he could never escape the comparisons with Ozzie Smith, the greatest defensive shortstop of all time and a first-ballot Hall of Famer.

# Rebound

AFTER SUCH A dreary season, 1982 showed little promise. But a few surprises were in store.

In yet another managerial change, Frank Howard and his entire coaching staff were fired. Howard was replaced by Dick Williams, the team's sixth manager in just over five years. He was the Padres' eighth manager overall.

Born May 7, 1929, Dick Williams came up as a rookie with the Brooklyn Dodgers in 1951. He played with Brooklyn, the Baltimore Orioles, Cleveland, the Kansas City A's, and Boston. For his career he hit .270 with 70 home runs.

One of the winningest managers in baseball history, Williams first skippered the Red Sox in 1967. His Sox lost a heart-breaking seven-game World Series to St. Louis that year. Williams managed Boston for three seasons, but he was fired after a feud with Carl Yastrzemski and other players. It was not the first time a personality conflict cost him a job.

His next stop was Oakland. Williams led the Athletics to a first-place finish in the A.L. West in 1971, and then guided the A's to world championships in 1972 and 1973. But he quit immediately after the '73 World Series over a dispute with owner Charles O. Finley. Williams then spent two years as manager of the California Angels.

Williams headed the Montreal Expos from 1977-81, where he posted two second-place finishes and one division title. But despite his successes, he was fired. The Padres hired him for the 1982 season, and he worked his magic to guide the Friars to their first "glory years".

Williams led San Diego from 1982 through 1985. He compiled a record of 337-311, which makes him the second-winningest manager in team history. The Padres became the third team Williams led to the World Series, which ties the major league record. For his career, he had a managerial record of 1,571 wins and 1,451 losses over 20 seasons. Williams was hard-edged, stubborn, and emotional, and often butted heads with his players. But few could argue with his results.

Williams led the Padres to at least a .500 record in each of his four years at the helm. No other manager in team history can claim such an accomplishment.

**Assembling a winner** The Padres reached the .500 mark in 1982, rebounding impressively from their disastrous '81 campaign. Templeton anchored the infield at short, with Broderick Perkins at first, Flannery at second, and Salazar at third. In the outfield were veterans Lezcano, Richards, and Ruppert Jones—all solid but not spectacular players.

Jones was the Padres' lone representative on the '82 All-Star team, ending the year at .283 with 12 HRs and 18 stolen bases. But the real star of the team was Kennedy, who followed up his stellar rookie performance with a huge year (.295, 21 HRs, 97 RBIs). He had 42 doubles on the season—40 as a catcher, which tied Johnny Bench's record.

Speedster Alan Wiggins originally came up as an outfielder/first baseman in 1982. Wiggins was blessed with enormous natural talent, but his career was plagued by persistent problems with drug abuse. The rookie was arrested on July 21 for cocaine possession. He agreed to enter treatment and was suspended for one month.

"The thing that's sad is here's a young athlete who has made tremendous progress in the last year, and now he's involved in a career-threatening activity...We're not going to condone this behavior," said team president Ballard Smith.[30]

The pitching staff was headed by Tim Lollar, who won 16 games with a fine 3.13 ERA in 1982, coming back from a dreadful '81 season. After his big year, Lollar looked like an emerging star, but he developed elbow problems and he was never the same.

Another promising young pitcher of the early-80s was Dave Dravecky. Acquired as a minor leaguer in a steal from Pittsburgh, Dravecky went 5-3 as a rookie in 1982. In '83 the southpaw won 14 games and represented San Diego in the All-Star game. Rookie pitcher Eric Show (which rhymes with 'how') won ten of sixteen decisions to go with an excellent ERA of 2.64. Between Lollar, Dravecky, and Show, the Padres had one of the brightest young staffs in the game.

Show eventually became the winningest pitcher in Padres history, totaling 100 victories from 1981-90. He finished his career with Oakland in 1991. That year, he may have become the first player to go on the disabled list for biting his nails and infecting his thumb.

**Mr. Padre** 1982 also saw the debut of Mr. Padre: Anthony Keith Gwynn.

Tony Gwynn was born May 9, 1960. "For me, it's a challenge. I don't care, lefty, right-hander, soft thrower, hard tosser, I don't care, I'm going to go up there and take my hacks and see what I can do. It's still fun and it's still the greatest job in the world."[31]

Gwynn attended Long Beach Polytechnic High School and San Diego State University. He hit .423 in 1980 and .418 in '81, when he was an NCAA All-American.

Tony Gwynn was an outstanding point guard at San Diego State. He was drafted by the Padres and the NBA's Clippers on the same day. (Courtesy, Hall of Champions)

In addition to baseball, he was an outstanding point guard on the San Diego State basketball team. He set Aztecs records with 590 assists, including 221 assists in a season. To this day, he is the only athlete in WAC history to be recognized as All-Conference in two sports.

On June 9, 1981 Gwynn was drafted by teams in two sports on the same day—the Padres and the NBA's Clippers. Fortunately for the Padres, Tony chose baseball. In rookie ball he won a batting title and the MVP award, and by mid-1982 he was wearing a Padres uniform.

Tony made his major league debut on July 19, 1982. Facing the Phillies' Sid Monge in the bottom of the eighth inning, Gwynn smoked a 1-2 curveball for a double—the first hit of his major league career. Pete Rose was playing first base for Philadelphia, and as Gwynn rounded first Rose shouted to him, "Don't catch me in one night!" Rose, who'd soon become baseball's all-time hit leader, went to second base to shake Gwynn's hand.

The list of Tony Gwynn's accomplishments could easily fill the remainder of this book:

- *Eight batting titles (1984, 1987, 1988, 1989, 1994, 1995, 1996, 1997). Those eight titles tie him with Honus Wagner for the N.L. record.*
- *Five other seasons finishing in the top five in batting (1985-86, 1991-93).*
- *A sixteen-time All-Star (1984-87, 1989-99, 2001). He was voted to start the All-Star game 11 times, the most ever by a N.L. outfielder.*

- *Five Gold Gloves (1986-87, 1989-91).*
- *Seven times finishing in the top-ten in N.L. MVP voting.*
- *Seven-time team MVP.*
- *The highest single-season batting average in 53 years.*
- *Five of the top eleven single-season averages since World War II.*
- *Nineteen straight seasons of .300 or better—another N.L. record.*
- *The Padres' all-time leader in virtually every offensive category, except home runs, where he's third behind Colbert and Winfield.*
- *Ranked number 39 on SABR's (Society for American Baseball Research) list of the 100 Greatest Baseball Players of all time.*
- *Placed 49<sup>th</sup> on the Top-100 list compiled by The Sporting News.*

Gwynn possessed excellent speed early in his career. He stole a high of 56 bases in 1987 and has over 300 lifetime steals. He tied a record with five stolen bases in one game.

Only in his rookie season did Gwynn strike out more times than he walked. For his career, he fanned an average of only once every 22 at bats. (By way of comparison, Hall of Famer Reggie Jackson struck out once for every four at bats.)

The term "5.5 hole" was coined by Gwynn to refer to the spot between the third baseman (which is designated, for defensive scoring purposes, as the number-five position), and the shortstop (the number-six position). The left-handed Gwynn excelled at taking pitches the other way, through the "5.5 hole" into left field.

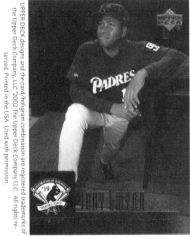

Considered one of the greatest pure hitters of all time, Tony Gwynn leads the Padres in virtually every offensive category. (Courtesy, Upper Deck)

Gwynn works at his hitting incessantly. He spends hours studying videotapes of his previous at-bats against individual pitchers. Nicknamed "Captain Video" by his teammates, he paid almost $100,000 to install a state-of-the-art videotape facility in the Padres clubhouse. He encouraged teammates to study and analyze tapes of their at-bats as well. He spent countless hours counseling teammates, especially younger players, on the art of hitting, freely sharing the wisdom of 20 years in the major leagues.

Tony Gwynn is widely regarded as one of the greatest pure hitters of the modern era. Were it not for a number of stints on the disabled list, including injuries to his wrists, knees, feet, hamstrings, Achilles' tendon, and other various ailments, Gwynn might well have approached 4,000 hits and, just possibly, Rose's record.

What's most remarkable is that Tony has done it all with one team, the San Diego Padres.

Tony has not only been faithful to his club, but he's also contributed generously back to the community. He and his wife Alicia have benefited numerous causes in the San Diego area for two decades. The Tony and Alicia Gwynn foundation focuses on helping children in need. In 1999, Tony was inducted into the World Sports Humanitarian Hall of Fame.

Tony Gwynn is, indeed, Mr. Padre.

**Meeting Tony Gwynn** Earlier I mentioned my friend Isaac, a lifelong Padres fan. While he was in college, Isaac was working at Cal's Sporting Goods when Tony Gwynn walked in. Tony was exhausted, having undergone another day of grueling rehab. He came to buy shoes for everyone on his son's basketball team.

Isaac recalls: "When he walked in, I was in awe…I said to a co-worker, 'My God, that's Tony Gwynn!' But he didn't *act* like a star—he was a modest man.

"He was obviously exhausted. His eyes were bloodshot from lack of rest, but he was still friendly. He needed basketball shoes for his son's team. No matter how tired he was, he found time to laugh and joke with us. And even though he must have been very busy, you could tell he took an active part in his son's team."

**I look like a taco** The Padres exceeded all expectations with their 81-81 season in 1982. They posted an identical 81-81 record the next season, even scoring the same number of runs as they allowed (653). In each year the Padres finished in fourth place, eight games behind Atlanta in 1982, and ten in back of Los Angeles in '83. The team's slow-but-sure recovery was bringing fans back to the park.

Players witnessed several personnel changes which laid the foundation for the Padres' World Series appearance a year later. The first of those blockbuster moves was the signing of free agent first baseman Steve Garvey.

Garvey's major league career spanned nearly twenty years. He came up with the Dodgers in 1969 and became part of the longest-running infield in baseball, with Davey Lopes at second, Ron Cey at third, and Bill Russell at shortstop from 1973-81.

1974 was Garvey's finest all-around major league season. That year he collected 200 hits, 21 HRs, and 111 RBIs to go with a .312 average. He won his first Gold Glove and made the All-Star roster as a *write-in* candidate. Garvey was named MVP of the All-Star game and was also the National League MVP in 1974, leading the Dodgers to the pennant.

STEVE GARVEY 1B

Signed as a free agent prior to the 1983 season, Steve Garvey's dramatic home run won game four of the '84 NLCS.
(Courtesy, Donruss)

From there on, Garvey was an All-Star with the Dodgers every year until 1981, and then with the Padres in 1984-85. He won four Gold Glove awards. Upon joining the Padres, Garvey enjoyed six seasons in which he hit .300 or better, five seasons of 100 or more RBIs, and six years with at least 200 hits.

On December 21, 1982, one day before his 34th birthday, Garvey signed a five-year, $6.6 million contract with the Padres. The Padres had reached the .500 plateau in 1982, and management felt that the best way to build on that was to add experienced, proven marquee players like Garvey.

"I had to go by my heart," he said. "I decided this was where I wanted to play…All I am is one player who has been consistent through the years. I've been on a winning team; I know what it takes to win."[32]

After trying on the Padres trademark brown, yellow, and orange uniforms (in contrast to the Dodgers' red, white and blue) Garvey joked, "I used to look like the American flag. Now, I look like a taco."

Williams praised Garvey's winning attitude and his reputation for hitting in the clutch. He called his new first baseman the 'All-American boy.'

Dodgers fans were shocked. When Garvey played his first game at Dodger Stadium as a visitor, he took out a full-page ad in the *Los Angeles Times* thanking fans for their support. In part, the ad read:

"It is 1983 and the uniform is no longer the same, nor are the colors or the name. But the man inside remains simple, dedicated, principled and with the same realization that you have been with me through the good times and bad for 13 years now…You taught me the power of hope, the virtue of patience, and the strength of dignity. I would like to dedicate the National League consecutive game record to you, not only for the past but also the present and future. With love and dedication—Steve Garvey."

In his first month as a Padre, Garvey played in his 1,118[th] consecutive game, breaking the National League record held by Billy Williams. Ironically, or perhaps fittingly, the event occurred at Dodger Stadium. *Sports Illustrated* featured Garvey on its April 25 cover beneath the heading, "The Iron Man".

Just three months later, Garvey's streak crashed to a halt. In a July 29 doubleheader against the Braves, the first baseman dislocated his thumb in a collision at home plate. He was forced to sit out the second game, thus ending his streak. The injury limited Garvey to 100 games in his first season in San Diego, when he hit .294 with 14 home runs.

Garvey's streak lasted a total of 1,207 games (September 3, 1975 through July 29, 1983). It still stands as the National League record. Among all major leaguers, only Lou Gehrig and Cal Ripken Jr. have played in more consecutive games.

**Bruce Bochy** Catcher Bruce Bochy joined the Padres in 1983. He was born April 16, 1955 in France, but grew up in the United States.

Bochy came up with the Houston Astros in 1978. In his first major league game he greeted the N.L.'s ERA champ, the Mets' Craig Swan, with two base hits. Bochy was Houston's backup catcher for three seasons before being dealt to the Mets. He spent 1981 in the minors and was called up to join New York for 17 games in 1982.

Needing a backup to Kennedy, the Padres acquired Bochy in 1983. Though used sparingly, he displayed occasional power at the plate. 'Boch' played with San Diego from 1983-87, hitting .232 with a respectable .420 slugging percentage.

After his playing days were over, Bochy's affiliation with the Padres was just beginning. Like Dick Williams, he'd be better known as a manager than a player.

**RAK** 1984 began on a sad note when Padres owner Ray A. Kroc passed away on January 14. He was 81. The team dedicated the season to the man who saved major league baseball in San Diego. A banner bearing Kroc's initials, 'RAK', flies atop Qualcomm Stadium today.

Joan Kroc continued to operate the club until 1990. She carried on her late husband's tradition of philanthropy throughout the community.

Ray Kroc did see his Padres reach respectability, but unfortunately he wouldn't live to see them make the postseason. In his honor, players wore the initials "RAK" on their sleeves throughout the 1984 season, all the way to the World Series.

# The First Pennant!

IF YOU WANT to elicit a nostalgic smile from any longtime Padres fan, just mention the year 1984. After 15 frustrating seasons, the Padres finally made it to the postseason. The Padres won 92 games against 70 losses, easily winning the National League West. San Diego was the only team in the division with a record over .500.

Statistically, the Padres didn't dominate the league. The team was fifth in ERA, batting, home runs, and stolen bases. They were also fifth in attendance, drawing a shade under two million—an increase of almost 25% over the year before, as San Diegans shed their reputation for indifference and caught baseball fever that magical summer.

While the Padres had their best year to date, Garvey experienced his weakest season at the plate in 1984. He hit .284 with 8 HRs and 86 RBIs, playing in all but one of the Padres' games. Though his range at first base was limited, he did not commit an error all season. His ability to scoop the ball out of the dirt saved his infielders numerous errors. Garvey was voted the starting first baseman in the All-Star game at Candlestick Park.

Tony Gwynn, who was quickly establishing himself as one of the game's superstars, led the Padres offense. Gwynn was voted to start the All-Star game that year, playing rightfield and batting leadoff for the National League. For the season, Tony collected a league-best 213 hits and won his first batting title with a .351 average. He also stole 33 bases and struck out only 23 times. He was second runner-up in the National League MVP voting.

Wiggins found a home at second base in 1984. He became the team's catalyst that season, drawing 75 walks and scoring 106 runs. Wiggins broke his own team record for stolen bases with 70.

The Padres were buoyed by other new faces that pushed the team over the top. Outfielder Kevin McReynolds was a homegrown talent who caught on full time in 1984. He hit .275 with 20 HRs and 75 RBIs in his first full season.

McReynolds was joined by another new face in the outfield, Carmelo Martinez. San Diego acquired Martinez before the season in a three-team trade involving the Cubs and Expos, in which the Padres also obtained reliever Craig Lefferts for pitchers Gary Lucas and Scott Sanderson. Summarizing his defensive capabilities, Martinez said (half-jokingly), "I only have trouble with fly balls."

Though slow-footed and hardly the game's greatest defensive player, Martinez was a patient hitter and showed occasional pop at the plate. He hit .250 with 13 HRs and 66 RBIs in 1984. Carmelo is the cousin of long-time Seattle DH Edgar Martinez.

**The Goose** Another veteran who had a tremendous impact on the Padres' surge was reliever Rich Gossage, better known as the "Goose". Gossage broke in with the Chicago White Sox in 1973 and spent a total of 22 years in the major leagues. His explosive fastball ranked with Nolan Ryan and other great power pitchers of the era.

After the 1977 season, Steinbrenner dug deep into his pockets and signed Gossage to a six-year free agent contract. The Goose didn't disappoint, leading the Bronx Bombers to a world championship in '78, winning his first Fireman of the Year award. During his six years in New York, no American League reliever registered more saves than Gossage.

But by then, Gossage had enough of the Steinbrenner's antics. Entering the free agent market once again, he signed a five-year contract with the Padres for roughly a million dollars per year, making him baseball's highest-paid relief pitcher.

Though several teams were bidding for the services of baseball's premiere closer, Gossage cited manager Dick Williams as a main reason he opted to sign with the Padres. Gossage also believed the Padres were close to making a run for a divisional title. His instincts were correct, of course.

In 1984, Goose went 10-6 for San Diego with a 2.90 ERA and 25 saves, fifth in the NL. He was another important key to the Padres' newfound success.

During his career Gossage was an All-Star nine times, including twice as a Padre. He recorded the save in the '84 All-Star game at Candlestick Park, retiring three of the four batters who faced him (Winfield connected for a two-out double). Gossage ended the game by striking out Rickey Henderson. It was Henderson's ninth strikeout in nine career at-bats against the Goose.

**"Balls"** Third baseman Graig Nettles, a native San Diegan, came home prior to the '84 season and made an enormous contribution to the pennant drive. Nettles was a fixture at third base with the Yankees for over a decade, leading the league in home runs in 1976, appearing in five All-Star games, and winning two Gold Gloves.

Summarizing his tenure with Steinbrenner's Yankees, Nettles made the famous statement, "Some kids dream of joining the circus, others of becoming a major league baseball player. As a member of the New York Yankees, I have gotten to do both." Nettles ended up in owner George Steinbrenner's doghouse after writing his autobiography *Balls*, which was highly critical of Steinbrenner.

At the end of spring training Steinbrenner, incensed by the book, retaliated by shipping Nettles to San Diego for pitcher Dennis Rasmussen. Yankees fans were shocked by the deal. *Newsweek* wrote, "Never before…has a book resulted in the sudden trade of its author." Steinbrenner denied trading Nettles because of the book, but to Yankees fans the motives were obvious. As a five-and-ten player, Nettles could not be traded without his consent, and he would only agree to go to San Diego, his hometown.

Although his offensive numbers tailed off somewhat, the 40-year old Nettles brought his veteran presence and postseason experience to the Padres clubhouse. "Puff" hit .228 with 20 HRs and 65 RBIs in less than 400 at bats, bringing his steady glove to the hot corner and solidifying the Padres infield.

**Basebrawl** The Padres' glorious season was marred by perhaps one unpleasant incident—the infamous brawl in Atlanta on Sunday, August 12, one of the ugliest in baseball history. The Padres had soundly beaten the Braves the previous night, opening up a ten-and-a-half game lead.

Atlanta's Pascual Perez drilled leadoff hitter Alan Wiggins on the first pitch of the game. The previous day, Wiggins had beaten out two bunt singles and stolen a base, and it looked like a clear case of payback.

Perez was known as a hot dog, jumping around the mound and pointing his finger like a gun after striking out a batter. "There isn't enough mustard in Georgia to cover Pascual Perez," said Padres manager Williams.

Ed Whitson started for the Padres. When Perez came to bat, Whitson threw a pitch behind him, which resulted in a warning for both sides. Late umpire John McSherry told Williams and Braves manager Joe Torre that the next brushback pitch would result in the ejection of the manager and pitcher.

In the fourth inning, Whitson threw three inside pitches at Perez, missing each time. On the third try, Whitson and Williams were ejected.

Rookie Greg Booker came on in relief. When Perez came to bat again in the sixth, Booker threw a pitch behind his back, but he also missed his intended target. McSherry immediately ejected Booker and acting manager Ozzie Virgil.

Tensions were mounting. Perez added to the atmosphere when he fielded a grounder in the seventh inning and made a gesture to the crowd before throwing to first.

Perez came to bat for a fourth time in the eighth inning. This time Craig Lefferts, now pitching for the Padres, finally found his target, drilling Perez on the left arm. That set off a ten-minute bench-clearing brawl. Six players and acting Padres manager Jack Krol were ejected.

Tony Gwynn was pulled away from the melee by batting coach Deacon Jones, who wrapped the league's leading hitter in a bear hug to protect him from injury.

In the ninth, the Braves' Donnie Moore nailed Nettles in the back. Nettles did what he had to, charging the mound, which set off a second bench-clearing brawl. It was one of the most brutal fights in baseball history, resulting in ten more ejections. Fans pelted Padres players with various objects and some even came onto the field, getting the police involved.

During the melee, Perez scampered back to the safety of the Braves' dugout. The Padres' Champ Summers came after him, but five Braves wrestled him to the ground before he got there. Injured Braves first baseman Bob Horner even came down to the dugout to protect Perez.

"There was one guy on the field who didn't forget that Perez was in the dugout," said Summers.

"Why would they throw at me?" asked Wiggins. "Maybe it was frustration on their part. I hadn't tried to show anyone up."

"These guys care for each other," said Flannery. "I've been on other teams that didn't stick up for each other."

Players on both sides escaped with no serious injuries. Kurt Bevacqua had scratches on his arms and chest, Flannery a puffed lip, and Lefferts several welts on his face. Templeton slightly twisted a knee and Nettles bruised his shoulder. "I was on the bottom of four different piles," joked Nettles. "I won't know how I am until tomorrow."

"There was no question in our minds that Perez hit Wiggins on purpose," said Williams. "He hit only two batters in 135 innings this year. It was totally deliberate. We know who started what and we were going to finish it. We weren't going to be intimidated."[33]

In all, the league handed out 17 ejections. Williams was slapped with a $10,000 fine and was suspended for ten days. Torre received a three-game suspension. The incident wasn't pretty, but it showed that the Padres were tough, resilient, and willing to stand up for one another.

**Celebration!** On September 20, 1984, the long wait was over. For the first time, the San Diego Padres were officially champions of the National League West!

The setting was Jack Murphy Stadium; the opponent was the San Francisco Giants.

The Padres scored all their runs in the second inning. Nettles singled, McReynolds walked, and Martinez was hit by a pitch to load the bases. Templeton then stroked a single, putting the Padres ahead, 2-0.

Lollar, the Padres starting pitcher and no easy out, did the rest of the damage. He hammered a three-run homer into the rightfield seats to put the Padres up, 5-0. It was Lollar's third homer of the year, and it proved decisive.

Dravecky struggled to hold the lead in relief. The Giants chipped away and sliced the margin to 5-4 in the ninth. Finally, with two out and the tying run aboard, Steve Nicosia grounded out to Wiggins at second base. The ballgame was over, guaranteeing the Padres at least a *tie* for the division.

"I looked around," said Nettles, a veteran of several postseason victories in New York, "and realized that there were no police on the field or no fans waiting to jump out of the stands. There's just a different atmosphere than there was in New York."

Bevacqua called the moment a dream come true. But he added, "We're missing one guy who should be with us, a man I really respected. I wish Ray (Kroc) was here to enjoy this."[34]

It was a surprisingly small crowd (16,760) that saw the Padres make history.

Still, the division wasn't won just yet. The Padres would have to wait another three hours for the end of the game between the second-place Astros and the Dodgers. The players gathered for a party at Gossage's house to await the outcome. Sure enough, the Dodgers disposed of the Astros behind rookie Orel Hershiser. The Astros' loss officially clinched the division for the Padres. The *real* celebration finally began!

Ray Kroc's widow, Joan, and her son-in-law, Ballard Smith attended the party. As the Houston loss was announced, Mrs. Kroc made the rounds to congratulate the players.

Gossage was enjoying his champagne, relaxing in the pool. The immaculately dressed team owner reached down to shake his hand. Gossage took Mrs. Kroc's hand and yanked her into the pool.

**The unfriendly confines** Garvey was the recipient of the 1984 Lou Gehrig Memorial Award. The award was established in 1955 to recognize the player who best exemplified the character of Lou Gehrig, both on and off the field. The first winner of the award was Alvin Dark, future Padres manager. Tony Gwynn won the honor in 1998.

The Padres had been in first place every day since June 9, finishing the season 12 games ahead of Atlanta and Houston. Reflecting the parity that existed in baseball at the time, from 1979-87 every team in the National League won at least one divisional title.

In the East, the Chicago Cubs outlasted the Mets to capture the divisional title. The tough-luck Cubs had not won a world championship since 1908, and hadn't even played in a World Series since 1945, setting the standard for futility. But 1984 finally looked like their year. Led by Cy Young winner Rick Sutcliffe and MVP Ryne Sandberg, the Cubs coasted to 96 wins, taking the division over New York by six and a half games.

The stage was set for a showdown between the Padres and Cubs in the N.L. Championship Series. The "experts" almost universally picked the Cubs, and indeed they looked formidable: Chicago easily led the league with 4.73 runs scored per game (San Diego was fourth with 4.23), and the Cubs would have their ace Sutcliffe going twice. Sutcliffe, who was later a Padres broadcaster, went an amazing *16-1* and helped spark the Cubs' turnaround after he was acquired from Cleveland in a midseason trade. The rest of the Chicago staff was average, with only Steve Trout (13-7, 3.41 ERA) winning more than ten games.

Ironically, the Padres' McKeon wanted to acquire Sutcliffe the previous winter, but he backed away when Cleveland demanded McReynolds in return. Back in 1978, the Dodgers offered Sutcliffe and other young players to the Padres for Dave Winfield, to no avail.

Second baseman Ryne Sandberg had a monster season, batting .314 with 200 hits, 19 HRs, 84 RBIs, 19 triples, and 32 steals. He also won his second Gold Glove. The rest of the Cubs' lineup were no slouches either: Although aided by the 'friendly confines' of Wrigley Field, the Cubs' lineup was devastating from start to finish.

The series featured two of the most intimidating closers in the game, Gossage and Lee Smith. Smith recorded 33 saves in 1984, en route to becoming baseball's all-time career leader.

**Blowout**  The Cubs were baseball's lovable losers, but the decades of frustration never kept the faithful from coming in droves to Wrigley Field—truly one of America's great sports landmarks. At the time, Wrigley still didn't have lights (that would come four years later), and all games were played in the afternoon. All year the Cubs' improbable race for the divisional title rocked Chicago, and the Padres faced daunting odds coming into Wrigley for the first two games. The fans made a huge difference in games one and two, but the Padres would later benefit from the 'tenth man'.

Major league umpires went on strike just before the start of the playoffs and wouldn't return until the World Series. The championship series were called by high school and college umpires. As it turned out, there were no controversial plays that could have decided a game, though players grumbled about several calls, particularly the strike zone.

"The only people who think we're going to win this thing are me, my players, and coaches," said Williams of his underdog Padres.[35]

Game one of the NLCS was played on October 2, 1984 before a packed house at Wrigley Field. Sutcliffe was opposed by the Padres' Eric Show. It was one of the ugliest games of the year. Chicago blew the Padres away, 13-0. It was the largest margin of victory in a shutout in postseason history. Show was relieved by the ambidextrous Greg Harris, who tied a playoff record by giving up seven earned runs.

The Cubs scored two in the first, which turned out to be all they needed. They added three more in the third inning, then exploded for six runs in the fifth and a pair in the sixth. Bob Dernier and Ron Cey homered, and Gary Matthews connected twice. Even Sutcliffe joined the parade with a home run, his first in five years. It was the first time in league championship series history that a team hit five home runs in one game.

During the game, fans threw a smoke bomb at Gwynn. The rightfielder took it in stride: "When you come to Chicago, you have to expect to get ragged on. It's a tradition."[35]

**At the brink**  The Padres came back with Mark Thurmond in game two. The 28-year old southpaw went 14-8 with a fine 2.97 ERA for San Diego during the regular season. But before a raucous crowd at Wrigley, Thurmond was outpitched by Steve "Rainbow" Trout.

The Cubs scored all their runs in the first four innings. "I was getting behind in the count, and that's something I can't afford to do," said Thurmond, the second Padres starter to take an early shower.[36]

Andy Hawkins, Dravecky, and Lefferts shut the Cubs down the rest of the way, but the damage was already done. San Diego managed just two runs off Trout.

The Padres nearly tied it in the ninth. With McReynolds at first, the Padres down 4-2, and Lee Smith on in relief, Kennedy hammered a drive deep to left field.

The previous afternoon, with the wind blowing out, the ball would have carried for a game-tying two-run homer. But this day, without the benefit of the wind, Kennedy's drive was caught by leftfielder Henry Cotto against the wall to end the game. The final score was Chicago 4, San Diego 2. The Padres stood at the brink of elimination.

At the time, the NLCS was a best-of-five affair (today, it is best-of-seven), so the Cubs needed just one more victory to wrap it up. Only one team in history, the 1982 Brewers, had rebounded from a 2-0 deficit to win a five-game playoff series.

"It's not an impossible situation," said Wiggins. "We just have to be more aggressive. For some reason, we're not getting the breaks."[36]

Cubs fans were convinced that their decades-long drought was over. To take the series, San Diego would have to win all three remaining games, and they'd still have to face the indomitable Sutcliffe once more. Fortunately for the Padres, the rest of the series was to be played before the hometown faithful, as opposed to the hostile crowds in the windy city.

**Comeback** Thousands of frenzied fans were waiting for the Padres as the team jet landed back in San Diego. That night Dick Williams, Gossage, and other players led pep rallies at the airport and the stadium. San Diego was on fire with pennant fever, a new experience for the community. Suddenly the impossible—winning three straight against the Cubs—appeared inevitable.

Garry Templeton, acquired in the controversial trade for Ozzie Smith, was the Padres' catalyst and cheerleader in game three of the 1984 NLCS. (Courtesy, Hall of Champions)

"I'm an emotional person," said Gossage. "When I saw all those people, I told the guys on the bus I felt like we were 2-and-0 instead of 0-and-2...I saw a lot of love and appreciation in peoples' eyes."[37]

Game three featured Whitson for the Padres and Dennis Eckersley for the Cubs. The contest was witnessed by the biggest baseball crowd in San Diego history. Before the game Templeton played cheerleader, waving his cap to get the fans to their feet. The Padres shortstop wanted to break the tension and he took the initiative to pump up the crowd.

Templeton was indeed the Padres sparkplug in game three, leading with his glove and his bat. After making a sensational catch to snuff out a Cub rally in the first inning, Tempy stroked a two-run double in the fifth to give San Diego its first lead of the series.

The Padres scored three runs in the fifth inning and four more in the sixth, capped by a McReynolds home run. Whitson and Gossage combined on the 7-1 win. The Cubs' lead in the series was now two games to one. Not only were the Padres still alive, but the momentum seemed to shift overnight.

**"Gar-VEY!"** Game four, played before 58,346 on October 6, 1984, was one of the most dramatic and memorable games in playoff history. Scott Sanderson (8-5, 3.14) started for the Cubs. The Friars countered with southpaw Lollar (11-13, 3.91).

San Diego came out swinging in the first inning. Wiggins and Templeton singled, and Gwynn's sacrifice fly brought in the first run. Garvey's two-out double delivered the second run, giving the Padres a 2-0 lead.

But Lollar was unable to hold the lead. The Cubs went ahead 3-2 in the fourth inning on home runs by Jody Davis and Leon Durham.

In the San Diego fifth, pinch hitter Flannery singled, was sacrificed to second by Wiggins, and scored on a two-out single by Garvey. That chased Sanderson with the score even at 3.

In the sixth inning, McReynolds slid hard into second base, trying to break up a double play. He jammed his left wrist and had to be removed from the game. X-rays later revealed that the wrist was broken. The Padres' co-leader in home runs spent the rest of the postseason on the bench, his left arm wrapped in a cast. It was a devastating blow.

Despite the setback, the Padres appeared to have the game in the bag in the seventh. McReynolds' replacement, reserve outfielder Bobby Brown, drew a walk against reliever Tim Stoddard and stole second. Gwynn was intentionally passed, which brought up Garvey. The Padres first baseman was locked in that day, delivering a single to score Brown for his third RBI in as many at bats. Gwynn later scored on a passed ball by catcher Jody Davis. The Padres went up, 5-3, and the crowd could smell victory.

Relievers Hawkins and Dravecky held the Cubs in check through the middle innings, and the ball was handed to Gossage in the eighth.

But the seesaw battle continued as Chicago scored twice off the Goose to knot the score at 5.

The key out in the game was in the top of the ninth. With Lefferts on the mound, third baseman Ron Cey stepped in with two outs and the bases loaded. As the crowd held its breath, Cey grounded out to thwart the rally. The stage was set for a dramatic bottom of the ninth.

Lee Smith was summoned from the bullpen to preserve the tie and, hopefully for the Cubs, send the ballgame into extra innings. The Cubs' ace retired the first man he faced, but Gwynn came through with a single. Up stepped Garvey, the hottest man on either team. He'd already driven in runs in the second, fifth, and seventh innings. What further heroics could be in store for the Padres' 35-year old iron man?

With the count 1-and-0, Smith uncorked a 95-mph fastball down the heart of the plate. Garvey leaned into the pitch and deposited the ball over the right-centerfield wall. Game over, *Padres win 7-5!*

The series was tied up, two games apiece. Utter pandemonium ensued. The crowd chanted "Gar-VEY! Gar-VEY!" Garvey's teammates mobbed him even before he reached home plate and carried him triumphantly off the field. The scene could have been straight from a fantasy movie. It remains a memory forever etched in the minds of Padres faithful.

"I don't remember anyone, in one day, doing what Steve Garvey did today," said Williams. "Unbelievable."

The usually reserved Garvey could hardly conceal his excitement, pumping his fist as he rounded the bases. "This was very special. I came here with two goals. First, to help build a winner, a championship team. The second was to build a tradition."

"Did you see the Garv? I mean, usually all you get out of him is a little clap or a little fist, but he was going wild out there!" said Gwynn.

"These were probably as emotional a two games as I have experienced, except for the three-game sweep of Houston in Los Angeles in 1980," Garvey said. "The fans here this season got educated as to what a winner looks like, and they're responding to it."

Added Gwynn: "My legs are weary, my head's spinning, I can hardly speak. Can there be anything better than this?"[38]

Series finale  The fifth and final game of the series was held Sunday, October 7 in San Diego. Game five would determine which team—the Padres or the Cubs—advanced to the biggest prize of all, the World Series.

To get there, the Padres had to find a way through the seemingly invincible Sutcliffe. For San Diego, 15-game winner Eric Show took the mound, hoping to rebound from his drubbing in game one.

The game didn't start well for the Padres. Durham touched Show for a two-run homer in the first and Davis blasted another in the second, staking the Cubs to a 3-0 lead. For the second time in the series Show was given an early hook. Hawkins entered in relief.

Sutcliffe looked dominating, holding San Diego scoreless into the sixth inning. Down 3-0 and missing their leading power hitter, the Padres were 12 short outs from elimination.

But the Cubs' ace appeared to be tiring. Wiggins set the table in the home half of the sixth with a bunt single. Gwynn followed with a single and Garvey worked Sutcliffe for a walk. The bases were loaded with no outs. Nettles and Kennedy followed with consecutive sacrifice flies to cut the lead to 3-2.

Martinez drew a walk to start the seventh inning. He was on second base when pinch-hitter Flannery bounced a routine grounder to first. The Padres caught a huge break when the ball rolled through Durham's legs, which allowed Martinez to score the tying run. Wiggins followed with a single. With two runners on base, up stepped the last man the Cubs wanted to see in this situation, Tony Gwynn. It was the most clutch situation of the game, and probably of the season.

Gwynn chopped a hard ground ball up the middle. His immediate response was that he'd hit into a double play, and he put his head down to try to beat it out. But a few steps out of the box, he heard a sudden roar from the crowd. The ball bounced just past the reach of Sandberg into right-centerfield for a double. Flannery and Wiggins scored, and the Padres had a 5-3 lead.

Hawkins, Dravecky, and Lefferts didn't allow a run from the second inning on. The Padres added an insurance run and Gossage pitched the final two innings for the save. The Padres had accomplished the impossible, defeating the heavily favored Cubs 6-3, taking the series three games to two.

Garvey was named MVP of the series. Having previously won the award in the 1978 NLCS between the Dodgers and Phillies, Garvey became the first player to earn the distinction twice (Dave Stewart and Orel Hershiser later matched his achievement).

"The fans were the turning point," said Gwynn. "I don't think we believed we could come back. I know I didn't."

"The fans beat Sutcliffe down. He's only human; he could only take so much. It was deafening out there," said Thurmond.

"He (Sutcliffe) looked like he was going to blow us away," Gwynn said. "We knew we were in trouble if we didn't get something going in the sixth inning."

"I started to jump into Goose's arms, and remembered we still have some games left to play," said Kennedy. Those 'games left to play' were the 81st World Series!

"The involvement and the madness of the fans was a big part today and our tenacity was also a key. The fans were our tenth player. They were worth three runs to us. What a feeling to see the fans get involved the way they did in the sixth inning, when we were down and needed a lift."[39]

The San Diego Padres, once baseball's laughingstock who endured six straight last place finishes and were nearly driven out of town a decade earlier, were, at long last, champions of the National League!

# 1984

# The World Series!

THE PADRES SUCCEEDED in befuddling the 'experts' by upsetting the heavily favored Cubs. But they'd find themselves underdogs one more time, facing an even more formidable opponent in the Detroit Tigers, who were widely regarded as the best team of the decade. The Tigers were well rested, having dusted off Kansas City in a three-game sweep, while the Padres' draining series with the Cubs had gone the distance. Though the Reagan-Mondale presidential election was in full swing, San Diego fans set their focus on the city's first World Series.

The Tigers finished with a record of 104 wins and only 58 losses on the season, an amazing .642 winning percentage. Jack Morris, the master of a devastating split-finger, headed Detroit's pitching staff. Morris won more games during the 80s than anyone in major league baseball. He threw a no-hitter the first week of the season, and finished the year with 19 wins.

Detroit had its share of other stars, including Willie Hernandez, who won both the A.L. Cy Young and MVP awards in 1984. Hernandez's record on the season was 9-3 with 32 saves (and only two blown saves) to go with a 1.92 ERA, easily his finest season. Aurelio Lopez went 10-1 in relief, giving the Tigers the best lefty-righty bullpen duo in baseball. Starters Dan Petry and Milt Wilcox went 18-8 and 17-8 respectively, illustrating the tall order facing San Diego batters.

As imposing as their pitching was, the Tigers' batters were equally intimidating. Catcher Lance Parrish clouted 33 home runs during the regular season. Kearny High graduate Alan Trammell and "Sweet" Lou Whitaker provided one of the longest-running double-play combinations in baseball. Trammell would spend 20 years in the majors—all with the Tigers—and hit .314 in 1984. Whitaker, who spent 19 seasons with Detroit, hit .289 and won his second Gold Glove award in '84.

Kirk Gibson anchored the Tigers' outfield with a combination of power and speed (27 HRs and 29 stolen bases). Chet Lemon (20 HRs) and Darrell Evans (16 HRs) gave the Tigers a powerful lineup, backed by reserves Johnny Grubb and Ruppert Jones, both former Padres All-Stars.

Some called it the 'Fast-Food' series, McDonald's versus Domino's. (The Tigers were owned by Tom Monaghan, owner of Domino's Pizza.) Games one and two were played in San Diego; games three, four, and five in Detroit. The series would return to San Diego, if necessary, for games six and seven.

On October 9, 1984, before 57,908 screaming fans at Jack Murphy Stadium, Detroit manager Sparky Anderson, onetime Padres coach, exchanged scorecards at home plate with San Diego skipper Dick Williams. Anderson and Williams were teammates on the 1955 Fort Worth Cats, and they managed against each other in the 1972 World Series, with Williams' Athletics besting Anderson's Reds that year.

The designated hitter (DH) rule was implemented in the American League in 1973. In the World Series, the DH was used in even-numbered years, while pitchers had to hit in odd-numbered seasons. (The format has since changed—now, pitchers hit in games played in N.L. parks, while the DH is employed in A.L. venues.)

As 1984 was an even-numbered year, the Padres had to find a DH. They turned to veteran Kurt Bevacqua, a pinch hitter and utility man used sparingly during the season, to fill the bill. "He couldn't hit water if he fell out of a boat," said Tommy Lasorda of Bevacqua's offensive skills. Bevacqua once joked that he holds the record for "most games watched, career". He was perhaps best known for winning $5,000 in Topps' bubble-gum blowing contest a decade earlier, and for another stunt in which he caught five balls thrown off a 25-story building in downtown San Diego. The DH rule gave Bevacqua his one moment in the national spotlight, and he made the most of it.

**Helpless** Morris was the Tigers' starter for game one. Williams countered with lefty Thurmond, who was roughed up at Wrigley Field the week before.

This time out Morris was not his usual dominating self. After the Tigers took a 1-0 lead in the first on a Trammell RBI, the Padres came scrapping back. Garvey and Nettles banged out singles off the Tigers' ace and scored on Kennedy's two-run double. Kennedy was stranded at third when Bobby Brown (who had a dreadful series subbing for the injured McReynolds) grounded out. The Padres were up, 2-1.

The lead held until the fifth. But by then Thurmond had already thrown over one hundred pitches, and the Padres starter began to tire.

Thurmond surrendered a two-out double to Lance Parrish, bringing Larry Herndon to the plate. Everyone remembers the name Kirk Gibson from this series, but it was Herndon who provided the big blow for the Tigers in the first game. Herndon, a part-time leftfielder who hit only seven home runs on the season, deposited Thurmond's 110th pitch of the ballgame into the rightfield seats. With one swing of the bat, Detroit had a 3-2 lead, which remained the final score.

The Padres had chances to come back, most notably in the sixth and seventh innings. Nettles and Kennedy both singled to lead off the sixth. Salazar ran for Nettles, and Bobby Brown was called on to bunt them over. He struck out. Martinez was up next, and he also failed on a sacrifice attempt, striking out.

Morris then fanned Templeton, striking out the side to end the threat. Templeton said Padres hitters were overanxious at the plate, which was causing them to go after bad pitches. He could think of no one in the National League who possessed Morris' wicked split-finger, except perhaps for Bruce Sutter.

The Padres' most squandered scoring opportunity came in the seventh. Leading off the inning, Bevacqua drilled a shot down the rightfield line. The ball found its way into the 'Bermuda Triangle'—the stadium's uniquely-shaped bullpen area, where outfielders sometimes have to reach under chairs to fetch balls in play.

It was an easy double, but the Padres DH, never fleet of foot, tried to stretch it into a triple. In so doing, he was breaking one of baseball's time-tested rules: never make the first or third out at third base. Third base coach Ozzie Virgil, who waved Bevacqua around to third, was certain that he had an easy triple.

However, Bevacqua stumbled as he rounded second base. Whitaker, who had his back to the infield waiting for Gibson's throw, said the roar of the crowd told him that Bevacqua was probably trying for third. Gibson hit the cutoff man perfectly, and Whitaker turned and made a strong relay to nail the runner at third base.

"Did it feel helpless?" Bevacqua lamented. "As helpless as the people on the Titanic felt."[40]

Morris went the distance, scattering eight hits as the Tigers hung on for a 3-2 win. It was up to Ed Whitson, the Padres game two starter, to turn things around. It was a game San Diego had to win; no team had ever lost the first two games at home and came back to win a World Series.

**Bevacqua's fifteen minutes** Unfortunately, Whitson wouldn't survive the first inning. Whitaker, Trammell, and Gibson greeted the Padres starter with successive singles. Gibson stole second, and a sacrifice fly by Parrish scored Trammell. Third baseman Darrell Evans singled to plate Gibson, giving Detroit a quick 3-0 lead. Williams had seen enough; after just two-thirds of an inning Whitson was pulled. Andy Hawkins was called on once more to staunch the bleeding.

In fact, the bullpen shut out the Tigers the rest of the way; Hawkins threw 5 1/3 stellar innings, allowing just one hit and no walks. Lefferts threw scoreless one-hit ball over the last three innings.

The bullpen's heroics gave the offense time to claw back. Wiggins led off the bottom of the first with a bunt single against Tiger starter Dan Petry. Gwynn followed with a walk, then Garvey surprised everyone in the stadium with a sacrifice bunt, moving both runners over. Nettles drove in Wiggins with a sacrifice fly.

The Padres added another run in the fourth when Bevacqua singled to left, moved to third on a Templeton single, and scored when Bobby Brown grounded into a force at second.

The home team went ahead for good in the fifth. Nettles walked with one out, and Kennedy slapped a hard shot to second that looked like a double play. But the ball took a high hop and bounced off Whitaker's chest, putting runners at first and second. That brought up the man of the hour, Bevacqua.

Bevacqua had hit just .200 with one home run during the regular season, but he caught fire at the right time. Petry delivered an 0-and-1 slider, which Bevacqua drove deep over the leftfield wall for a three-run home run.

Bevacqua leaped high in the air as he reached first base. When he crossed home plate, he blew a kiss to his wife as he was mobbed by his teammates. The Padres took a 5-3 lead, which remained the final score. Anderson later revealed that he was annoyed by Bevacqua's demonstrative celebration as he rounded the bases. The Tigers' loss snapped Anderson's personal 12-game postseason winning streak.

In the series' first two games, Hawkins, Lefferts, and Dravecky had combined for 12 1/3 scoreless innings. Dating back to the Chicago series, the entire bullpen had logged 21 consecutive scoreless innings. Hawkins recorded the win in game two, Lefferts the save.

"They've shown us great relief pitching, and we haven't even seen the Goose yet," added the Tigers' Parrish.[41]

**The Motor City**  With the series split 1-1, the scene shifted to Tiger Stadium in Detroit for the next three games. Game three was played Friday night, October 12. Lollar was the starter for the Padres.

Yet again, another San Diego starter was rocked; Lollar, in his final appearance as a Padre, was the latest victim. He and two relievers tied a playoff record by issuing eleven walks.

The Detroit scoring began with two out in the second when Lemon singled. To the plate stepped third baseman Marty Castillo, who'd connected for just four home runs all season. With the count 1-and-2, Castillo smoked a fat fastball over the heart of the plate for a two-run homer. For the second time in three games, a light-hitting semi-regular burned the Padres with the longball.

In that same inning, still with two outs, Trammell doubled home Whitaker. Detroit loaded the bases against Lollar, ending his evening after he'd retired just five batters. Williams summoned rookie Greg Booker, who hadn't pitched in ten days. Booker hit Herndon with a pitch, forcing in a run and extending Detroit's lead to 4-0.

The Padres got one of those runs back in the third. Wiggins and Gwynn singled, and Garvey grounded out to score a run.

In the home third, Detroit loaded the bases against Booker on three walks. In came Greg Harris, who hit Gibson to force home the fifth Tiger run. In back-to-back innings, the Padres gave away two runs by hitting a batter with the bases loaded.

Harris held the Tigers scoreless for the rest of the game, giving the Padres a chance to climb back from their 5-1 deficit.

It looked like the visitors might mount a comeback in the seventh. Gwynn reached on an infield hit, moved to third on Garvey's double, and scored on Nettle's sacrifice fly. Lefthander Willie Hernandez came on with Garvey at third and the lefty-swinging Kennedy at bat. With the count full, Kennedy slammed a long fly to center. The ball seemed to elude centerfielder Lemon, who turned the wrong way but recovered in time to make a sensational catch.

"I was running with my head down. I didn't see the catch," said a dejected Kennedy. "It didn't surprise me in the least, the way my season has been going."[42]

The Tigers' relief ace closed the door the rest of the way; 5-2 was the final score. The crowd of 57,908 rocked ancient Tiger Stadium as the Tigers took a two-to-one series edge. Between the two teams, 24 runners were left on base, which set a record for a World Series game. The Padres tied the record by issuing eleven walks, while the Tigers tied the mark by leaving 14 runners on base.

"We'll have our hands full here now, with Morris and Petry," added Kennedy. "We'll have to work to win one game here (to bring the series back to San Diego). I'm looking for Show or Thurmond to pitch a strong game."

Williams stated the obvious: "Our starting pitching has been very poor."

Said pitching coach Norm Sherry, "It was like a bad dream. You expect 11 walks in a rookie league, not in the majors."

Show, who like the other Padres starters was having a dreadful postseason, was on tap for game four. "It's going to be tough to win at Tiger Stadium, no doubt about it," he said before his start. "They've got a tough park, with that short fence in right field, and they can stack a lineup with left-hand hitters against a right-handed pitcher. My work is definitely cut out for me."[42]

**Mr. Trammell** Anderson opted to go with a three-man rotation, so Show was paired against Morris. For the third straight time in the postseason, the Padres ace was shellacked.

Eric Show won 100 games as a Padre, the most in team history. He was roughed up in the '84 postseason, allowing 11 runs in eight innings of work. (Courtesy, Topps)

The Tigers' hero this time was Trammell, who connected for a two-run homer on a 2-and-0 fastball from Show in the first inning. The Tigers' All-Star shortstop repeated the feat two innings later with another two-run blast off the Padres starter. In three postseason games, Show had given up seven home runs in just eight innings of work. Show's night ended in the third inning, and relievers Dravecky, Lefferts, and Gossage pitched scoreless ball the rest of the way.

Trammell's two home runs accounted for all of the Detroit scoring. Kennedy had a solo shot in the second but the Padres never caught up. The final score was 4-2. Morris threw another complete game, notching his second series victory.

"If we knew what the problem was with our starters, we'd correct it," said Williams. "Maybe I should be starting my relievers.

"He (Morris) was even stronger against us today than he was against us in San Diego. We have our backs to the wall. I don't have to say a word to my players. They know what they have to do. Maybe we'll win three in a row again."[43]

**The Goose is cooked** The situation looked bleak: the Padres were down, three games to one, a game away from elimination, just as they'd been in the NLCS.

McReynold's bat was dearly missed; his replacement, Bobby Brown, was 0-for-14 to that point, failing to come through in several critical situations. Martinez was just 1-for-13.

The Tigers were batting .408 as a team against the Padres' four starters. By contrast, their average against Padres relievers was a scant .118. The San Diego bullpen allowed just one run in 24 innings.

Game five, October 14, 1984, was do-or-die. The weight of the season fell on the shoulders of Mark Thurmond. But *again*, Tiger batters mauled a Padres starter: Thurmond retired just one of the six batters he faced, surrendering three Detroit runs. One of the hits was a two-run homer by Gibson. After just a third of an inning, Williams was forced to tap into his exhausted bullpen one more time. Hawkins did the job yet again, holding the Tigers in check until the fifth.

Garvey singled home a run in the third, and the Padres tied it in the fourth on a sacrifice fly by Brown and a Wiggins single. That chased Petry in favor of Bill Scherrer. The score stood at 3-3.

In the fifth inning, the Padre bullpen finally began to show some cracks. Gibson singled, and then Hawkins allowed a walk to Herndon. Hawkins had done yeoman's work throughout the series, but the big Texan was clearly tiring. Lefferts came on and walked Lemon, bringing up utility man Rusty Kuntz.

Kuntz batted only 140 times during the season, but once again, a seldom-used backbencher delivered for the Tigers. It actually turned out to be one of the series' more bizarre plays.

With the bases loaded, Kuntz plunked a shallow fly toward right field. When second baseman Wiggins realized that Gwynn lost sight of the ball, he hustled back and made the catch with his back to the plate. Gibson tagged from third and came racing for the plate. With Wiggins' momentum taking him away from the infield, he could get little on his throw as Gibson slid home safely, breaking the tie.

"I lost the ball when it went up in the clouds. I was having trouble all night," said Gwynn.[44]

Indeed, Tiger Stadium was engulfed in fog and clouds the entire series, and many Tigers confirmed that during overcast conditions, outfielders can easily lose sight of the ball. Gwynn acknowledged that if he'd picked up the ball, Gibson wouldn't have scored.

Gibson's hustle—along with a little luck—gave Detroit a 4-3 lead. Lefferts turned in another stellar performance: 2 innings with no runs allowed, giving him ten scoreless innings for the postseason.

With one out in the seventh Williams played the odds, lifting Lefferts and calling on Gossage to face the right-handed Parrish. The strategy backfired: Parrish greeted the Goose with a solo home run, extending Detroit's lead to 5-3.

Bevacqua, continuing his postseason heroics, negated that run in the top of the eighth with his second round-tripper of the series, shaving the lead to 5-4. The Padres were still in it, down by just a run as the Tigers came to bat in the bottom of the eighth.

It wasn't the night for the Goose, who opened the bottom of the eighth by walking Castillo. Looking for insurance runs, Whitaker laid a sacrifice bunt down the third base line. Nettles gloved the ball and rifled it to second, but Templeton was off the bag and both runners were safe. Templeton accepted blame for blowing the play, admitting that he was looking for Nettles to throw to first.

Trammell then advanced both runners with a successful sacrifice. That brought up Gibson, setting up the ultimate power confrontation, and the moment of high drama of the series.

With first base open Williams held up four fingers, the sign for an intentional walk. Gossage wanted to pitch to Gibson, and shook off the sign. That brought Williams out for a conference.

"Gossage said he wanted to pitch to Gibson because he'd had good success against him in the past," said Williams. "He thought he could strike him out. He (Gossage) has done the job all year, but I take full responsibility."[44]

For his part, Gibson said he couldn't remember ever getting a hit off Gossage. Earlier in the series Gossage confided in teammates that he dominated Gibson in the American League.

Williams reluctantly agreed to let his veteran ace pitch to Gibson. Gibson subsequently launched Gossage's second pitch, a high fastball, into the upper rightfield bleachers. The Padres stood in stunned silence as Gibson circled the bases, fists clenched in the air. With that swing of the bat, the series was all but over.

In the top of the ninth, just as the rain began to fall, leftfielder Herndon gloved a fly ball off the bat of Tony Gwynn for the final out. The final score was 8-4, with the Tigers taking the series four games to one. Ravenous Tiger fans poured onto the field as players scurried for the safety of the clubhouse.

**Back to paradise** "No one gave us much chance to win our division," said Williams. "No one gave us a chance in the playoffs against the Cubs. I'm proud. I thought we did quite well. We have a lot of young players who matured during the playoffs. Our starting pitchers had trouble in the series, but they had done an outstanding job the rest of the year."[44]

Bevacqua led the Padres offense for the Series, batting 7-for-17 (.412) with 2 doubles, 2 home runs, and 4 RBIs. Wiggins (.364) and Templeton (.316) were the only other Padres to have a solid offensive series. Nettles hit .250 but walked five times for a .471 on-base percentage. Gwynn hit .263 with 3 walks.

Bochy came to bat one time and delivered a hit, giving him a perfect one-for-one (1.000). "I led off the eighth and singled," he later recalled. "But I didn't get to enjoy the moment. As soon as I got to first Ron Roenicke was already headed out from the dugout to run for me. And he wasn't that much faster than I was."[45]

Kennedy had some less-than-kind words about the Motor City: "This place is what San Diego would look like after a nuclear war."[46]

The Padres desperately missed the offensive spark of McReynolds, as replacement Bobby Brown went just 1-for-15 (.067). Kennedy hit .211 with one HR, and Garvey (.200) failed to repeat his NLCS heroics. Martinez batted just .176. The Padres actually outhit the Tigers .265 to .253, but it wasn't enough.

Martinez fanned nine times in his 17 at bats, establishing a record for a five-game World Series. Whitaker and Trammell each tied records—Whitaker with six runs scored; Trammell with nine base hits. Anderson, who led the Reds to world championships in 1975-76, became the first manager to win a title in each league (had the Padres won, Williams would have claimed the same distinction). As it was, Williams became the first manager in history to lead three different teams to the World Series.

Two separate Series MVP awards were given: Morris won the Babe Ruth award, while Trammell, who became a Padres coach after his playing days were over, won *Sport* MVP honors. The Tigers became the only team besides the 1927 Yankees to win the World Series after leading the race wire to wire.

Detroit fans were celebrating their victory in the streets outside Tiger Stadium when the celebration turned ugly. Rioters set fire to a police car and a taxicab, and when they saw the Padres' team bus pull out of the stadium parking lot, they began shaking it violently. Only the intervention of police officers on horseback prevented them from tipping it over, and the Padres made it, safe and sound, back to paradise.

# Back to the Cellar

THE PADRES ROSTER was essentially intact for 1985, and the veteran team was favored to return to the postseason. McKeon made one major move during the winter to bolster the starting rotation: the acquisition of pitcher LaMarr Hoyt from the White Sox.

Hoyt established himself as a proven winner with Chicago. He turned in back-to-back 9-3 seasons in 1980-81, then led the league with 19 wins in '82. He had a breakout season in 1983 when he posted a 24-10 record, capturing the Cy Young award.

1984 saw him fall to 13-18, and trade rumors persisted throughout the year. After the season, the White Sox sent Hoyt and two minor leaguers to San Diego in exchange for Lollar, shortstop prospect Ozzie Guillen, and third baseman Salazar.

The trade looked like a steal for Trader Jack, at least after the first year. In 1985, Hoyt went 16-8 for the Padres and was named the starting pitcher in the All-Star game.

Managed by Dick Williams, the National League All-Star squad featured *seven* Padres in 1985: Hoyt, Kennedy, Gwynn, Nettles, Gossage, Templeton, and Garvey. It was the final All-Star game for all except Gwynn (who still had 13 more) and Kennedy (who played one more, with Baltimore). Williams named Hoyt as the National League's starting pitcher.

The American League starter was Jack Morris, who tormented the Padres in the World Series the previous October. But this time, a Padre extracted a measure of revenge; Hoyt was the winning pitcher and MVP of the game, becoming one of just six pitchers to win the award.

LaMarr Hoyt was at the top of his game, and it looked as though the Padres had finally found the one true stopper they'd been lacking. But tragically, his career was nearing the end.

**Talent wasted**  San Diegans were still delirious with pennant fever in 1985. Attendance topped the two million mark for the first time as fans had visions of a repeat trip to the World Series. Indeed, the Padres were only a game and a half behind the Dodgers at the All-Star break, but the team slipped badly in the second half. Despite the acquisition of Hoyt, the Padres fell to 83-79, tied for third place, a disappointing 12 games behind Los Angeles. Martinez paced the team with 21 homers. Gwynn led the Padres in batting with a .317 average—an off-year for him, but still good for fourth in the league.

Whitson signed a free agent contract with the Yankees after the World Series. Hawkins took his place in the rotation and picked up where he left off in the postseason, turning in the best year of his career (18-8, 3.15). Show and Dravecky were just above .500. Thurmond dropped to 7-11 and would never regain the form he'd shown during his fine '84 campaign.

Out of the bullpen Gossage sported a 1.82 ERA with 26 saves. It was his last truly dominant season as a closer.

The team's overall decline was compounded by problems off the field. Wiggins continued to lose his battle with drugs. He relapsed early in 1985 and entered rehabilitation for the second time. The talented switch-hitter finally wore out his welcome: After the incident, management declared that Wiggins would never again play for the Padres. The ballclub had to decide whether to pay off his contract or find another team willing to take him.

Clearly the Padres would never get market value for Wiggins. Teams knew that taking on a man with two drug offenses was a risk; they also knew the Padres were backed into a corner and were forced to make a trade.

On June 27, 1985, the Padres sent their catalyst, the man who'd stolen 70 bases and scored 106 runs the year before, to Baltimore for pitcher Roy Lee Jackson. They might as well have given Wiggins away; Jackson appeared in just 22 games in a San Diego uniform.

Wiggins consented to the Orioles' demand to spot-test him for drugs. In his place, Flannery and Jerry Royster manned second base.

"Thankfully, it's over with," said Hawkins. "It was real bad publicity for the team. Now it's a closed chapter."[47]

Alan Wiggins had the potential to become one the great stars in baseball. But sadly, he could never overcome his self-destructive off-field behaviors. He played just two more seasons with the Orioles and was out of baseball by 1987.

His personal problems continued even after his career ended. On January 9, 1991, at age 32, Wiggins died of complications from AIDS.

**Sitting down on the job**  One of the Padres' low points of the 1985 season occurred on September 11 at Cincinnati's Riverfront Stadium. Pete Rose, now player-manager of the Reds, was completing his remarkable run at Ty Cobb's career hits record, having tied the mark of 4,191 when the Padres came to town. On the mound for San Diego was Eric Show.

Rose wasted no time delighting the sellout crowd of 47,237. In the bottom of the first, he slapped a 2-and-1 pitch from Show to left center, just in front of Carmelo Martinez. Charlie Hustle had finally broken the record he'd been chasing for 23 years.

Rose was congratulated at first base by Garvey, who was also on the field when Hank Aaron broke the career home run record. The Reds held an elaborate ceremony complete with confetti, fireworks, presentation of the ball, an emotional embrace by Rose's son, and several long ovations. It was the moment Reds' fans, and all baseball fans, were looking forward to all season.

Show, evidently annoyed by the lengthy interruption, sat down on the pitching rubber.

The next day's papers focused as much on Show's act of indifference as Rose's accomplishment itself. Show claimed he was simply resting during the intermission but he was widely criticized, even by teammates, for his apparent lack of respect. Today, Show's creditable career is remembered as much for this incident as anything else.

**Prohibition**  The Padres plunged in the standings for a number of reasons. During its pennant-winning season the team showed remarkable unity and cohesion, combining a near-perfect blend of veteran experience with youthful talent. Wiggins' problems and subsequent trade were certainly a distraction, but that was only the beginning of the Padres' steady decline.

The players were well aware that a feud was simmering between McKeon and manager Dick Williams. After fighting with the front office most of the year, Williams resigned at the end of the '85 season. The Padres were the fifth club from which he departed under less-than-ideal circumstances.

To his credit, Williams inherited a last-place team and turned it around. Under his leadership for four seasons (1982-85), the Padres never finished below .500. Williams was a winner everywhere he went, but he attracted controversy like a lightning rod.

Steve Boros was hired as manager in 1986. Boros had an unremarkable playing career with the Tigers, Cubs, and Reds in the late-50's and early-60's. He previously managed the Oakland A's to a fourth-place finish in 1983.

Another off-field controversy became a distraction to the Padres in the mid-80s. Several members of the team, led by Show, became active members of the ultra-conservative John Birch Society. They distributed literature at shopping centers and attempted to recruit teammates to their cause. Their persistence caused a conflict with some of the free spirits on the team (sometimes referred to as the 'Bingers'). The rift came to a head in 1986, when the Birch members persuaded management to ban beer from the clubhouse.

Gossage was furious. He reeled off several unflattering, highly publicized remarks about the team's management and even took a shot at McDonald's. Gossage decried the beer ban, declaring (among other things) that the team was "only interested in signing choirboys." For his tirade, the team suspended Goose without pay for the rest of the 1986 season.

His teammates—including the Birchers—rallied to his defense, and eventually Goose was reinstated, after apologizing and agreeing to pay $25,000 to the Ronald McDonald House.

With the ban on beer in the clubhouse, players were forced to take their post-game spirits to the stadium parking lot.

As the 80's drew to a close, Eric Show, the leader of the 'Birchers', waged a battle with substance abuse and other emotional disorders. In 1994, at age 37, he passed away at a drug-rehabilitation center. Show won more games (100) as a Padre than anyone in team history. Tragically, he became the second member of the Padres family lost to substance abuse.

**Another lost talent** LaMarr Hoyt was arrested on drug possession charges in February 1986. He was arrested a second time just days later. The Padres ace entered rehabilitation and missed most of spring training. Hoyt's problems affected his performance on the field, and it turned into another high-profile embarrassment to the club. After his spectacular 1985 campaign, Hoyt plummeted to 8-11. He never threw another pitch after the 1986 season.

Shortly after the season, Hoyt was arrested at the San Ysidro border crossing for attempting to carry illegal narcotics into the United States. He had 490 pills wrapped in plastic and concealed in his pants. He was sentenced to 45 days in jail.

Commissioner Peter Ueberroth banished Hoyt from baseball for 12 months and the Padres severed all ties with him. He attempted a comeback with the White Sox in 1988, but he was arrested yet again when agents found marijuana and cocaine in his apartment. His career was over.

For a time, LaMarr Hoyt was one of the best pitchers in baseball. But like Wiggins and Show, he ultimately succumbed to the demons within.

**Getting rusty**  The lineup for the 1986 Padres was essentially unchanged from the '84 team, minus Wiggins. But by now, the veterans were all a couple years older and it began to show. Gwynn was the team's leading hitter with a .329 mark, third best in the league. He also won his first of five Gold Glove awards that season, which he lists as one of his proudest accomplishments.

McReynolds led the team with 26 home runs and 96 RBIs. Gwynn was tops on the Padres with 37 steals. Offensively, no one else on the club had a standout season.

Boros led the Padres to a disappointing record of 74-88 in 1986, good for a fourth-place finish, missing last place by a scant game and a half. Replacing the experienced and successful Williams was a tall order for any new manager, and the comparisons were inevitable. While seven players represented the Padres at the 1985 All-Star game, Gwynn was the team's lone representative in '86. The World Series seemed a lifetime ago.

In mid-season the Padres reacquired Whitson from the Yankees for reliever Tim Stoddard. Whitson struggled under the media glare in New York and feuded with Billy Martin, once getting into a fistfight with the pugnacious Yankee manager. Whitson resurrected his career after returning to San Diego and enjoyed several productive years back on the west coast.

Lefferts led the majors with 83 games pitched in 1986. Today, the German-born Lefferts ranks second all-time in appearances among Padres pitchers.

Rookie Jimmy Jones made his major league debut on September 21, 1986. In his first major league start, he threw a one-hitter against the Houston Astros. The no-hitter was spoiled by the unlikeliest man in the lineup, pitcher Bob Knepper (a career .099 hitter), who tripled in the third inning. It was another close-call for a Padre hurler in search of the team's elusive first no-hitter.

**Separate ways**  1986 was the final season in San Diego for Nettles, Kennedy, and McReynolds. Nettles was traded to Atlanta, where he spent one season before moving to Montreal. He retired in 1988 with a total of 390 home runs, placing him in baseball's top fifty.

With rookie sensation Benito Santiago waiting in the wings, Kennedy was the subject of trade talks all season. On October 30, 1986 he was traded to Baltimore for pitcher Storm Davis. (Davis never made an impact with San Diego, and was dealt to Oakland soon after for prospects.)

"What can you say?" pondered Kennedy. "I gave them 110 percent for six years, and they gave me the same thing. Those six years weren't wasted—any of them."[48]

While with Baltimore, Kennedy would become just the second catcher to start an All-Star game in both leagues. He wrapped up his career with the Giants before calling it quits in 1991. Terry Kennedy has crouched behind the plate for more games than anyone else in Padres history.

**"I ain't an athlete"** McReynolds was traded to the Mets for outfielders Stanley Jefferson and San Diegan Kevin Mitchell. McReynolds continued to provide pop at the plate, averaging 26 homers a year over the next four seasons in New York. Mitchell, who grew up in the violent San Diego gang culture, was a Padre just a few months before being packaged in a major trade with San Francisco.

The wholesale changes didn't stop with the players: Boros was fired after the '86 season, his sole year as Padres skipper. He was replaced by the fiery Larry Bowa.

Bowa was born December 6, 1945, making him one of the youngest managers ever. He broke in with the Phillies in 1970 and played for 16 seasons in the major leagues. A five-time All-Star and two-time Gold Glove shortstop, Bowa was an intense competitor on and off the field. He was a sparkplug for the division-winning Phillies four different seasons, including their world championship year in 1980. He also played with the Cubs in the '84 NLCS against the Padres. Bowa was regarded as one of the great shortstops of his era, but his managerial career wouldn't prove as successful.

Outfielder/first baseman John Kruk made his debut in 1986. Kruk batted .309 as a rookie before taking over for the injured Garvey in 1987. He had his finest season that year, hitting .313 with 20 home runs and a surprising total of 18 stolen bases. The portly Kruk was popular with teammates and fans alike.

Though he didn't look the part of a professional athlete, the scraggly first baseman hit consistently, year in and year out. The West Virginian stood 5'10", 210 lbs., and made no attempt to hide his vices: smoking, drinking, and chewing tobacco. When a woman told him he didn't look like an athlete, Kruk gave his famous response: "I ain't an athlete, lady, I'm a baseball player."

The Pirates' Andy Van Slyke once quipped: "If someone from Germany, who had no idea what baseball was, saw Kruk play, he'd wonder why the beer truck driver was playing first base."

**First-to-worst** The Padres had come full-cycle by 1987. In a span of just six years, they'd gone from last place to the World Series and back to last place again. They ended the season with a record of 65 wins and 97 losses, a full 25 games behind San Francisco. Not surprisingly, the crowds also shrunk; only two teams in the league drew less in 1987.

Much of the blame for the Padres' dismal season rested with Bowa. His extreme intensity and aggressiveness became an irritation to many on the team, particularly the younger players. Bowa had a habit of nervously pacing in the dugout during games, visibly displaying his emotions. After one loss in L.A., he stormed into the clubhouse and overturned the food table, screaming, "You guys stink! You don't deserve to eat!"

At one point Gwynn and Kruk had to forcibly carry outfielder Jefferson from the clubhouse to keep him from coming to blows with his manager. Bowa directed one of his tirades directly at Jefferson, questioning his manhood.

1987 marked the end of Steve Garvey's long and prestigious career. Injuries limited the veteran to just 27 games during the final year of his contract, and with the young Kruk establishing himself at first base, Garvey didn't fit into the Padres' plans for 1988. He discussed returning to the Dodgers, but approaching 40 years of age and suffering an arm injury, he finally announced his retirement.

**Dravecky's challenge** Former N.L. president Charles "Chub" Feeney was named Padres team president on June 10, 1987. Ironically, fourteen years earlier, Feeney favored the move of the Padres from San Diego to Washington.

Trader Jack swung another blockbuster trade on July 4th with the Giants which involved future Cy Young and MVP winners. In need of a veteran starting pitcher to help in their drive to the division title, the Giants sought left-hander Dave Dravecky. Mired in last place, the Padres had nothing to lose.

San Diego sent pitchers Dravecky and Lefferts and third baseman Kevin Mitchell to San Francisco in exchange for pitchers Mark Davis, Mark Grant, and Keith Comstock, along with third baseman Chris Brown. Two years after the trade, Davis won the Cy Young award for San Diego. Mitchell captured MVP honors the same season for San Francisco.

"You always anticipate the possibility of a trade, but I never thought it would come true, to be honest with you," said Dravecky.

"I'm going to miss San Diego…This has been my life in the major leagues—San Diego."[49]

McKeon acknowledged that it was difficult to trade Dravecky, but he was high on young Brown, who was regarded as the Padres third baseman of the future. Feeney went so far as to label him one of the league's best third basemen,

But Brown, an All-Star the previous year with the Giants, never came close to stardom again. He'd play a total of 124 games for the Padres, batting just .234 during his time in San Diego. Brown infuriated Bowa with his lackadaisical attitude and complaints of minor, nagging injuries. The moody third baseman was a major disappointment, and his career was over two years after the trade.

Lefferts was an effective closer for the Giants before returning to San Diego in 1990. Mitchell was named league MVP after turning in a monster performance in 1989 (.291, 47 HRs, 125 RBIs), leading the Giants to the World Series.

An all-star in 1983, Dave Dravecky's career ended in 1989 when cancer was found in his arm. (Courtesy, Hall of Champions)

Soon after the trade, Dravecky faced one of the most heart-rendering stories in baseball. In 1988 he made only seven starts for the Giants when, complaining of a sore arm, he was placed on the disabled list. Doctors discovered a soft-tissue cancer in the deltoid muscle of his pitching arm, placing his career, and his life, in jeopardy.

Dravecky underwent surgery in 1988 to remove the tumor. Amazingly, he returned to the mound in 1989 and won his first game back. He won a second victory but paid the price: While throwing a pitch against Montreal, his weakened left arm broke. The snap was so loud it could be heard in the stands. Dravecky would never pitch again.

The former Padres All-Star had a total of three operations to remove cancerous tumors. On June 13, 1991, doctors were finally forced to amputate his arm.

For his career, Dravecky posted a record of 64-57 with an excellent 3.13 lifetime ERA. As a member of the Padres from 1982-87, he compiled a mark of 53-50. Since his ordeal, Dave and his wife Jan authored the books *Comeback*, *Do Not Lose Heart*, and *Stand By Me*, which are targeted to people fighting cancer or have had limbs amputated.

Said the former Padre: "While I was in the hospital, I received thousands of cards and letters from people who offered me hope and encouragement. Some of the letters were written by people who were having similar problems as I. When I got home, we formed the *Dave Dravecky Outreach of Hope* to help answer those letters, as well as others that continued to come in."

"Cancer is a family's disease, because everyone in the family is affected when a member is diagnosed. They need encouragement as much as the person who has the cancer."[50]

The Draveckys are committed Christians, and Dave says his faith was strengthened by the ordeal. Today he makes his living as a motivational speaker, offering hope and encouragement to those in need.

**Rookie sensation** There were actually a few bright spots for the Padres in an otherwise-dreary 1987 season. On April 13 against the Giants, the Padres' first three batters—Wynne, Gwynn, and Kruk—all homered. The feat had never been accomplished.

Infielder Randy Ready, who was obtained from the Brewers, batted .309 with an excellent .423 on-base percentage. Jefferson stole 34 bases despite a .230 average.

Gwynn enjoyed one of baseball's greatest offensive seasons of the '80s, batting .370 with 218 base hits in 1987. He set career-highs with 119 runs scored, 56 stolen bases, 13 triples, 82 walks, and another Gold Glove. Somehow, despite Gwynn's awesome season, the Padres managed to lose 97 games; the team's last-place finish probably cost him the MVP award. For the second straight year, he was the only Padre named to the All-Star team.

Another shining star in 1987 was catcher Benito Santiago, the unanimous choice for N.L. Rookie of the Year. Santiago had an amazing rookie season, batting .300 with 18 HRs, 33 doubles, and 79 RBIs. He even stole 21 bases. Defensively, he threw out one-third of all base runners and developed the knack for rifling the ball to any base from his knees.

The highlight of Santiago's standout campaign was his 34-game hitting streak, which set the major league record for both rookies and catchers. The streak finally ended October 3 against L.A.'s Hershiser.

By 1987 the Cubs and Padres, who faced each other in the playoffs just three years before, fell to last place in their respective divisions and were ready to deal. The Padres bullpen was becoming crowded, with youngsters Lance McCullers and Davis making Gossage expendable.

Prior to spring training 1988, Gossage was dealt to the Cubs for Keith Moreland. Goose was outstanding as the Padres closer in 1984-85, but his performance declined over the next two seasons.

Chicago, having lost closer Lee Smith that off-season, took a chance that Gossage might find some of his old zip again.

Moreland hit 27 home runs in his final year with Chicago, and the Padres were anxious to add power to their punchless lineup. Unfortunately, Moreland's career was nearing the end: playing first base and outfield, he produced just 5 home runs for the Padres in 1988.

Likewise, Gossage never regained the form that made him baseball's dominant closer for ten seasons, but he pitched effectively enough to make contributions wherever he went. He finally retired in 1994, boasting 310 saves over 22 major league seasons. 83 of those saves came as a member of the Padres, which ranks third on the team's all-time list.

**Bye-bye Bowa** With the team off to a 16-30 start in 1988, the Padres finally severed ties with Bowa. Not surprisingly, Bowa was furious. He aired his criticism of Padres management, particularly Feeney.

"I managed aggressive. What few runs we did score were because we put men in motion."[51]

Bowa was replaced by McKeon himself. Trader Jack also retained his position as general manager. The strain of holding down two full-time jobs at once would eventually catch up with him.

# Two Races In One

THE PADRES BOUNCED back after McKeon took the helm in 1988. After a horrible start, they went 67-48 the rest of the way, finishing a surprising third in the division.

Starting pitching was the team's strength in 1988. Show led the way with a 16-11 record. Hawkins and Whitson won 14 and 13 games, respectively.

The surprise of the rotation was Dennis Rasmussen. The Padres originally traded the 6'7" righty for Nettles before the '84 season, and got him back in a trade with the Reds in 1988. Rasmussen (14-4, 2.55) became the team's best starter.

Davis represented the Padres on the '88 All-Star team. This was the only year from 1984-99 that Gwynn was not a member of the squad. Gwynn, who'd gotten off to a horrendous start, got his average up to .313 by season's end, earning a third batting title.

Davis emerged as the Padres bullpen ace, garnering 28 saves with a 2.01 ERA. He headed a solid bullpen which included McCullers, Dave Leiper, Greg Booker, and Mark Grant.

Booker pitched from 1983-90. The 6'6" righty spent nearly his entire career with the Padres, being used mainly in long relief. Booker was McKeon's son-in-law and later became a Padres coach.

Grant had an affable personality that made him popular with fans and teammates alike. "Mud" split his two-plus seasons with San Diego between the starting rotation and the bullpen. In 1988 he went 2-8, but turned those numbers around (8-2, 3.33) as a setup man for Davis in 1989.

Grant's major league career lasted eight seasons, including stops with five other teams. After his retirement in 1995 he moved into the broadcast booth, where he shares his fun-loving spirit and baseball expertise with Padres fans.

Kruk and Ready were traded to Philadelphia during the 1989 season for outfielder Chris James. It was another move that didn't work. James played a total of 87 games for San Diego, while Kruk led the Phillies to the World Series four years later, becoming the dominant personality on the team and the clubhouse leader.

Padres fans missed Kruk's colorful personality and easy-going irreverence. He ended his career in 1995 with a .300 lifetime average.

An up-and-comer who made an immediate impact in 1988 was 20-year old Roberto Alomar. As a rookie he batted .266 with 24 steals, and just got better with age. Alomar hit .295 with 42 steals in '89, although he led all second basemen with 28 errors. He worked hard on his glovework and after that season was regarded as the premiere defensive second baseman in baseball, eventually winning nine Gold Gloves. His father, Sandy Alomar Sr., was a major league ballplayer from 1964-78. The elder Alomar had the distinction of briefly coaching both his sons on the same team.

**Bruce Hurst and Jack Clark** Following the 1988 season, Moreland and underachieving third baseman Chris Brown were dealt to Detroit for pitcher Walt Terrell. It didn't accomplish much for either side: Moreland and Brown were both out of baseball by the following season, while Terrell went just 5-13 for the Padres in 1989. He was sent midseason to the Yankees for third baseman Mike Pagliarulo.

McKeon pulled off a couple of key acquisitions before the '89 campaign which paid enormous dividends. The Padres lured pitcher Bruce Hurst, one of the top left-handers in the game, from Boston with a three-year free agent contract. The Bosox actually offered him more money to stay, but Hurst preferred San Diego, which was closer to his home in Utah.

Hurst gave the Padres their money's worth and more. In his first National League campaign he went 15-11, finishing fifth in the league in ERA (2.69) and strikeouts (179). He showed his impact early, throwing a one-hitter against the Braves on April 10. Hurst formed a solid one-two punch with Ed Whitson (16-11, 2.66) in 1989.

McKeon also obtained slugging first baseman Jack Clark, a four-time All-Star, in a deal sending McCullers, Jimmy Jones, and Stan Jefferson to the Yankees. Clark led the team with 26 homers and 94 RBIs in his first season as a Padre. The only true power bat in the lineup, Clark didn't see many pitches around the zone. He drew 132 bases on balls, leading the league and establishing a team record. Clark set a record in July by fanning nine times in two games.

**Rising stars** Santiago threw out an amazing 45% of runners who attempted to steal. His average fell to .236, but he made his first All-Star appearance and won his second Gold Glove.

22-year old Leon ("Bip") Roberts, a Rule V draft pick, joined the Padres for good in '89, batting .301 with 21 steals in a part-time role. The Padres tried to find a place for Roberts' potent bat, trying him at second, third, short, and the outfield. That was the story of his career wherever he went—splitting time between the infield and outfield, but never catching on at any one position. Roberts' versatility made him especially valuable throughout his twelve-year career.

The Padres' climb back to contention in 1989 would not have been possible without Mark Davis' sensational year out of the bullpen. Davis led the league with 44 saves (one short of the then-N.L. record) and posted a sterling 1.85 ERA, en route to winning the Fireman of the Year award. Davis also captured Cy Young honors, becoming the fourth reliever in history to do so. He placed sixth in the N.L. MVP voting.

1989 saw the debut of rookie Andy Benes, who made a big contribution down the stretch. Benes went 6-3 with during the last two months of the season, his first of six with the Padres. Calvin Schiraldi, acquired from the Cubs for the pennant drive, went 3-1.

Two races came down to the final days of the 1989 season: the race for the batting title between Gwynn and the Giants' Will Clark, and, more importantly, the race for the National League Western division, which, coincidentally, was also between the Padres and Giants.

San Francisco boasted N.L. MVP Kevin Mitchell and first baseman Clark, the MVP runner-up. The Giants held a big lead most of the summer, but the Padres climbed back into the race with a 29-10 tear the last six weeks of the season.

**Scoreboard watching** The Padres were very much in contention in mid-September, trailing the Giants by just five games. San Diego fans caught a glimpse of pennant fever for the first time in five years; Gwynn even admitted to sneaking peaks at the scoreboard.

With 16 games left to play, the standings in the N.L. West were:

| Team | W | L | G.B. | Pct. |
|------|------|------|------|------|
| Giants | 84 | 62 | --- | .575 |
| Padres | 79 | 67 | 5 | .541 |
| Astros | 77 | 69 | 7 | .527 |

The next two weeks were excruciating for scoreboard-watchers. Every Padre win seemed to be matched by a Giant win, and vice versa. On

September 13, the Padres bested the Braves 3-2, and fans stayed at Jack Murphy to watch the end of the Giants-Reds game on the stadium scoreboard. Cincinnati took a 7-5 lead over San Francisco in the 13th, but the Giants came up with three runs in the bottom of the inning to take the ballgame, 8-7. That game exemplified the frustration of the '89 race.

The Padres lost to Atlanta the next day, while Bob Brenly's bloop hit gave the Giants a 4-3 win over the Reds. The Giants always found ways to win the close ones.

The Padres and Giants prepared for a showdown the weekend of September 15-17 at Candlestick Park. It was the biggest series of the season so far; if the Padres could manage a sweep, they'd be at the doorstep of first place.

In the series' first game, Templeton doubled home Chris James to give San Diego a 3-2 lead, bringing Santiago to the plate. The hot-hitting backstop came through with a two-run homer off Bob Knepper to put the visitors up, 5-2. The Padres held on to win 5-3, behind Dennis Rasmussen. Greg Harris (not the same Greg Harris who pitched in the '84 postseason) threw the final four innings for the save.

The Padres got a scare during the game when Roberts suffered chest pains and had to be carried away on a stretcher. He was flown back to San Diego for tests and missed the remainder of the Giants series. Roberts was the team's sparkplug down the stretch, hitting .406 in his last ten games.

Fortunately the ailment was not life-threatening. Roberts was suffering gastroenteritis which, along with a muscle tear in his rib cage, caused the pains. He was cleared to rejoin the team after the Giants series.

"This game was really important to us," said Gwynn, who had three hits to inch past Clark in the batting race, .341 to .339. "It keeps you hungry. It keeps you in the right frame of mind."[52]

3,000 fans watched the game on the JumboTron back at Jack Murphy Stadium. The promotional event was called the "Giants Bustin" party, arranged by the Padres and KFMB radio.

Saturday's game was rained out, setting up a doubleheader for Sunday, September 17. The twinbill was dubbed "Super Sunday". The weather was wet and cold, standard fare for Candlestick. In the first game, Jack Clark staked the Padres to a 2-0 lead with a two-run home run. But in the third inning, Schiraldi strained his forearm and had to leave the game. Mark Grant was summoned in relief, and was victimized by shoddy defense.

The score was 3-3 in the sixth when Mitchell slugged a two-run HR, his second homer of the game, propelling the Giants to a 5-3 win. It was a serious blow to the Padres' hopes of catching San Francisco.

The Padres came back in the nightcap, jumping immediately on veteran Rick Reuschel. Alomar led the game off with a home run and Bruce Hurst notched his 15th win as San Diego prevailed, 6-1. Jack Clark was the offensive hero of the day, going 5-for-7 with two HRs against his former team.

The Padres ended up taking two out of three in the series, inching to within five games of the Giants. The two teams were scheduled to face off in a season-ending series at Jack Murphy Stadium, so the Padres hoped to stay close enough to control their own destiny.

**Close but no cigar** San Diego did what they had to do, sweeping a three-game series from Cincinnati. Unfortunately, they wouldn't gain any ground; San Francisco also took three straight from the Dodgers. The Giants' three wins over L.A. were all by one run, including a dramatic win where San Francisco scored five runs in the bottom of the ninth.

San Francisco still held a five-game lead with just nine games left. The Padres couldn't seem to find a break, and time wasn't on their side.

In the next series, the Padres continued their valiant effort, taking two out of three from the Dodgers, but the Giants also grabbed two of three from Houston. The Padres played well, but they hadn't gained ground in over a week.

San Diego won the next two from Cincinnati, while the Giants split a pair with L.A. Now four games out with four left to play, one Padres loss or one Giants win would clinch the division for San Francisco.

The next night the Dodgers shut out the Giants 1-0, keeping the Padres' slim hopes alive. But the Reds played the role of spoiler as Eric Davis stroked a two-out RBI double off of Schiraldi in the 13th inning, dealing the Padres a 2-1 loss. The race was finally over, one day before the Giants were scheduled to visit San Diego.

Davis had worn out the Padres all year (over one-fifth of his RBIs for the season came against San Diego). Faced with the option of walking Davis, Schiraldi and McKeon chose to pitch to him—a decision which ended the Padres' season.

"Let's give the Giants credit," said McKeon. "I think we surprised a lot of people when we went down to the last three games."[53]

Had the Padres held on to win that ballgame, San Francisco would be coming to Jack Murphy Stadium for a decisive season-ending series. But with the division already decided, the season's final three games were now anticlimactic. But there were other reasons to come to the park for that final weekend.

Tim Flannery

Saturday night, September 30, was Tim Flannery day. The gritty utility man, who endeared himself to fans during his decade with the team, was retiring. When Flannery stepped to bat, he was given such an ovation that play had to be halted. In the fifth inning Roberts came out to second base to replace Flannery, who walked off the field to a standing ovation. With that, his playing days were over.

Tim Flannery at the San Diego Hall of Champions. (Courtesy, Hall of Champions)

The game featured an emotional JumboTron tribute, showing highlights from Flannery's career. Flannery, his wife Donna, and their 4-year old son Daniel swayed to "Like a Rock" as they watched the clips.

"Ninety-nine percent of the guys leave this game bitter, because they've either been released or they continue to play too long," said the 32-year-old Flannery, who retired voluntarily after spending a decade with the Padres.

"I'm overwhelmed by the way my teammates and this city have embraced me over the last couple months—well, for the last ten years." [54]

A consolation prize

Another memorable moment from the final weekend was the duel between Gwynn and Will Clark for the batting title. Going into the final game, Sunday, October 1, Clark held the slightest advantage: .3339 to .3333. The race came down to the eighth inning. Gwynn was 2-for-3 on the day while Clark had one hit in three attempts. This gave Tony a slight edge (.3349 to .3339), but each man had one last at bat.

With two out in the eighth, Clark stood in against relief ace Mark Davis. He swung at the first pitch and lofted a high fly ball—right to centerfielder Shawn Abner. Clark's final average was .3333 which, barring a rally or extra innings, eliminated him from the batting race.

In the home half of the eighth, Gwynn grounded a 2-and-1 pitch from ex-teammate Lefferts past the diving lunge of second baseman Ernest Riles for an RBI single. The race had come down to each man's final at bat, and Gwynn came out ahead. He looked to his wife and children in the stands as the crowd gave its hero a long ovation.

As Gwynn stood at first base, Clark extended his hand in congratulations. Tony finished the afternoon 3-for-4, good for a .3361 average and another batting title—his closest ever. Gwynn finished eighth in the league MVP voting.

The Padres won that final game, taking two of three from the Giants to finish 89-73, three games behind. The Giants went on to be swept by the A's in the World Series, which was remembered for the devastating earthquake in San Francisco prior to the start of game three.

"He does it every year, and that's why he's the best hitter in the National League," said Clark.

Gwynn, who also stole 40 bases that season, won his fourth batting crown in six years. But he confessed afterward: "It didn't feel right...I won the batting title, but Will went to the playoffs. I'd have traded places with him."[55]

# The Strange Changes

DESPITE THE PADRES' rejuvenation, 1990 saw still more changes at the 'Murph. Most surprising was the departure of Davis, the 1989 Cy Young winner.

A free agent after his sensational campaign, Davis became one of the highest-paid relievers in history when he signed a four-year, $14 million contract with Kansas City. The Royals' high-priced gamble didn't paid off, as Davis never came close to the form he'd shown in San Diego. The Padres briefly reacquired Davis in 1993, but his career was effectively over by then.

Attempting to replace their departed stopper, the Padres signed Lefferts as a free agent for 1990. Lefferts, one of the heroes of the '84 postseason, was handed the role of closer. He did an adequate job filling Davis' shoes, notching 23 saves with a 2.52 ERA.

The Padres also signed free agent outfielder Fred Lynn for the 1990 season. The nine-time All-Star had a productive career over the past decade and a half, but he was well past his prime when he arrived in San Diego. Lynn hit just .240 with 6 homers as a Padre, mostly in a pinch-hitting role. 1990 was the end of his distinguished career.

**The Werner era** The dawn of the 90s also saw the biggest change of all—the end of the Kroc era. Joan Kroc, who owned the team since her husband's death six years earlier, announced that she was selling the club to a group headed by television producer Tom Werner. A press conference was scheduled for April 2, 1990 to announce the sale.

The Krocs and C. Arnholt Smith were the only owners the Padres had known. Ray Kroc bought the team for $12 million in 1974. Sixteen years later, the asking price was a staggering $75 million.

Mrs. Kroc nearly sold the team to George Argyros three years earlier, but she decided that his notorious penny-pinching was not in the team's interest. Mrs. Kroc retained ownership of the team six years after her husband's death, mainly out of respect for his memory.

Mrs. Kroc's statement read, "While I will be relinquishing ownership of the Padres, I will not be relinquishing my status as a loyal and enthusiastic supporter of the team. Being identified with the Padres for the past 15 years has been one of the special privileges of my life and a source of the deepest pride."

Werner, the new majority owner, planned to buy a home in San Diego and cancel his Dodgers season tickets. "This (San Diego) is a terrific place to live and to watch a baseball game," he said. "Who wouldn't want to be leaving the smog of Los Angeles?"

"You hate to see her (Mrs. Kroc) go, but obviously this is what she wanted to do," said Gwynn, when told of the sale. "She wants to spend more time with her family, and you have to respect that."[56]

Werner was the producer of "The Cosby Show", "Roseanne", and other television hits. His tenure with the Padres started on a rocky note when he invited one of his stars, Roseanne, to sing the national anthem before a home game against Cincinnati.

Roseanne made a mockery of the anthem, screeching and screaming the words. She concluded by spitting and grabbing her crotch.

**Joe Carter** Sandy Alomar Jr. was voted Minor League Player of the Year in both 1988 and 1989, and he played briefly with the Padres at the end of each year. But with Santiago as the incumbent backstop, Alomar had nowhere to go. Before the 1990 season, McKeon traded Alomar, Chris James, and minor league infielder Carlos Baerga to Cleveland for outfielder Joe Carter.

The trade paid immediate dividends for the Indians, while, over the long term, the Padres were left to rue the deal. Alomar became the first rookie to start an All-Star game in 1990 and was the unanimous choice for Rookie of the Year. Baerga became a three-time All-Star with Cleveland.

After finishing a close second in 1989, the Padres were favored to win the division in 1990. To do so, they'd need strong production from Carter, their prize off-season acquisition. But Carter turned in a sub-par performance, hitting just .232, the lowest mark of his career. He hit 24 HRs with 115 RBIs and 22 stolen bases. Considering what Padres surrendered to obtain him, Carter's performance was a major disappointment.

That year, Carter became the fourth Padre to play in every game of the season (Winfield, 1980; Garvey, 1985; and Smith, 1981 were the others).

By early July, the Padres were a disappointing 37-43. With his team failing to play to expectations, McKeon resigned as manager. He resumed his position in the front office on a full-time basis. McKeon was replaced by coach Greg Riddoch, who never played in the major leagues. Riddoch, who held a Master's degree in Education Administration and once taught high school, managed the Padres from mid-1990 until late in the '92 season.

The strain of holding two such demanding jobs finally proved too much for the 59-year-old McKeon. "It's time to move on and give it to a younger guy who has a lot of enthusiasm," he said. McKeon retained his title as General Manager (officially, 'Vice President of Baseball Operations').

"It was just a case where I was wore out. Believe me, I didn't have the time to devote to both jobs."[57]

Gwynn and Roberts tied for the team lead in hitting in 1990, each concluding the year with a .309 average (Roberts actually finished half a point higher—.3094 to Gwynn's .3089). Aside from his rookie season, it was the lowest average of Gwynn's career. Roberts came into his own that season, swiping 46 bases while splitting duties between the infield and outfield.

Pagliarulo was another disappointment, hitting just ten home runs after averaging almost 25 a year with the Yankees. After the season, "Pags" signed a free agent contract with Minnesota.

On August 9, Templeton recorded his 2,000th career hit, 14 years to the day that he collected his first major league hit. 1990 was Tempy's last full season with the Padres.

Clark again led the team in homers with 25, upping his average to .266. The Padres first baseman walked 104 times in just 334 at bats, giving him a colossal .441 on-base percentage to go with his .533 slugging average. On July 30, Clark belted his 300th lifetime home run.

Whitson turned in another solid performance, notching 14 wins against 8 losses with a 2.60 ERA, third in the league. Hurst, Rasmussen, and Benes all finished around the .500 mark.

The Alomar brothers were briefly reunited in the 1990 All-Star game at Wrigley Field. Sandy was the starting catcher for the A.L. while Roberto was named to the N.L. squad. Gwynn and Santiago were also named to the team, though the latter had to be replaced due to an injury.

The Padres ended the 1990 season with a disappointing record of 75 wins and 87 losses, despite scoring the same number of runs (673) as they allowed. Cincinnati easily won the N.L. Western division en route to the world championship. San Diego tied with Houston for fourth place, 16 games out.

After highly-publicized feuds with Gwynn and his manager, Clark did not fit into the Padres' plans for 1991. He signed a free-agent contract with the Red Sox and had one more productive season before he retired in 1992. Clark was forced to declare bankruptcy that year, listing debts of over eleven million dollars.

**Parting ways** 1990 also saw the end of the decade-long relationship between McKeon and the Padres. Just two months after he resigned as field manager, McKeon was fired as general manager. McKeon went on to skipper the Reds in the late-90s, winning Manager of the Year honors in 1999.

Throughout his tenure in the front office, McKeon left an indelible stamp on the ballclub with his frequent wheeling and dealing. Below is a recap of Trader Jack's biggest deals as general manager of the Padres:

- *December 8, 1980: Traded pitchers Rollie Fingers and Bob Shirley and catchers Gene Tenace and Bob Geren to St. Louis for catchers Terry Kennedy and Steve Swisher, IF Mike Phillips, P Al Olmsted, P Ken Seaman, and P John Urrea. Advantage: Both parties benefited.*
- *April 5, 1981: Traded OF Bobby Mitchell to Pittsburgh for minor league P Dave Dravecky. Huge advantage to San Diego.*
- *February 11, 1982: In a swap of shortstops, sent Ozzie Smith to St. Louis for Garry Templeton. Advantage: Cardinals.*
- *December 21, 1982: Signed free agent Steve Garvey. The Padres wouldn't have made it to the World Series without him.*
- *January 6, 1984: Signed free agent Goose Gossage. See above.*
- *March 30, 1984: Traded pitchers Dennis Rasmussen and Derrin Cloninger to the Yankees for 3B Graig Nettles. Again, see above.*
- *December 6, 1984: Traded OF Ozzie Guillen, IF Luis Salazar, and pitchers Tim Lollar and Bill Long to the White Sox for P LaMarr Hoyt and two minor leaguers. The deal looked great the first season, but Hoyt's career fizzled soon after. Advantage: Neither.*
- *July 9, 1986: Swapped pitcher Tim Stoddard to the Yankees for Ed Whitson, who was making his second tour with the Padres. Advantage: San Diego.*
- *December 11, 1986: Traded OF Kevin McReynolds, IF Adam Ging, and P Gene Walter to the Mets for 3B Kevin Mitchell, outfielders Shawn Abner and Stan Jefferson, and two minor league pitchers. Advantage: New York.*

- *July 5, 1987: The Padres sent Mitchell, Dravecky, and Lefferts to San Francisco for 3B Chris Brown and pitchers Mark Davis, Mark Grant, and Keith Comstock. Advantage: a slight edge to Frisco, as Mitchell led the Giants to the World Series. The deal involved the trade of Davis, a future Cy Young winner, for Mitchell, a future MVP.*
- *October 24, 1988: Dealt OF Stan Jefferson and pitchers Lance McCullers and Jimmy Jones to the Yankees for 1B Jack Clark and P Pat Clements. Advantage: Padres.*
- *December 6, 1989: Traded C Sandy Alomar, OF Chris James, and IF Carlos Baerga to Cleveland for OF Joe Carter. Advantage: Cleveland.*

Most players expressed regret at McKeon's firing. "Jack has always been like a father figure to me," said Roberts.

"He was always faithful to this team," said Templeton. "He's one of those great individuals from the old school."[58]

**Fernandez and the Crime Dog** Joe McIlvane was the Padres' new general manager, and his first major deal was a major bust. On December 5, 1990, reflecting their penchant for dealing away promising young players, the Padres traded Carter and Roberto Alomar to Toronto.

Carter, who'd just bought a house in San Diego, was shocked by the deal. "Fans in Toronto are going to see the real Joe Carter," he vowed, acknowledging his off-year.

"I just feel real disappointed because not only did I love the Padres, but I loved the people around the club, the fans, and San Diego," said Alomar. "I love this community and I'm going to miss it all."[59]

The elder Alomar had been fired at the end of the season. One year earlier, there were three Alomars on the Padres. Now there were none.

Carter and Alomar went on to form the core of a two-time world champion team in Toronto. Alomar became a perennial All-Star and gold glover, leading his teams (Toronto, Baltimore, Cleveland) to several postseason appearances. His image took a hit in 1996, when as a member of the Orioles he spat at umpire John Hirschbeck after being called out on strikes. The boo-birds hounded Alomar for a while, but he eventually won fans over again, winning election almost every year to the All-Star team.

In return, San Diego received first baseman Fred McGriff and short-stop Tony Fernandez. McIlvane felt the ballclub needed to fill holes at first base and shortstop, as Clark was lost to free agency and Templeton's playing days were clearly numbered.

Nicknamed "Crime Dog" for the canine character who advised viewers to "take a bite out of crime", McGriff averaged 35 homers in each of his last three seasons in Toronto. He continued his hot hitting after moving west: With the Padres in 1991, he turned in a sensational year (.278, 31 HRs, 106 RBIs), helping fans forget the loss of Alomar—for the time being.

Fernandez, who appeared in three All-Star games and won four gold gloves with the Blue Jays, was one of the game's premiere short-stops when he joined the Padres. He routinely hit around .300 and averaged over 20 steals a season with the Blue Jays. Fernandez came through with a decent season, hitting .272 with 23 stolen bases for the Padres in 1991.

Neither McGriff nor Fernandez remained with San Diego for long. As with the trade of Smith a decade earlier, Padre fans would be haunted by the ghosts of infielders past.

**Templeton's farewell** Fighting knee and back problems through the late-80s, Templeton's 15-year career finally came to an end in 1991. His speed was gone and his offensive production had dropped off considerably. With the arrival of Fernandez, Tempy's time in San Diego was nearly through.

Templeton was the Padres' regular shortstop for over nine years (1982-91). Today, he ranks behind only Gwynn in team history in games, at bats, hits, and doubles. His lifetime average as a Padre was .252.

On May 31, 1991, Temply was hitting just .193 when he was traded to the Mets for another veteran infielder, Tim Teufel.

After the trade, Templeton aimed some of his verbal shots at Riddoch. He had also clashed at various times with Williams, Boros, and Bowa.

Many of Templeton's former teammates heaped praise on the one-time team captain, however. Gossage called him the MVP of the '84 N.L. championship team. Flannery praised him as the team's leader.

Templeton played just 80 games with the Mets before he retired at the end of the '91 season. Throughout his career, he could never escape the inevitable—and frequently unfavorable—comparisons with the man for whom he was traded, future Hall of Famer Ozzie Smith.

**Temper tantrums** After grounding out against the Dodgers in July, Santiago threw his helmet in disgust as he headed back to the dugout. The helmet bounced up and struck Riddoch in the temple, giving the Padres manager a mild concussion. Santiago was fined $300.

The moody backstop hit .267 with 17 homers and 87 RBIs in 1991. He drew only 23 walks while striking out 114 times. For the first time in his three major league seasons Santiago didn't win the Gold Glove, though he was named to his second All-Star team.

Santiago spent much of the 1991 season angry, primarily at his manager. He was taken out of a game in May for not running hard on a ground out. Riddoch said it was the third time in a week that Santiago failed to run out a ground ball. McKeon and Bowa had previously benched him for similar reasons.

**Combined no-hitter** Another veteran, Ed Whitson, retired in 1991. To this day, Whitson ranks third in team history in wins (77), innings pitched, and game starts. Like Templeton, he was a key member of the 1984 pennant-winning club. Whitson's career spanned a total of 15 seasons.

The Padres crept back above .500 in 1991 with a record of 84-78, ten games behind the surprising Braves. Teufel, the former star of the Mets and Twins, hit just .232 during his brief time in San Diego. Gwynn hit .317 in 1991—a sensational season for most other players, but a sub-par year by his standards. Outfielder Darrin Jackson, used largely in a pinch-hitting role, belted 21 home runs. Gerald Clark, the third outfielder, provided little offensive help, hitting .228.

The pitching staff was led by Hurst (15-8, 3.29), Benes (15-11, 3.03), and converted reliever Harris (9-5, 2.23). Lefferts went 1-6 with 23 saves.

On September 11, the Braves' Kent Mercker, Mark Wohlers, and Alejandro Pena combined for a no-hitter against the Padres. With two out in the ninth inning, Jackson almost broke up the no-hitter. He was safe on a grounder between third and short which looked like a hit, but (as the game was played in Atlanta), the official scorer ruled it an error. It was the fourth of six no-hitters thrown against the Padres, and the first combined no-hitter in N.L. history.

**Gary Sheffield** The Padres' 1992 season was nearly identical to the previous year. The team dropped back two games to finish at 82-80.

Prior to the season, Bip Roberts was traded to Cincinnati for Randy Myers, who'd established himself as a fine reliever with the Mets and Reds. Handed the closer's position by the Padres in '92, the lefty notched 38 saves, second in the league, despite a high ERA of 4.29.

Another key acquisition in 1992 was third baseman Gary Sheffield. At the end of spring training, the Padres sent three prospects—pitcher Ricky Bones, shortstop Jose Valentin, and outfielder Matt Mieske—to the Brewers for the 23-year old Sheffield.

All three youngsters surrendered by the Padres had solid careers throughout the decade, but the trade had enormous short-term *and* long-term consequence for San Diego. In a roundabout way, it helped lay the foundation for the pennant drives of the late 90s.

McIlvaine had been pursuing Sheffield for two years, despite concerns over his attitude and clubhouse presence in Milwaukee. The Padres predicted he'd become an All-Star one day, and they were right. After hitting less than .200 with the Brewers, Sheffield injected immediate muscle into the Padres lineup, combining with McGriff to form the best one-two punch in the game. Sheffield had a breakout year (.330, 33 HRs, 100 RBIs) in 1992. He fanned just 40 times and finished third in the N.L. MVP voting.

His .330 average earned Sheffield the N.L. batting title, making him the only Padre other than Gwynn to lead the league in hitting. Sheffield's .580 slugging percentage is the Padres' third-best mark for a single season.

From 1992-2000, either a Padre or a Rockie led the National League in batting: San Diego's Sheffield ('92) and Gwynn ('94-'97), and Colorado's Andres Galarraga ('93), Larry Walker ('98-'99), and Todd Helton ('00) all claimed the batting crown during that span.

McGriff had another outstanding season in 1992, pounding a league-high 35 homers to go with 104 RBIs and 96 walks. Crime Dog is the only Padre to win a home run crown. He also became the only player to win a homer title in both leagues, having led the A.L. in round-trippers in 1989. To this day, McGriff ranks second in slugging percentage (.519) among players with at least 1,500 at bats as a Padre.

The 1992 All-Star game was played at Jack Murphy Stadium, the second time the mid-summer classic came to America's Finest City. Five Padres—Gwynn, Fernandez, McGriff, Santiago, and Sheffield—represented the home team before the crowd of nearly 60,000.

The Chicken made a surprise appearance during the game. Giannoulas was asked to give advance notice when he planned to make an appearance, but this time he showed up unannounced. Before he could do his routine, he was escorted back to his seat by security.

Former Padre Bip Roberts returned to Jack Murphy Stadium and received a long ovation during the introductions. "That hit me inside big-time," he said.

Gwynn tied an All-Star record by throwing out two runners at second base. "Truthfully, I'd rather have a good defensive game than a good offensive game," he said. "People associate me with hitting, so doing something like that is a kick."[60]

**Pepe Le Peu**  Gwynn missed 34 games due to injuries in 1992, and hit .317 for the second straight year. His lower-body ailments also affected his speed; he stole just three bases, a career-low.

Fernandez attempted to steal 40 times during the season. He was successful 20 times and *un*successful 20 times, the worst stolen base percentage of any player with at least 20 steals since 1923.

Lefferts was converted from a reliever to a starter, and the southpaw responded with a mark of 13-9 with a 3.69 ERA. Just before the trading deadline of August 31, Lefferts was dealt to Baltimore for a minor leaguer who never saw action with the Padres. With his departure, only Gwynn remained from the National League championship team of eight years ago.

Hurst led Padres starters in 1992 with a 14-9 mark. He punctuated his season with a one-hit shutout over the Mets on May 18—his second one-hitter as a Padre. When the season ended, Hurst underwent surgery for a torn rotator cuff in his shoulder. He would appear in just 13 more major league games.

The most humorous moment of the season occurred when a skunk wandered on the field during a game in July. The skunk apparently made its nest in the tarp, which, of course, is rarely used in San Diego. The nervous grounds crew spent several minutes trying to catch the animal; the incident is still a mainstay on blooper films.

The JumboTron showed a close-up of the critter with the subheading, "Pepe Le Peu".

Not much else was funny about 1992. Despite boasting the league's batting and home run champs, the Padres were mired in third place, 16 games behind the Braves. With the team underachieving once more, Riddoch was fired on September 23. He was replaced by Jim Riggleman. Through no fault of his, under Riggleman's stewardship, the Padres saw their darkest hours.

**The path less traveled**  Pittsburgh slugger Barry Bonds was eligible for free agency at the end of the '92 season, and he openly stated that his first choice was to play for San Diego. Having the perennial All-Star and first-ballot Hall of Famer in a lineup with Gwynn, Sheffield, and McGriff would have made the Padres the most feared team in baseball.

Indeed, the Padres reached a fork in the road. They could pursue superstars like Bonds, who were willing to come to San Diego for less money, which would make the Padres heavy favorites in the National League.

Instead, management chose the other path: cut payroll to the bone.

Within the blink of an eye, the Padres' marquee players were shipped to contending teams for untested prospects and minor leaguers. Convinced that the team had no hope of competing, the Werner group decided to dump salary.

It was known as the "Fire Sale".

# The Darkest Days

THE FIRE SALE began immediately after the 1992 season and continued through mid-1993. The following are the moves which forever altered the face of baseball in San Diego:

1) *October 26, 1992*: Shortstop Tony Fernandez was traded to the Mets for two prospects—pitcher Wally Whitehurst and catcher Raul Casanova. Fernandez went on to enjoy a successful career through the 90s, appearing in several playoffs and World Series games, and eventually becoming the all-time hit leader from the Dominican Republic.

Whitehurst posted back-to-back 4-7 campaigns for the Padres before he retired in 1995. Casanova never played for the Padres and was included in a noneventful trade with Detroit in 1996.

2) *December 9, 1992*: Middle reliever Jose Melendez was sent to the Red Sox for Poway High alumnus Phil Plantier. This wasn't one of the blockbuster moves of the Fire Sale, but it did pay dividends for the Padres. Melendez pitched in just 19 more major league games, while Plantier had a career year for San Diego in 1993 (34 homers, 100 RBIs).

Plantier was also part of the huge trade with Houston in 1994 which laid the foundation for the pennant drives of 1996 and '98.

3) *December 9, 1992*: Closer Randy Myers signed a three-year free-agent contract with the Chicago Cubs.

4) *December 16, 1992*: Catcher Benito Santiago signed a free-agent contract with Florida.

Santiago wanted to remain in San Diego and even offered to take less money, but management wasn't interested in retaining the temperamental receiver. Santiago went on to play with several more teams during his career, including stops in Cincinnati, Toronto, Chicago, Boston, and San Francisco.

5) *March 30, 1993*: In a straightup swap of outfielders, Darrin Jackson was shipped to Toronto for Derek Bell.

This deal worked out nicely for San Diego. Jackson became a journeyman reserve, never catching on again as a starter. Bell turned in two solid seasons with the Padres, averaging .284 with 18 HRs and 25 steals a year. Along with Plantier, Bell was later included in the blockbuster trade with Houston.

6) *June 23, 1993*: The Padres sent setup man Tim Scott to Montreal for infielder Archi Cianfrocco. Cianfrocco would play with the Padres for the next six years, mostly as a reserve infielder and pinch hitter.

7) *June 24, 1993*: Defending batting champ Gary Sheffield and pitcher Rich Rodriguez were dealt to the expansion Florida Marlins for three young pitchers, one of whom was reliever Trevor Hoffman.

Rodriguez was a solid middle-reliever with the Padres from 1990-93, but he was eligible for arbitration after the season. His 1994 salary was projected at $1 million, and the Padres were looking for another taker. Sheffield was due $3.11 million in 1993 and $4 million the following year.

Despite his reputation as a less-than-ideal presence in the clubhouse, Sheffield had an enormously successful career after leaving San Diego. He moved to the outfield in Florida and Los Angeles and appeared in several All-Star games. But this deal proved that a trade can't always be measured in the short run. Today, fans can appreciate how important the Sheffield-for-Hoffman trade was for the Padres' future.

Sheffield didn't want the trade. "I'm going home to Florida to play," said the native Floridian, "but that doesn't erase the fact that I don't want to leave. My heart's always been here."[61]

Randy Smith, the new general manager, pointed out that Sheffield would be eligible for free agency after the following season, and there was no way the Padres would be able to meet his salary demands. The front office reasoned that obtaining three prospects for Sheffield now was more desirable than getting nothing in eighteen months. The Padres were especially high on young Hoffman, who was expected to improve the bullpen immediately.

Cost-cutting changes were even ordered in the front office. McIlvane was relieved of his duties as general manager, replaced by Smith, who made half of McIlvane's $500,000 salary. At 29, Smith became the youngest GM in major league history. Like his predecessor, he was given the unenviable task of paring the payroll even further. The Sheffield-Hoffman deal was Smith's first major transaction.

8) *July 18, 1993*: In the most disappointing move of all, first baseman McGriff was traded to Atlanta for three minor leaguers, none of whom panned out for the Padres. The Padres were particularly excited about obtaining outfielder Melvin Nieves, who played in only 108 games as a Padre.

The trade of the league's defending home run champ was expected for days while the two teams haggled over the details. The Padres had their sights set on three of the Braves' young prospects—infielder Chipper Jones, catcher Javier Lopez, and particularly outfielder Ryan Klesko, but the Braves refused to part with any of them.

Gwynn and other players were upset that management didn't hold out for more in return for McGriff. Locked in a tight pennant race, the Braves were desperate for a power-hitting first baseman. McGriff was the best around and the most readily available. But Smith settled for less than market value, to the chagrin of the players.

After arriving in Atlanta, McGriff remained one of the league's most prolific power hitters. His arrival in Atlanta helped turn the Braves' season around, enabling them to catch San Francisco in a race that went down to the wire. The McGriff deal probably ranks as the most lopsided trade in team history. But the mission was accomplished: his $4.25 million salary was no longer the responsibility of the Padres, absorbed instead by Ted Turner and all his millions.

9) *July 26, 1993*: In a five-player trade, San Diego sent Bruce Hurst, who was recovering from shoulder surgery, and pitcher Greg Harris to the Rockies for catcher Brad Ausmus and pitchers Doug Bochtler and Andy Ashby.

Though the Padres couldn't have known it at the time, this was a steal, partially making up for the disappointing McGriff trade. Harris was a reliable starter and setup man for the Padres for five seasons, but after the trade, he posted a woeful mark of just four wins against twenty-five defeats for the rest of his career. Hurst won only two more.

Ausmus took over starting catching duties for the next two seasons. He would ultimately be involved in the trade for Chris Gomez—yet another important piece to the two division-winning teams. Bochtler was a key setup man in the '96 pennant race. Ashby became a cornerstone of the Padres pitching corps from 1993-99.

After being fleeced so many times themselves, the final move in the Fire Sale was actually one of the Padres' best.

**Giving up?** To many fans, management simply gave up on fielding a contender. General managers McIlvaine and Smith were ordered to dump all high salaries—save only the untouchable Gwynn, who continued to take less money to play in San Diego. To no one's surprise, the Padres plummeted to the bottom of the National League West in 1993. Devoid of their veteran talent, they finished with a disastrous record of 61-101, 43 games behind Atlanta. Accordingly, attendance was also worst in the league.

The Fire Sale left a sour taste in the community. Fans toted banners in protest, some of which read "Trade Werner" and "Welcome to Kobey's". Two season-ticket owners even filed a class-action lawsuit seeking a refund for their seats plus unspecified punitive damages. Lawyers even circulated the stadium handing out business cards to season ticket owners, encouraging them to join the litigation.

Worse, some wondered whether Werner and his so-called 'Gang of 15' might even sell the club to an out-of-town buyer. But Werner and the minority owners, many of whom were local businessmen, insisted that was never an option.

Andy Benes pitched for San Diego from 1989-95. He is the team's all-time strikeout leader. (Courtesy, Topps)

Looking back nearly a decade later, the Fire Sale left a mixed legacy. On one hand, Hoffman, Ashby, Ken Caminiti, Steve Finley, and Chris Gomez, all of whom played key roles in the team's successes in 1996 and '98, rose (directly or indirectly) from the ashes of the Fire Sale. However, the negative publicity surrounding the team for two years damaged the credibility of the franchise, alienating thousands of fans in the process.

Through all the madness, Tony Gwynn remained the Padres' one constant in 1993. Still enduring nagging injuries, Tony rebounded from two sub-par seasons to hit .358—second in the league to Andres Galarraga, whose stats were padded by the high altitude of Denver.

Gwynn and Benes (15-15, 3.78) represented the Padres in the '93 All-Star game. That season, Benes was the winning pitcher in nearly one-fourth of the team's victories. The Padres' workhorse of the early-to-mid 90s, Benes went 59-54 in his first five seasons with the club, never with an ERA over 3.78.

Pitcher Tim Worrell made his debut in 1993. Worrell was used mainly as a starter, going 2-7 with a 4.92 ERA. He was used sparingly the following two seasons before catching on in 1996-97, primarily as a reliever. Worrell pitched for the Padres for a total of five seasons, compiling an overall mark of 16-23.

Gwynn, Bell (21 HRs, 26 steals), and Plantier (34 HRs, 100 RBIs) represented the offense in '93. But beyond that, the cupboard was bare. Was there anything on the horizon for long-suffering Padres fans to look forward to? Unfortunately, things actually got worse (if that was even imaginable) before they got better.

**Werner's legacy** 1994 brought about another format change in baseball, one which angered some purists. Major League Baseball planned to divide the leagues into three divisions each—the east, central, and west. In addition to the three division winners, a fourth team, the 'wild card', would also advance to the playoffs.

The reformatting was pushed by Werner. He successfully pitched the idea of doubling the number of teams that made the playoffs, thereby increasing fan interest. Werner, a television man, believed that television revenues would increase substantially under such a format.

The Eastern and Central divisions had five teams apiece, whereas just four teams—San Diego, San Francisco, Los Angeles, and Colorado—comprised the western division. A fifth team was added to the N.L. West when Arizona entered the league in 1998.

**Distant memory** Gwynn described the 1994 mid-season classic in Pittsburgh as one of his two greatest All-Star memories (the '99 game at Fenway Park was the other).

With the N.L. down 7-5 in the bottom of the ninth, McGriff tied the score with a pinch-hit two-run homer. That set the stage for Gwynn's heroics in extra innings. Gwynn, who played the entire ballgame, singled in the tenth. Houston's Moises Alou drove the ball into left-centerfield for extra bases. Gwynn slid under the tag of catcher Ivan Rodriguez with the winning run, barely ahead of the throw from Cal Ripken Jr. The win ended the National League's seven-year losing streak.

Unfortunately, the exciting mid-summer classic soon became a distant memory.

**Stee-rike 2**  Players began the 1994 season without a contract. Team owners insisted on a salary cap in order for small-market teams to survive, claiming that free agency tipped the scales disproportionately in favor of big cities and large-market franchises. Revenue sharing was also an issue.

Both sides were equally intractable. The threat of a work stoppage loomed like a dark cloud over the entire season.

In December 1975, players won the right to free agency, which became a source of chronic friction between players and owners, leading to a series of lockouts and strikes.

Bip Roberts, reacquired from Cincinnati in the off-season, hit .320 with 21 steals in 1994. Bell had another fine season (.311, 14 homers, 24 stolen bases). Plantier belted 18 homers but hit just .220. Australian-born Craig Shipley banged out a .333 average in part-time duties at third base. Ricky Gutierrez manned shortstop but provided little power or speed. The shortstop position remained a weakness for the Padres since the trade of Fernandez.

Benes went just 6-14 in 1994 but led the league in strikeouts, becoming the only Padre hurler to do so. He threw a one-hitter July 3 against the Mets (the Padres still lacked that elusive no-hitter, despite so many close calls). Benes was the Padres player representative and took a hard line during the strike.

Rookie Joey Hamilton anchored the pitching corps. The 23-year old Georgian went 9-6 with a sharp 2.98 ERA on the year. Hamilton averaged over 200 innings for the Padres from 1995-98. He'd be a mainstay of the rotations in the playoff seasons of 1996 and '98.

Batting was not one of Hamilton's strengths. While most pitchers have difficulty at the plate, Hamilton took it to the next level, going hitless in his first 57 major league at bats.

Through the specter of a strike and amid all the front-office maneuvering, it was difficult for players to concentrate on baseball. The Padres were mired in last place with an abysmal 47-70 record at the time of the strike.

**Gameless...**
**will play for free**  The lights went out August 12, 1994, when major league ballplayers officially went on strike.

It was the eighth work stoppage in baseball history and by far the most destructive. In all, the strike lasted 232 days (Aug. 12, 1994—March 31, 1995). Owners lost an estimated $800 million in revenue and players lost around $600 million in wages. No price tag could be placed on the loss of prestige of America's pastime.

Major league baseball was in jeopardy. With no resolution in sight to the endless conflict between players and management, the season was lost. All the while, the average fan simply couldn't sympathize with the petty bickering between millionaires. Some fans toted signs reading, "We'll play for free."

How many fans can name the teams that were in first place when play was halted? On August 12 the Dodgers, at three games over .500, led the N.L. West. In the Central the Reds led Houston by a half game, and Montreal actually led Atlanta by six in the East.

The Padres were also last in attendance. Between the Fire Sale and the labor dispute, fans who felt betrayed found other ways to spend their time and money. It was a dark time for professional baseball in San Diego—and all over the nation, for that matter.

"I'd like to see the two sides lock themselves in a room and get it done," said Gwynn. "But I've been around long enough to know that it doesn't happen that way."[62]

The strike accomplished what even wars, a depression, an earthquake, and terrorist attacks could not: cancellation of the World Series.

"There cannot be joy on any side," said acting Commissioner Bud Selig on September 14, the day the Series was officially cancelled. "This is a sad day. Nobody wanted this to happen, but the continuing player strike leaves us no choice but to take this action."

**Three hits short** The strike destroyed another dream in San Diego. Gwynn had an excellent shot at becoming the first player in 53 years to hit .400. He was hitting .394 (including an unbelievable *.475* clip during August) at the time of the strike. The mark was the highest since Ted Williams' .406 in 1941, and was the highest average in the National League since Bill Terry's .401 in 1930.

Gwynn fell three hits short of .400.

Without the strike, most observers felt he would likely have achieved the goal. Riggleman noted that he was getting stronger as the season went on. Gwynn walked 48 times (against just 19 strikeouts) for a .454 on-base percentage, which led the league and established a team record. The batting crown was his fifth.

Surprisingly, despite his flirtation with .400, Gwynn finished just seventh in the MVP voting, probably owing to the Padres' sad circumstance. After the Fire Sale, devoid of their star talent and mired in last place, the Padres simply fell off the radar screen.

**Andy Ashby and Trevor Hoffman** The strike was finally settled toward what would have been the end of spring training. The late start cut 18 games from the 1995 season.

Andy Ashby was acquired by San Diego in the final move of the Fire Sale. He was a product of the Philadelphia organization, going 1-5 as a rookie and 1-3 his sophomore season, posting high ERAs. Obtained by the Rockies in the expansion draft, he went 0-4 with a still higher ERA in '93 before his trade to the Padres.

Having acquired a pitcher with a career 2-12 mark and a 7.44 ERA for accomplished veterans Hurst and Harris, it appeared the Padres had gotten the short end of another trade.

But while Hurst and Harris combined for a total of just six career wins after the trade, Ashby became a cornerstone of the Padres starting rotation over the next six seasons. In the strike-shortened '94 campaign, he went 6-11 with a 3.40 ERA. It was in 1995 that Ashby developed a cut fastball, and established himself as a true staff ace. Ashby later appeared in two All-Star games and earned a reputation as one of baseball's true good guys.

It's hard to picture Trevor Hoffman in any other uniform, but he garnered two wins and a pair of saves in 28 games for the Marlins in '93. Trevor is the younger brother of infielder Glenn Hoffman, who played in the majors from 1980-89 and later became a Dodgers manager and coach.

Originally drafted as a shortstop, Hoffman was obtained in the Sheffield deal in 1993. He appeared in 39 games for the Padres that season, posting a record of 2-4 with three saves. It was in 1994 that he assumed the role of closer, and he's never looked back. Hoffman was named to the All-Star team three straight seasons (1998-2000) and won the Fireman of the Year award in 1998. He was second in the Cy Young voting that season.

In June 1997, Hoffman recorded his 109th save as a Padre, surpassing Rollie Fingers as the team's leader. Today, Trevor has over 300 saves for his career. The master of the nastiest changeup in the game is still going strong, ranking as one of the great closers in baseball history.

When the game's on the line and Trevor gets the call, with "Hell's Bells" blaring and fans on their feet, there may not be a noisier, more exciting park in America than Qualcomm Stadium.

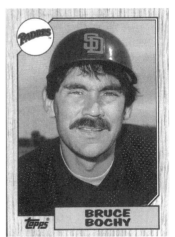

Bruce Bochy was a backup catcher for the Padres for five seasons. He later became the winningest manager in team history. (Courtesy, Topps)

**"Boch"** During the off-season the Padres made several more moves—but this time the

148

Fire Sale was over, and the club was actually posturing to become a legitimate contender once more.

The first major transaction occurred on October 21, 1994, when Bruce Bochy was hired to replace manager Jim Riggleman. Bochy's playing career lasted from 1978-87. After his retirement, he was hired as a minor league manager for the Padres and became third base coach for the major-league club in 1993. 'Boch' provided long-needed stability and sensibility to the clubhouse, ultimately becoming the winningest manager in team history.

The next big overhaul took place in the front-office. Padres fans, remember the name John Moores, who may have saved baseball in San Diego, just as Ray Kroc did twenty years prior.

# A New Owner, A New Era

ON DECEMBER 21, 1994, the $81 million sale of majority ownership of the Padres was finalized. The transfer of the club to more progressive owners led by John Moores and Larry Lucchino—owners sincerely interested in the long-term success and stability of the franchise, who were willing to make financial commitments to ensure that success—may have saved professional baseball in San Diego again.

Ray Kroc would be tipping his cap.

"Part of the mistake we made was, the average fan doesn't care about the problems of running a small-market team," said outgoing owner Werner, who retained a minority ownership in the team.

Addressing the Fire Sale, he said, "What we were doing was regrettable, but we were doing it to keep the franchise afloat, to keep from losing $15 million a year."[63]

After founding Houston-based BMC Software, Moores built a reported net worth of $400 million. The native Texan and his wife Becky are well-known philanthropies, contributing generously to causes throughout the community, including a $20 million donation to the UCSD Cancer Facility.

Moores readily admits that buying the Padres, who continue to lose millions each year, was a financial blunder. But the fan within keeps him attached to the game he loves, and though other cities have expressed interest, he has dedicated himself to keeping the Padres in San Diego.

By the mid-90's, the Padres were already hinting at the need for a new facility, which was necessary from both a financial and a practical standpoint. For twenty-five years, they'd shared a multi-purpose stadium with two football teams, and economic realities finally made that situation unworkable. "The demonstration made in Cleveland and

Baltimore [with their new downtown stadiums] makes the case for doing it by fact, not just argument," wrote syndicated columnist George F. Will.

In both those cities, where baseball was once barely hanging on, tickets to home games sell out for the entire year; three million tickets to Indians games at Jacobs Field were gone before this season even started. The Padres will enjoy enormous new revenue streams once they move into their own downtown ballpark, enabling them to compete financially with the rest of the division. It is to this end that the Moores/Lucchino team has committed itself.

Despite his monetary losses, Moores says there is no price tag on the pleasure that the Padres give him, year in and year out. Fortunately for San Diego, John Moores is a different breed of corporate cat. Which is why, as Will says, "He is the best team owner in sports."

**Wow!**  One of the most important dates in Padres history was December 28, 1994. With the players still on strike, the Padres and Houston Astros pulled the trigger on baseball's biggest trade since 1957. The Astros they felt certain that Cal State Fullerton's Phil Nevin, their first overall pick in the 1992 draft, was their third baseman of the future. That left Ken Caminiti, an outstanding fielder with decent production at the plate, expendable. The Padres had need of a third baseman, which set the stage for a blockbuster trade.

The Padres also needed a centerfielder and shortstop. Randy Smith's father was president of the Astros, which made for a natural working relationship between the clubs. Smith and Astros GM Bob Watson first discussed a four player deal. Then it grew to five or six. The teams discussed various scenarios over a period of two months.

When the Padres new ownership group took over, Smith was given the green light to add salary. With that, the wheels were in motion. The deal ultimately involved twelve players. It was the final step in the team's rise from the dark days of the Fire Sale to legitimate contender status.

The Padres sent pitcher Pedro Martinez (not the same as Boston's Cy Young pitcher), outfielders Bell and Plantier, and infielders Shipley and Gutierrez to Houston. In return they received Caminiti, centerfielder Finley, shortstop Andujar Cedeno, first baseman Roberto Petagine, pitcher Brian Williams and a player to be named (pitcher Sean Fesh).

In completing the trade, the Padres were assuming an additional $5.5 million in payroll. The deal dramatically altered the dynamics of the National League West.

Bochy's reaction to the news: "*Wow.*"

"I don't think there's any question (the Padres are contenders)," added Gwynn. "Now it falls into the players' laps to get it done."[64]

Said ESPN's Peter Gammons: "To their credit, when Tom Werner and Randy Smith began trading during the fire sale, they pledged they were doing it in order to rebuild for 1995, and they absolutely fulfilled their promise. You don't see that very often in baseball these days."

**The scorecard** So who got the better of the trade?

Plantier played in a total of just 22 games for Houston. He briefly returned to the Padres, but by 1997 his career was through. Plantier never came close to his fine '93 campaign, in which he lead the Padres in home runs and RBIs. Likewise, Shipley and Martinez had minimal impact after leaving San Diego.

Bell provided modest power for the Astros over the next five seasons, averaging 15 home runs a year with an average close to .300. Gutierrez was the Astros' semi-regular shortstop for the next four seasons. He was consistent, if nothing else (he hit .261 three years in a row). His offense improved when he took over as the Cubs' full-time shortstop in 2000.

From the Padres' end, Cedeno was not the answer to their problems at shortstop. His greatest claim to fame was striking out ten times in three games, tying a major league record. Cedeno hit just .210 in 1995 and was shipped to Detroit in the Chris Gomez deal in mid-1996.

Petagine played only the '95 season with San Diego, hitting .234, mostly as a pinch hitter. Williams also spent just one year as a Padre, going just 3-10. Fesh never played in the majors.

So the biggest trade in team history essentially boiled down to Bell and Gutierrez for Finley and Caminiti. The Padres were smiling all the way to the bank.

**Steve Finley and Ken Caminiti** Steve Finley broke into the majors with the Baltimore Orioles in 1989. After two mediocre seasons in Baltimore, his bat came alive with Houston, where he averaged .281 with 28 steals from 1991-94. In Finley the Padres saw a combination of speed and emerging power.

In his first season as a Padre, Finley hit .297 with 36 steals and 104 runs scored. It was the following season, 1996, that Finley blossomed into one of the best outfielders in baseball, finishing in the top ten in N.L. MVP voting.

Caminiti came up as a 24-year old rookie with Houston in 1987. Like Finley, his early career showed scant indication of his future stardom. He hit under .250 with limited power during his first five seasons.

Centerfielder Steve Finley was acquired from Houston in a mammoth twelve-player trade on December 28, 1994. (Courtesy, Hall of Champions)

Caminiti raised his average by 1992 and showed more pop at the plate. His best year with Houston was the strike-shortened '94 season, when he hit .283 with 18 HRs and 75 RBIs. The switch-hitting Caminiti made his first All-Star appearance that year, which was his final season in Houston.

Cammy came into his own as a bonafide superstar after arriving in San Diego. In 1995, the third baseman hit .302 with 26 homers, 94 RBIs, and 33 doubles—all career highs. He also won the Gold Glove award. By solidifying the defense on the left side of the infield, Caminiti improved the confidence of Ashby and Hamilton, who were primarily groundball pitchers. He had finally emerged as one of the best all-around third basemen in the game.

Caminiti's hard-nosed brand of play, even while battling chronic injuries throughout his career, won the hearts of Padres fans. He brought heart and soul to the ballclub, and he emerged as the unquestioned leader of the Padres' division-winning teams.

In a span of just four days (Sept. 16-19), Caminiti homered from both sides of the plate in three different games. The feat set a record: No one had ever switch-hit homers three times in an entire season—and Caminiti managed it in just four games.

Finley and Caminiti won Gold Gloves in 1995, despite what Caminiti called 'one of my worst years' defensively. Plagued by chronic back pain, the Padres third baseman committed a career-worst 27 errors. The pain was so severe that even sitting down after games was difficult.

**Padre Scholars** In its ongoing effort to give back to the community, the new ownership established the Padres Scholars Program in 1995. The program awards $5,000 college scholarships to 25 disadvantaged, academically-deserving middle school students in San Diego County each year. The program is the only one of its kind in Major League Baseball. Players contribute funds each year, which are matched dollar-for-dollar by ownership.

**Finishing touches** In April 1995, the Padres further upgraded the ballclub by signing veteran Jody Reed, the best-fielding second baseman in baseball during the previous season. Reed hit around .280 most of his career before joining the Padres.

Reed batted .255 with San Diego in 1995, showing a sharp eye at the plate and fielding a solid second base. He committed only four errors that season, and his .994 fielding percentage tied for best among N.L. second basemen.

Ausmus was the Padres' regular backstop, hitting .293 with 16 steals. Bip Roberts, again splitting his time between the infield and outfield, batted .304.

**Around the corner** Another important pickup for the Padres was someone who needed little introduction to southern Californians, pitcher Fernando Valenzuela. Fernando pitched for the rival Dodgers from 1980-90, winning Rookie of the Year honors *and* the Cy Young Award in 1981. His heroics incited "Fernando-Mania" throughout Los Angeles, and for most of the 80s, the Dodgers ace didn't disappoint. But by the early-90s, it looked as though his career was on the decline.

The Padres decided to take a chance on Valenzuela, and the veteran rewarded their confidence. In 1995, Valenzuela appeared in 29 games for the Padres, starting 15, posting an 8-3 mark. His ERA was high that year (4.98), but he would make a significant contribution to the club's pennant drive the following season.

Ashby (12-10, 2.94) led the staff in wins. Hamilton's ERA was close to Ashby's, but he posted just a 6-9 record.

Benes, who was coming off the worst year of his career, was just 4-7 in July when the Padres dealt him to Seattle. In return, the Padres received pitcher Ron Villone and outfielder Marc Newfield. Benes posted a 7-2 mark the rest of the way, helping the Mariners overtake the Angels and win the A.L. West by one game.

Benes pitched for the Padres from 1989-95, and today ranks as the team's all-time strikeout leader. He is also fifth in team history in wins (69), fourth in starts, and fourth in innings pitched. Benes had a solid career after leaving the Padres, winning double-figures for St. Louis and Arizona through the 2000 season.

Hoffman had his first outstanding season as the Padres closer in 1995 with a 7-4 mark and 31 saves. Willie Blair, pitching for his fifth team in six seasons, went 7-5, splitting time between the rotation and the 'pen'.

Gwynn was the only Padre named to the 1995 All-Star team. At age 35, Gwynn won his sixth batting title with a .368 mark. Tony struck out only 15 times in 535 at bats, an incredible rate of just one whiff every 36 times up—compared with the league average of one K for every five at bats.

The 1995 version of the Padres rebounded from consecutive last place seasons to finish in third place, 8 games behind L.A. They were just four games under .500, an amazing improvement from the previous year. Fans still took some convincing before coming back to the park; despite the team's advances, attendance in San Diego was second-worst in the league. But under a new manager and new ownership, fans could see that something was happening. Good things, very good things, were just around the corner.

# A Weekend for the Ages

JUST THREE YEARS after baseball hit rock bottom in San Diego, the Padres completed their astonishing rise to first place.

Prior to the 1996 season, the Padres hired another youthful general manager, 34-year old Kevin Towers. Towers pitched for seven years in the Padres farm system but never made the majors. Former GM Randy Smith moved on to Detroit but maintained his friendship with Towers, and the two became frequent trading partners.

The Padres made an aggressive attempt to sign free agent Craig Biggio in the off-season, offering the All-Star second baseman the largest contract in team history, but he chose to re-sign with Houston.

San Diego reached the postseason once again in 1996, ending a twelve-year drought and completing a meteoric climb from worst-to-first within the span of just two years. Entering the season, the nucleus of the club was already in place.

The Padres needed one more quality starter to complete their rotation. Though San Diego rarely went the free agent route, they signed control artist Bob Tewksbury on December 18, 1995. The ten-year veteran was a reliable starter for the Cardinals throughout the 90's, and he was the starting pitcher in the 1992 All-Star game in San Diego. Tewksbury signed a one-year contract for $1.5 million, with a club option for 1997.

The Padres also needed a first baseman, and the venerable Bip Roberts became trade bait once more. The Padres already had a table-setter in Finley, and with Roberts' salary and frequent stays on the disabled list, he was deemed expendable. On December 21, 1995, the Padres sent Roberts to the Kansas City Royals for veteran Wally Joyner.

It was the second time in four years that Roberts had been dispatched by the Padres, and the news of the trade devastated him. He went on to play three more years, spending time with Kansas City,

Cleveland, Detroit, and Oakland. Roberts retired in 1998 with an excellent lifetime average of .294, with 264 stolen bases.

Joyner had a sensational rookie campaign with California in 1986, inheriting the first base job from Rod Carew and making an immediate impact on the Angels' pennant run. Wally hit .290 with 22 HRs and 100 RBIs in '86, finishing second in the Rookie of the Year voting to Jose Canseco. His finest all-around year was his sophomore season (.285, 34 HRs, 117 RBIs).

After 1987, Joyner never displayed the power he'd shown his first two years. He did continue to hit in the .290-.300 range, showing a good eye at the plate and becoming one of the best fielding first basemen in the game. Joyner played with the Angels from 1986-91 and with the Royals from 1992-95.

Nicknamed "Wally World" (after the fictional amusement park in National Lampoon's 'Vacation'), Joyner was 34 when he arrived in San Diego. He was a longtime friend of Kevin Towers, which helped ice the deal.

Joyner's slick glove saved infielders an untold number of errors. A practicing Mormon and devoted family man, Joyner plugged a gaping hole at first base in 1996, which was critical to the Padres' pennant run.

**Rickey** San Diego signed another free agent, future Hall of Famer Rickey Henderson, on December 29. Henderson (known simply as 'Rickey') had driven pitchers insane since his rookie season with Oakland in 1979. He broke Lou Brock's single-season stolen base mark with 130 in 1982, and then he shattered Brock's career record of 938 steals in '91. In the ceremony that followed, Rickey reminded the crowd, "Today, I am the greatest of all time."

Henderson played with the A's (four different times), Yankees, and Blue Jays before coming to the Padres. Born Christmas Day 1958, Rickey was named A.L. MVP in 1990. The ten-time All-Star may be known best for his flashy personality, making both friends and adversaries in his many stops around baseball. His lifetime statistics (stolen bases, walks, runs, and hits) rank him among the game's elite.

"I think he'll bring a little attitude to this ballclub," said Towers.

"We went from dumping guys to signing guys who we think can help us win," added Gwynn, who was Henderson's junior by one year. "The only bad thing is I have to give up my front seat on the bus now because he's the oldest guy."[65]

**Brothers Gwynn** Tony's brother, Chris, was an All-American baseball player at SDSU and a member of the 1984 U.S. Olympic team.

Chris played with the Dodgers from 1987-91. He moved to Kansas City for two years before returning to L.A. for the 1994-95 seasons. He signed as a free agent with the Padres in 1996. His signing gave rise to his brother's nickname 'T. Gwynn', so as to differentiate between the two.

The Padres were legitimate contenders, and fans realized once again there was a major league team in town. Nearly 2.2 million came to see the Padres battle for the title, a jump in attendance from thirteenth in the league to sixth.

**The makings** Towers sought to upgrade the shortstop position, and he went calling
**of a winner** on his friend Randy Smith in Detroit. The teams worked out a deal on June 18 which brought shortstop Chris Gomez and catcher John Flaherty to San Diego. The Padres sent Ausmus and the underachieving Cedeno in return.

Gomez, an alumnus of Long Beach State, first came up with the Tigers in '93. He hit .262 with the Padres for the rest of the 1996 season, providing steady defense at a crucial position. 'Gomey' was the Padres' regular shortstop until 1999, when knee injuries limited his playing time.

Padres starters were led by Hamilton (15-9 4.17) and Valenzuela (13-8, 3.62), who rewarded the Padres for their confidence. In his only season with the Padres, Tewksbury went 10-10, though he struggled down the stretch. Ashby won nine games against five losses and posted the best ERA among the starters (3.23).

Hoffman (9-5, 42 saves, and a sharp 2.25 ERA) appeared in a career-best 70 games, finishing third in the league in saves and fifth in the Cy Young voting. His 42 saves broke the team record set by Fingers in 1978.

Bochtler was second to Hoffman in games pitched with 63, appearing mostly in middle relief. Scott Sanders appeared in 46 games—30 in relief, 16 as a starter—posting a 9-5 mark with a 3.38 ERA.

While their starting pitching was only average, the '96 Padres were an offensive juggernaut. Leftfield was manned by Henderson, who hit just .241 but walked 125 times, giving him a .410 on-base percentage, fifth-best in the league. Rickey also stole 37 bases and scored 110 runs.

Joyner provided modest production, hitting .277 in 121 games with 8 HRs, 65 RBIs, and 69 walks. It was an off-season at the plate; Wally hadn't had such a poor offensive performance in four years. Still, he was highly regarded by teammates and fans, and his presence in the clubhouse contributed enormously to the team's turnaround.

Flaherty, acquired in the June trade with Detroit, became the Padres' regular catcher and hit .303 the rest of the season (by way of comparison, Ausmus hit under .200 after joining the Tigers—though he'd have better seasons ahead). Flaherty was backed up at catcher by Brian Johnson, who hit .272.

On July 27, the Padres became the sixth team to score twenty runs in a game. Flaherty belted a grand slam in a 20-12 win against the Marlins, which was also the 27th consecutive game in which he hit safely. It was the second-longest hitting streak by a catcher in history; former Padre Benito Santiago set the standard nine years earlier. Flaherty's streak was halted the next night.

An Achilles tendon injury limited Tony Gwynn's season to 116 games, but he managed a .353 average, which was good for his seventh batting crown. Because he had fewer than the required number of at bats (3.1 plate appearances per team game) a number of hitless at bats were added to his season total, but despite that penalty, he still led the league.

Finley came to bat 655 times and scored 126 times—both single-season team records. He had an all-around sensational year, hitting .298 with 45 doubles, 9 triples, 30 homers, 95 RBIs, and 22 steals. His defense in centerfield earned him another Gold Glove.

Gwynn and Caminiti represented the Padres at the 1996 All-Star game in Philadelphia, though the former was unable to play because of his Achilles' tendon injury. He came out for pregame introductions with his right leg in a walking boot.

Caminiti started the game in place of injured starter Matt Williams. He belted a solo home run leading off the sixth, leading the N.L. to a 6-0 victory. It is the only time that a Padre has homered in an All-Star game.

**Greg Vaughn** On the eve of the trading deadline, the Padres pulled off a major transaction, which solidified their status as serious playoff contenders. All-Star outfielder Greg Vaughn was acquired from the Milwaukee Brewers on July 31, 1996 in exchange for outfielder Marc Newfield and pitchers Bryce Florie and Ron Villone. Though they gave up three solid young players, the trade was huge for the Padres.

Villone and Newfield were acquired the previous year in the Benes deal. Newfield played just two more seasons in the major leagues. Villone pitched for Milwaukee, Cleveland, and Cincinnati, developing into a decent starter.

While pitching for Boston in 2000, Florie suffered every pitcher's worst nightmare. He was struck in the face by a line drive, suffering a fractured orbital socket and cheekbone. His career was never the same.

Greg Vaughn, cousin of the Angel's Mo, was born July 3, 1965. He played with Milwaukee from 1989-96, ranking fifth in Brewers history in home runs. Vaughn was having his finest season when he joined the Padres, hitting 31 HRs with 95 RBIs in just 102 games before the trade.

Vaughn was to be a free agent at the end of the year, and Milwaukee felt it could not afford to re-sign him. Padres fans heard that very statement so often through the years, but this time, San Diego was the beneficiary of another team's salary dump.

"I'm leaving a great organization," said Vaughn, "but I'm getting to go into a pennant race and a place where it's 75 degrees year-round."[66]

The move gave the Padres four outfielders, which put Henderson's status in jeopardy. But Vaughn had difficulty adjusting to the National League. He hit just 10 home runs and batted .206 after the trade, and toward the end of the season, Henderson was the full-time leftfielder.

Still, Vaughn's reputation kept opposing pitchers from pitching around Caminiti. His presence in the lineup may have cinched the MVP award for Cammy, who exploded after the acquisition of Vaughn.

Caminiti owned the 1996 season. Playing through constant pain, the Padres third baseman set team records of 40 HRs (since broken) and 130 RBIs. He had 37 doubles, 109 runs, a .326 average, and a .621 slugging percentage, the best in team history. And if that wasn't enough, he won the Gold Glove for the second straight year.

Amazingly, Caminiti injured the rotator cuff in his left shoulder in a game against Houston in April. Throughout the season he was unable to raise his left arm above his head, and the shoulder kept him from extending his arms while swinging. He underwent surgery after the season.

**IVs and Snickers** As one of its objectives, the new ownership group sought to extend the team's fan base south of the border. They made good on that commitment when the Padres and Mets squared off for a three-game series August 16-18 in Monterrey, Mexico. They were the first major league games played outside the U.S. or Canada.

In the midst of a pennant race with the rival Dodgers, there was some concern about the Padres relinquishing three home games, though the Padres were technically the home team for the series. Fans in San Diego watched the 'home games' on a one-hour tape delay.

Any questions about the Mexican fans' sentiments were answered when the Padres announced their starting rotation. Mexican native Fernando Valenzuela was given the start for game one. Never mind that his spot in the rotation was moved back a day: the fans chanted *Toro! Toro!* (the Bull), and cheered his every move. Clearly, the Padres became Monterrey's team, and with it, they had won over much of Mexico.

"I felt like I was at home," the 35-year old Valenzuela said. "It was a start in a regular-season game, and in my mind, I just wanted to do my job. But it was very emotional, and I felt a little hurried at times."[67]

Finley hit the first-ever home run outside the U.S. or Canada; Valenzuela recorded the first win. Valenzuela was lifted in the seventh after giving up three runs. The Mets scored seven more in the ninth off of three relievers before they finally slammed the door for a messy 15-10 win.

23,699 saw the first game of this historic series. The win also kept the Padres in a tie with L.A. for first.

The Mets came back to take game two, 7-3. Players on both sides complained about the dim lighting at *Estadio Monterrey*.

Lighting wasn't a problem in game three, which was played under the sun in Monterrey's searing Sunday afternoon heat. This game is remembered for the single-greatest individual performance of the season. If there was any microcosm of Caminiti's MVP season, this was it.

The heat affected several players. Caminiti was suffering a stomach bug, nausea, and dehydration. The Mets' Todd Hundley, suffering similar symptoms, skipped the game altogether. But with the Padres locked in a pennant race, Cammy proved himself tougher.

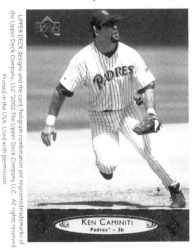

Prior to the game, two liters of liquid solution were pumped into his veins. Bochy was unsure whether to pencil his ailing third baseman into the lineup, but ten minutes before the game Caminiti told him he was ready to go. He ate a Snickers bar before taking the field.

In the second inning Caminiti delivered an opposite-field solo home run. He repeated the feat an inning later, this time with two men on base. He left after the fifth inning, the Padres safely ahead 6-0 en route to taking two out of three from the Mets. Caminiti required a second IV after leaving the game and was too weak to talk to reporters.

Ken Caminiti was the unanimous choice for National League MVP in 1996.(courtesy Upper Deck)

"We All started screaming for IV's and Snickers after that," joked Gwynn.

"That's the most incredible thing I've ever been around in baseball," added Tewksbury. "I thought there was no way this guy was going to play."[68]

**"Beat L.A.!"** On September 20, the Padres launched a program to build 60 baseball fields throughout San Diego County and Mexico. The 60 'Little Padres Parks' (honoring 60 years of professional baseball in San Diego) usually include an outfield fence, palm trees, scoreboards, seats, and landscaping.

The 'Little Padres Parks' represents one of the many efforts by the team to give back to the community.

By mid-September, the Padres and Dodgers were locked in a tight battle for the division title. Two Italians—Caminiti and the Dodgers' Mike Piazza—were considered the top candidates for league MVP to that point. Also, evoking shadows of his '89 showdown with Will Clark, Gwynn was locked in a close race with Piazza for the batting title.

The teams squared off in a four-game series in San Diego, beginning September 19, 1996. The series had everything: In the heat of a pennant race, the Padres' opponent was the rival Dodgers, which brought the excitement to another level. Los Angeles led the division by just a half game.

The Dodgers were managed by former shortstop Bill Russell, who took over after Tommy Lasorda suffered a heart attack in June. The offense was carried by catcher Mike Piazza (.336, 36 HRs, 105 RBIs). First baseman Eric Karros (.260, 34, 111), a San Diego native, and cannon-armed rightfielder Raul Mondesi (.297, 24, 88) joined Piazza in the heart of the order.

Japanese-born Hideo Nomo (16-11, 3.19) was the Dodgers' leading starter. (The following season, Nomo became one of the very few players that Tony Gwynn genuinely disliked. In 1997, Nomo sued Gwynn's wife, Alicia, claiming she used his name and likeness in a jigsaw puzzle without authorization. Gwynn made him pay: From then on, he stepped it up a notch every time the Padres faced Nomo.) Ismael Valdes (15-7, 3.32), Ramon Martinez (15-6, 3.42), and Pedro Astacio (9-8. 3.44) completed the rotation.

If Padres fans wanted to see the first game of the series, they had to be there in person. The biggest game of the season to date, featuring Valenzuela versus Martinez, wasn't televised.

Fans actually didn't miss much: Martinez threw a dominating six-hit shutout, fanning 12 batters as the Dodgers prevailed, 7-0.

Caminiti struck out three times and committed an error in the first inning that led to three Dodgers runs.

"I definitely noticed a little tension, and we've got to get rid of it," he said.

During the game he nearly snapped his bat in frustration, but held back. "That's a good bat; I don't want to break it."[69]

The Padres bounced back in the second game behind a strong outing by Hamilton. He exited with two out in the eighth and the Padres up, 3-2. Hoffman came on and retired all four batters he faced, saving Hamilton's fifteenth win of the year. The Padres added one more run on a home run by Caminiti for a 4-2 win. Finley was the offensive star of the game with two home runs.

The see-saw battle continued for the next two days. In the third game, the Dodgers pounded Scott Sanders for seven runs as Ismael Valdes cruised to a 9-2 win. It was the first time all season that Gwynn, Caminiti, and Finley each went hitless as starters.

Ashby got the call in place of the struggling Tewksbury to start the fourth and final game of the series. The score was 1-1 in the fifth, when Finley came to bat against Nomo with one man on base. The Padres centerfielder crushed his 28th home run of the season—his fourth decisive homer in September—to put San Diego on top, 3-1.

The Dodgers weren't finished. Piazza launched a second-deck homer in the eighth to bring L.A. within a run. But on came Trevor, in the midst of a streak of 15 saves in 15 chances. Hoffman shut down the Dodgers the rest of the way, and the final score was San Diego 3, Los Angeles 2. After the four-game split, L.A. still clung to a half-game lead.

"It would have been tough to come back from two-and-a-half games to this team," said Finley, referring to the scenario had the Padres dropped the final game.

"The pressure is still on them," cautioned Dodgers manager Bill Russell. "They still have to come to us."[70]

**Down to the wire** The Padres had five games remaining; the Dodgers six. The teams would face off in the final three games of the season at Dodger Stadium. During the Dodgers series, the Padres lost their starting catcher when Flaherty suffered a sprained ankle. He was expected to be out until the playoffs. Backup Brian Johnson would handle catching duties for the rest of the regular season.

As of September 20, Gwynn's average stood at .350; Piazza at .344. Even if Gwynn had the higher average by season's end, Piazza could still win the batting title if Tony didn't have enough at bats to qualify.

Despite the momentum of Sunday's win over L.A., the Padres dropped the next two ballgames to Colorado. It was exactly what they *couldn't* afford. The Dodgers seized the opportunity, taking two out of three from the Giants, opening up a two-game lead over the Padres. Going into the final weekend, the N.L. West standings were:

| Team | W | L | Pct. | GB |
|------|-----|-----|------|-----|
| Los Angeles | 90 | 69 | .566 | ~ |
| San Diego | 88 | 71 | .553 | 2 |

The only way the Padres could win the division now was to sweep the last three games from L.A. on their home turf, something they hadn't accomplished in five years.

Several scenarios loomed as the final weekend approached. Even if the Padres fell short of the divisional title, they held a one-game edge over Montreal for the wild card. If the Padres and Expos ended the season tied, Montreal would come to San Diego for a one-game playoff to determine the wild card winner.

If the Padres won the wild card, their opponent in the first round of the playoffs would be Atlanta, winners of the N.L. East. If they won the division outright they'd face St. Louis, central division champs, who had the lowest winning percentage of any playoff contender. Of the two teams, the Braves were clearly the tougher, particularly with their awesome pitching staff. Among the Braves' starters were John Smoltz, Greg Maddux, and Tom Glavine, with a total of seven Cy Young awards among them. In a best-of-five series, that rotation could be devastating.

"Winning the division is first in my mind, but getting in (the playoffs) is the first priority," said Gwynn. "Seems like every year somebody is clinching against us." It was the year before that the Dodgers clinched the division at Jack Murphy Stadium.[71]

For the Padres to avoid Atlanta in the first round, they'd have to sweep the Dodgers and capture the division flag. The Padres weren't necessarily guaranteed a wild card berth either, with the Expos just a game back. So the stakes were high entering the final weekend at Chavez Ravine.

**One down…** Scott Sanders (9-5) started game one of the series on Friday, September 27. Ismael Valdes, who'd dominated the Padres the previous weekend at Mission Valley, started for the Dodgers.

A number of Padres fans made the two-hour trek up the freeway, but a surprising number of seats were still empty at Dodger Stadium. Some players felt the Dodgers (and their fans) approached the series too casually.

Valdes cruised through seven innings, protecting a 2-1 Dodgers lead. To the plate came Caminiti, the Padres' most imposing hitter. The league MVP slammed a breaking ball from Valdes over the centerfield wall for his club-record 40th home run, tying the game.

The score remained 2-2 in the 10th. Finley greeted reliever Antonio Osuna with a single. He was driven home by—who else?—Caminiti, who doubled to left, putting the Padres up by a run. It was Caminiti's 130th and final RBI of the year, also a club record.

Joyner was intentionally passed, and Gomez singled to knock in Caminiti with the Padres' fourth run. On the play Joyner was caught between second and third, but centerfielder Todd Hollandsworth overthrew the ball, allowing Joyner to score.

Hoffman sealed the deal in the bottom of the tenth. The final score was San Diego 5, Los Angeles 2. The Dodgers still led by one game with two to play.

**Gwynn's heroics** In the second game, L.A. took an early 2-0 lead against Ashby. The Dodgers' Nomo carried a shutout into the sixth inning when the white-hot Finley stepped to the plate. Fins—an MVP candidate himself—led off the inning with his 30th homer of the year. Caminiti and Joyner then followed with back-to-back singles, and Gomez tied the score with a double to right. In the excitement surrounding this game and the next, Gomey's clutch hit is often forgotten.

With two out in the eighth and the score still tied at 2, Reed singled off reliever Darren Dreifort. Vaughn, pinch-hitting for Worrell, bounced a grounder deep in the hole at short. Reed slid into second and barely beat the force attempt by shortstop Gagne, thus keeping the inning alive. Henderson followed with a walk to load the bases. Mark Guthrie was summoned in relief.

To the plate stepped Tony Gwynn, the last man the Dodgers wanted to see in this situation.

Gwynn worked the count to 2-and-1 before utilizing his famous '5.5 hole', shooting the ball past the shortstop and into left field. Reed and Vaughn scored to put the Padres up, 4-2.

What was most remarkable about the hit was that third baseman Tim Wallach was playing far over toward shortstop to guard the 5.5 hole. Yet Tony still managed to punch it between Wallach and the shortstop. The hit also sealed Gwynn's sixth batting title.

"I wanted that hit bad," said Gwynn. "And they *didn't* want me to have it, just as bad."

"Tony is a special hitter," praised Dodgers manager Russell. "We had him defended well right there. The pitch was where we wanted it. And he placed the ball perfectly. I've never seen another hitter able to get hits like that."[72]

The lead held until the ninth, when Hoffman got the call. As he walked in from the bullpen, Trevor's thoughts were on his late father:

"I was thinking a lot about my dad there. It was like I was sharing it with him…like he was there. When I got to the mound, I was as calm as I've been all year."[73]

Hoffman inherited his love for baseball from his father, an usher at Anaheim Stadium. He recorded his 41st save, putting the Padres and Dodgers into a first place tie. With the San Diego win and an earlier loss by Montreal, the Padres clinched at least a wild card berth.

"Twelve years since I've been here," said Gwynn. "At times, it's seemed like 24.

"I've been on teams that were eliminated in July. It's amazing. Three years ago, I didn't know where we were going. In '93 and '94, there was me and a bunch of kids. I didn't think we'd turn it around this fast."[73]

**Another Gwynn delivers**   So going into the final game between the Padres and Dodgers, the situation was this: The winner claimed the western division crown and would travel to St. Louis for first round of the playoffs. The loser took the wild card, facing Atlanta. Though they preferred to play the Cardinals, the Padres were just thrilled to be in the postseason once more, regardless of the opponent.

The unique circumstance posed a dilemma for each manager. Do you try to win the division by going with your top pitcher and best players, or do you rest your regulars in anticipation of the playoffs?

Russell opted to go with Martinez, his number-one starter, for the final game—but only for two innings. For the Padres it was Hamilton's turn in the rotation, but Bochy chose to save him for the first game of the playoffs. He instead went with Tewksbury, who'd recorded just one win in his last eleven starts.

Sunday, September 29, 1996 was a day for three unlikely heroes. One of those was Tewksbury, who rewarded Bochy's confidence with seven scoreless innings. The Dodgers matched goose eggs, and the game remained scoreless through nine full frames. Game number 162, the season finale, was now in overtime.

Reliever Dario Veras was another surprise hero that afternoon. The rookie threw three scoreless innings, easily the biggest performance of his short career.

The Dodgers almost ended it in the bottom of the ninth. They had two men on with nobody out and the heart of the order due up. Bochy stuck with Veras, resisting the temptation to bring in Hoffman.

Once more, Bochy's confidence paid off. The rookie fanned Piazza, then induced Karros to hit into a double play to end the uprising. The game remained 0-0.

Finley led off the eleventh with a single. Caminiti followed with a sharp single to rightfield which was gloved by Raul Mondesi. Mondesi, who'd already gunned down Doug Dascenzo at the plate earlier in the game, owned the best arm in baseball. Finley nevertheless decided to challenge him, making a daring dash from first to third. He slid in barely ahead of the tag.

With runners on first and third and the pitcher's spot due up, Bochy made the call for Chris Gwynn. He stepped in against Korean phenom Chan Ho Park, now pitching in relief for the Dodgers. In a similar pinch-hitting situation five days earlier, Chris bounced into a game-ending double play against the Rockies. But despite his .169 average, Bochy stuck with him in another clutch situation.

What followed was one of the most memorable at bats in Padres history. Park delivered a 1-and-1 pitch, and Chris Gwynn, the unlikeliest Padre hero, smacked it into rightfield for an RBI double. Finley and Caminiti came around to score, giving the Padres a two-zip lead. It turned out to be the final regular-season at-bat of Gwynn's career, but by far the biggest.

At the Chargers game in San Diego, fans listening on portable radios let out a collective cheer when Gwynn's hit fell in. Players on the field couldn't figure out what was happening. The Chargers were in the midst of a touchdown drive, and had to motion for the fans to quiet down.

Hoffman was called on to protect the precious 2-0 lead in the bottom of the eleventh. True to form, Hoffy recorded his third save of the series and his 42nd of the season, fanning Chad Curtis for the final out.

With the improbable three-game sweep, the Padres won the National League Western division by one game. It was the second title in their 28-year history. The long-awaited celebration began at last!

"Bruce's belief in Chris Gwynn is the reason (he) got that hit," said third base coach Flannery. "The confidence he has in players is a reason why they play so hard for him."

"It's great," grinned Caminiti. "I wanted this feeling. They had this feeling last year. Now, I know the feeling."

"These three games against the Dodgers were more like the three playoff games against the Cubs," remarked Tony Gwynn. "We had to win three in a row then. We had to win three in a row here, and we did it. We got it done."[74]

# Three and Out

THE POSTSEASON FORMAT in 1996 was different from 1984. There was now an additional round of playoffs, called the National League Divisional Series (NLDS). It was a best-of-five affair, meaning the first team to win three games took the series.

The winner of each Divisional Series would face off in the N.L. Championship Series (NLCS), which was best-of-seven. The victor then advanced to the World Series. When the Padres made their last postseason trip, the league championship series was only five games.

St. Louis was without one of its most potent offensive threats, centerfielder Ray Lankford (a future Padre), who injured a tendon in his left rotator cuff. Lankford brought a combination of speed and power to the Cardinals offense (21 HRs, 35 stolen bases) and led the team with 100 runs scored.

St. Louis' best all-around performer in 1996 was rightfielder Brian Jordan, a former safety with the NFL's Atlanta Falcons. Jordan hit .310 on the season with 17 home runs, 104 RBIs, and 22 steals. Ron Gant (.246, 30 HRs, 86 RBIs) patrolled left, while 37-year old Gary Gaetti (.274, 23, 80) manned the hot corner. Five of Gaetti's 23 home runs during the season came at the expense of the Padres.

The rest of the Cardinals' regulars—first baseman John Mabry, shortstop Royce Clayton, second baseman Luis Alicea, and catcher Tom Pagnozzi—turned in solid but unspectacular seasons. In reserve were veterans Willie McGee and Ozzie Smith, playing in his nineteenth and final major league season.

The Cardinals' number-one starter was ex-Padre Andy Benes, who turned his career around after his struggles in San Diego the previous two seasons. The Cardinals obtained Benes from Seattle over the winter, and he went on to lead the team with 18 victories. He joined his brother Alan (13-10), Todd Stottlemyre (14-11) and Donovan Osborne

(13-9) in the rotation. Osborne, St. Louis' only left-hander, was questionable for the series, having gashed his left thumb on a broken champagne bottle during the Cardinals' division-clinching celebration.

Lurking in the bullpen was the oldest one-two punch in baseball, lefty Rick Honeycutt and right-hander Dennis Eckersley, both 42. Honeycutt and Eckersley were in their twentieth and *twenty-second* major league seasons, respectively. 'Eck' saved 30 games on the year, giving the Cardinals a closer almost—but not quite—on par with the Padres.

Managing the Cardinals was veteran Tony LaRussa, one of the winningest managers in baseball history. LaRussa, who also holds a law degree, guided the Oakland A's to three consecutive World Series appearances, including a championship in 1989.

On paper, San Diego looked like the better team, especially with the injury to Lankford. The Padres won three more games during the season, and they were riding a wave of momentum following the dramatic sweep of the Dodgers. But the Cardinals won eight of twelve head-to-head matchups during the season, including six out of eight at Busch Stadium. The consensus seemed to be that this was anyone's series.

**Gaetti 3,** "There's a love for everyone in this clubhouse that I've never felt be-
**Padres 1** fore," said Gwynn before the first game. "There is something special. You should cherish it, because it may never happen again."[75]

The series opened at Busch Stadium in St. Louis on Tuesday, October 1, 1996. LaRussa went with ace Todd Stottlemyre for game one. Hamilton got the call for the Padres.

Hamilton, who frequently struggled in the first inning, got two quick outs before plunking Ron Gant with an errant pitch. He got two strikes on the next batter, Brian Jordan, but the Cards' cleanup hitter banged out a single to keep the inning going. Up stepped Gaetti, who'd tormented the Padres all season.

Joey floated a change-up out over the plate and Gaetti made him pay: The ball landed just over the wall, beyond the outstretched glove of Finley in center field, for a three-run home run.

"I thought it was a fly ball out," said Gwynn. "It just kept going and going."

The hit batsman with two out was the key: "That kept the inning alive," Hamilton lamented.[76]

For television purposes, the game started at 3:20 local time, which meant that as the afternoon progressed, the shadows made it increasingly difficult to pick up the ball. The difficult conditions, along with the strong right arm of Stottlemyre, stymied Padres bats. San Diego managed only one run, a homer by Henderson leading off the sixth.

Hamilton and Padres relievers held the Cardinals scoreless after Gaetti's home run.

Once the lights took effect, the Padres scratched out six hits and two walks in the last three innings. It made for some dramatic moments, but 42-year old relievers Honeycutt and Eckersley snuffed out the rallies. The game ended when Eckersley snagged Gwynn's shot up the middle with two out and two men on. The final score was St. Louis 3, San Diego 1.

**Chess game** After an unusual off-day between games one and two, Bochy went with nine-game winner Scott Sanders to even the series. Andy Benes got the call for St. Louis. Benes started the year just 1-7 with a 5.92 ERA, and he was nearly dropped from the Cardinals rotation at one point. But he turned things around in June and went on a tear. The ex-Padre won 17 of his last 20 decisions, finishing 18-10 for the season.

Game two see-sawed back and forth for nine innings. The Redbirds struck first with a run in the third. Caminiti negated that with a home run leading off the fifth inning. It was the first ball Cammy put into play in the series.

St. Louis then reached Sanders for three runs in the bottom of the fifth. The inning started innocently enough when number-eight hitter Luis Alicea flew out. That brought up Benes, a .151 hitter. Sanders got ahead of him 1-and-2, but then the Cards' pitcher smoked a hard slider for a single.

Another former Padre, Ozzie Smith, followed with a single. Sanders walked Willie McGee to load the bases, bringing up Gant.

Sanders had retired Gant his first two times up, but Bochy came out with an early hook. The Padres skipper felt that Sanders was struggling with his command.

Exit Sanders, enter rookie Dario Veras, one of the heroes of the Dodgers series. But lightning wouldn't strike twice. The count to Gant was 1-and-1. Veras' next pitch was a slider which appeared to catch the plate, but umpire Gerry Davis called it a ball. The call was extremely critical to the outcome.

Veras and pitching coach Dan Warthen were adamant that the pitch was a strike. Indeed, Gant would have been retired when he swung and missed on the next pitch. Instead, he was still alive, the count now 2-and-2.

On the next offering, Gant provided the big blow of the game, a double over Finley's head to clear the bases and break the tie. Veras retired the next two hitters, but the damage was done. The Cardinals led, 4-1.

The Padres got two of those runs back in the sixth. Chris Gwynn, pinch-hitting for Veras, continued his heroics with a one-out single to center. Henderson legged out an infield hit, bringing up the other Gwynn. Tony singled to left center, scoring his brother. Henderson scored behind him on a throwing error by centerfielder McGee, making the score 4-3.

With Tony Gwynn on second and the heart of the order due up, it looked like the Padres might threaten for more. But Finley and Caminiti each grounded out, ending the rally.

In the top of the eighth, pinch-hitting specialist Scott Livingstone singled to left. Henderson drew a walk, which ended Benes' day. LaRussa summoned the veteran Honeycutt to face Tony Gwynn with two men on, nobody out, and the score still 4-3. October baseball doesn't get much better.

Gwynn and Bochy discussed a hit-and-run play, but that was thought to be too risky in this situation. Gwynn hadn't handled the sharp sliders from the left-handed Honeycutt well, popping out against him in game one. Bochy finally made his decision: He called on Gwynn, his best all-around hitter, to sacrifice the runners over.

Managers live with the knowledge that their decisions will be forever second-guessed, especially under the grueling spotlight of the postseason. This was no exception: Was it wise to take the bat out of the hands of your best hitter in a clutch situation such as this?

Regardless, the decision was defended by LaRussa, among others, whose Cardinals were caught completely off guard. Gwynn laid down a perfect bunt, putting the tying and go-ahead runs into scoring position with only one out. This again brought up the heart of the order, Finley and Caminiti, in a key situation.

Finley delivered a hard ground shot to first baseman John Mabry, and the Cardinals elected to give up the run for the out. Finley was retired at first but Livingstone scored to tie the game, 4-4. Henderson moved to third on the play.

LaRussa called for an intentional walk to Caminiti, which brought up the slumping Joyner. Bochy had a choice: let the left-handed Joyner bat against the lefty Honeycutt, or pinch-hit the right-handed Vaughn, which in turn would have brought on the right-handed Eckersley. Making his second excruciating decision of the inning, Bochy stuck with Joyner. The Padres first baseman was retired on a pop fly, ending the threat.

Bochy defended his decision: "With the score no worse than tied, we wanted to keep our best defensive player on the field."[77]

In the bottom of the eighth, Bochy was forced to make another decision: Bring on Hoffman to preserve the tie, or go with middle reliever Doug Bochtler. Providing more fodder to Monday-morning quarterbacks, Bochy passed over Hoffman in favor of Bochtler.

Bochtler was a reliable setup man during the season, and it seemed reasonable enough to bring him on in the eighth, with the idea of saving Hoffman for the ninth and possibly extra innings. But the pressure got to the young reliever. Bochtler began the inning by walking Jordan on four pitches. The count ran full on Gaetti, the next batter, who grounded sharply to Caminiti. Because the count was full, Jordan was running on the pitch, and Caminiti's only play was to first. Had the runner not been in motion, the Padres would have turned an easy double play.

Mabry was intentionally passed, which brought up Tom Pagnozzi. Bochtler's first pitch bounced away for a wild pitch, allowing both runners to advance ninety feet. The Cardinals had runners on second and third with just one out. Bochy finally made the call for Hoffman.

What followed was an unusual play, one which broke in the Cardinals' favor. Trevor delivered a change-up, which seemed to fool Pagnozzi. He swatted the ball like a cue shot back toward Hoffman, who stuck out his glove but could only deflect it. The ball caromed away and dropped in front of second baseman Reed. Jordan was running on contact, so if either Hoffman or Reed had made the catch, he'd have been doubled off of third. But by then, Reed's only play was to first, which allowed Jordan to score. The Cardinals took a 5-4 lead.

That was it for the scoring. Eckersley slammed the door in the ninth, putting an end to the hard-fought contest. The final score remained 5-4, and St. Louis took a two-zip lead in the series.

"I would have had it," said Reed of the ball off the bat of Pagnozzi. "I was kind of shocked when he (Hoffman) tipped it. Tough break."

"I really didn't see the ball too well," said Hoffman. "At first, it looked like a bullet. Then, it looked like a Bugs Bunny pitch. Then it was by me."

"This game is real simple," summarized Gwynn. "They got five runs. Three scored on walks. That's it as far as I'm concerned."[78]

With that, the series moved west to Mission Valley. St. Louis needed just one more victory to take the series. The Padres were now in the position of having to win the last three games—just as they'd done against the Cubs, twelve years earlier.

**Falling just short**  After two tough losses in St. Louis, sunny San Diego never looked more inviting. The Cards were ahead, but they'd have to beat the Padres on their own turf—and the fans were out in force.

The Cardinals were well aware of what the Padres had accomplished the previous weekend in Los Angeles. "It's not over yet," added Eckersley, who was a member of the '84 Chicago team that was swept three-straight in San Diego. "I don't want to re-live 1984. I know how precious it is to win and how devastating it is to lose."[79]

The breaks weren't going the Padres' way, but the series was filled with drama from the first pitch to the last. Game two had been decided in the eighth inning. The third game would go all the way to the ninth, and even then, it wasn't decided until every last drop of excitement was squeezed from it.

Game three was played in San Diego on October 5, 1996. The season was riding on the strong right arm of Andy Ashby, who allowed a run in the top of the first. Caminiti tied it in the third with a home run off Cardinals starter Donovan Osborne.

Seldom-used Archi Cianfrocco, who hadn't batted since September 18, was given the start at first base, spelling the slumping Joyner against the left-handed Osborne. The move seemed to pay off when Cianfrocco singled with one out in the second.

Johnson, still starting behind the plate in place of the injured Flaherty, followed with another single, sending Cianfrocco to third. Gomez then hit a chopper back to the mound, and on a daring play, Cianfrocco raced for home, sliding around Pagnozzi's tag to score the Padres' second run.

Reed followed with a double to left, scoring Johnson. With just one out, Gomez was held at third on the play. He was eventually stranded there: Ashby fanned and Henderson flew out, ending the inning. The Padres led, 3-1.

The Padres added to their lead in the fourth. Johnson and Gomez opened the inning with singles. Reed followed with another hit, driving in Johnson to give the Padres a 4-1 lead. Ashby sacrificed the runners into scoring position. It looked as though the Padres might break the game open, with runners at second and third and one out—and Henderson and Gwynn coming up.

But as happened so many times in the first two games of the series, the Padres failed to deliver with runners on base. Henderson and Gwynn were both called out on strikes, thus ending the threat.

Gant led off the sixth with a solo home run to slice the Padres' lead to 4-2. By this point, Ashby appeared to be faltering. Jordan followed with a single and stole second. Ash retired the dangerous Gaetti on strikes, but Mabry tripled into the rightfield corner, bringing home Jordan. Bochy then called for a double switch, bringing Worrell in relief with Joyner taking over at first.

Pagnozzi greeted the Padres reliever with a single, scoring Mabry from third to tie the ballgame at 4. Worrell got out of the inning without further damage. The game would be another nail-biter for Padres fans.

The injured Lankford made his first appearance of the series as a pinch hitter in the seventh. He delivered a single to center, and Royce Clayton followed with a walk. Pinch hitter Mark Sweeney (who joined the Padres the following season) laid down a sacrifice bunt that turned into an infield single. The bases were loaded.

Gant grounded into a double play, which scored Lankford and gave the Cardinals a 5-4 edge. The dangerous Jordan flied out to end the inning. He'd be heard from one more time in the series.

Leading off the bottom of the eighth against Honeycutt, Caminiti capped his sensational MVP season by clobbering his third home run of the series, which tied the game, 5-5. All three of his hits in the series were home runs. In the top of the inning, Cammy had made a sensational play to rob the Cards of another run, sliding to his knees and throwing out Royce Clayton to end a rally.

The Padres sought to take the lead that inning. Pinch hitter Vaughn went down on strikes, but Johnson delivered a double, his third hit of the game. Gomez fanned, but with two out, Reed drove a liner to right. The 54,000 people on hand held their breath, as it looked like the Padres would take back the lead…

Trevor Hoffman was the Padres' most successful "closer" and one of the greatest relievers of all time. (courtesy, Fleer/SkyBox International LP)

But this game belonged to Jordan. The graceful rightfielder made an airborne, backhanded catch of Reed's liner, preventing the go-ahead run from scoring and ending the inning.

"Three-quarters of the rightfielders in the National League never get to that ball," remarked Towers.[80]

Hoffman was summoned in the top of the ninth to preserve the 5-5 tie, setting the stage for the most dramatic moment of the series. Hoffman was the stopper so many times down the stretch, and the Padres needed his heroics at least one more time.

Pinch-hitter Ozzie Smith, making his final appearance in San Diego, started the inning by flying out to left. But Gant drew a walk, and the hottest hitter on either team, Jordan, stepped to the plate. The Cardinals rightfielder was less than one hundred percent; his neck and legs were sore from the catch he made the previous inning.

The count to Jordan ran full. Hoffman then delivered a slider, the biggest pitch of the season to date. Jordan deposited the ball over the leftfield wall, giving the Cardinals a 7-5 lead.

"I made the pitch," Hoffman said. "And he hit it out. I'll live with that mistake. I've got to tip my hat to him."[80]

The Padres made an attempt to come back in the bottom of the ninth. With one out and Henderson on second base, Gwynn lined out to the shortstop for what looked like a game-ending double play. But second baseman Alicea dropped the relay throw, giving the Padres one more chance. Finley, the next hitter, represented the potential tying run. If he could get on, Caminiti would get one more crack.

But Finley lofted an easy fly ball to (who else?) Jordan, ending the game. The Padres' storybook season was finally over.

"It happens that way," said Caminiti, who watched the final out from the on-deck circle. "Fins, in that situation, has been coming up big all year."

Said Gwynn: "It was a special year for us. We took a giant step forward. Hopefully, we'll be a better club next year and make it even better for the fans."[80]

Meanwhile, the Dodgers were swept by the Braves in their divisional series. St. Louis went on to lose to Atlanta in the NLCS, 4 games to 3.

Memorable though it was, the 1996 postseason was another heartbreaker for the Padres, who, with an occasional break, could have won any of the three games. The Padres always seemed to be just a clutch hit away.

# First-to-Worst

THE PADRES DEFIED all expectations in 1996, though the season had come to such an abrupt, disappointing end. The front office realized that the ballclub had to be upgraded if they hoped to return to the postseason, let alone advance beyond the first round. After analyzing the team's weaknesses during the divisional series, the Padres sought greater team speed, more punch from their second baseman, and an improvement in the starting rotation, especially from the left side.

Towers made the first major move of the off-season on November 26, 1996, when he dealt pitcher Dustin Hermanson to the Marlins for second baseman Quilvio Veras.

To make room for Veras, incumbent second baseman Jody Reed was traded to Detroit for class-A outfielder Mike Darr. Reed was an integral member of the '96 pennant drive, and the trade of the veteran upset several of his teammates. Reed provided exceptional defense during his two seasons in San Diego, but he hit just .244 and provided little power or speed. The switch-hitting Veras was nine years younger, and he possessed the speed that was lacking at the top of the order.

As it turned out, the move was to the ultimate benefit of the Padres. Reed batted under .200 with the Tigers, and after just 52 games in Detroit, his playing days were over. Meanwhile, Darr was twice named Minor League Player of the Year for San Diego.

The Dominican-born Veras became the Padres' leadoff hitter and top base stealer for three years (1997-99). 'Q' was a model of consistency, turning in three nearly identical seasons with the Padres.

On December 2, 1996, San Diego signed free agent catcher Carlos Hernandez. The native Venezuelan had spent the previous seven years with the Dodgers, backing up Mike Scioscia and then Mike Piazza. While in L.A., he yearned for the chance to play every day. Flaherty was the Padres' starting catcher, so Hernandez found himself playing backup for one more year.

Hernandez turned in a fine first season for the Padres in 1997, batting over .300 in part-time play. Sufficiently impressed, the Padres promoted him to the top job for the '98 season. Flaherty was thus expendable, and he was later involved in another pivotal trade.

The Padres elected not to pick up their option on Tewksbury, who turned 36 and struggled during the second half of the season. The team also wanted to add a top-flight left-hander in their rotation, and it happened that one was available. On December 6, the Padres traded Sanders to the Seattle Mariners for southpaw Sterling Hitchcock, who would inherit Tewksbury's spot in the rotation. Hitchcock, a ninth round draft pick of the Yankees in 1989, made a fraction of Tewksbury's $1.5 million salary, so the Padres also benefited financially.

The week before, the Padres were prepared to send Sanders to Boston for shortstop John Valentin, but at the last minute the Red Sox pulled out.

Sanders had been a .500 pitcher as a starter and reliever over four seasons in San Diego. He briefly returned to the Padres for their '98 pennant run, but by the 2000 season, he was playing in Japan. The Sanders-Hitchcock deal turned out to be another brilliant move by Towers.

Hitchcock had an immediate impact. On April 5, he combined with Hoffman for a one-hitter over the Phillies. 'Hitch' finished the season with a record of 10 wins and 11 losses, numbers similar to Tewksbury's the year before. Hitchcock later became the ace of the Padres staff, earning the opening day start in 2000.

**"Good riddance"** 1997 saw the curious case of Japanese star Hideki Irabu.

Still trying to solidify the starting rotation, Towers reached a negotiating agreement in January with a Japanese team, the Chiba Lotte Marines, for Irabu, their ace pitcher. The Yankees and Mets were both in hot pursuit of Irabu, but the Padres got there first: "Basically, he plays for us, returns to Japan, or sits out," said Towers, after completing the agreement.

At the time, the major leagues had only two Japanese players—Hideo Nomo of the Dodgers and Shigetoshi Hasegawa of the Angels. Described as the 'Japanese Nolan Ryan', Irabu led the Japanese major leagues in ERA for two seasons.

The Padres held the rights to one of Japan's top pitchers for six years—if he'd agree to sign with them. That was the rub.

"We're the only team with negotiating rights to him," said Towers. "We land this guy and we're going to be pretty strong."[81]

Despite the agreement, Irabu steadfastly refused to play for the small-market Padres. He stated that his boyhood dream was to pitch for the Yankees, and he demanded to play for a New York team.

Baseball's executive council ruled on February 27 that the rights to Irabu indeed belonged to San Diego. Irabu's agent likened his client's plight to a World War II internment camp. He threatened to sit out the season unless he was allowed to sign with the Yankees.

The Padres realized that they were left with no choice. On April 22, 1997, three months into the saga, they sold Irabu's negotiating rights to the Yankees for three million dollars. As part of the package, the Yankees also sent heralded prospect Ruben Rivera and minor-league pitcher Rafael Medina to the Padres. San Diego sent three minor leaguers to New York to complete the deal.

The Padres felt that they essentially received two potential impact players for free. "Good riddance" was the ballclub's attitude toward Irabu.

Rivera, the prize acquisition in the Irabu dealings, possessed exceptional speed and line-drive power, to go with an outstanding glove. Rivera posted an inordinate number of strikeouts while in the minor leagues, but the Padres felt that with his natural abilities and raw potential, he'd mature into a five-tool superstar. He was twice named the Yankees' number-one minor league prospect.

The Yankees went on to sign Irabu to a four-year contract, but he never became the sensation that they hoped. In three years in New York, he won 29 games against 20 losses with a 4.80 ERA. Referring to Irabu's work habits, Steinbrenner once called him a "fat (expletive) toad". It may be the ultimate baseball irony that the man who so adamantly refused to play in San Diego was shipped to the Montreal Expos at the end of the 1999 season.

**The "Q"** San Diego was on the vanguard of another trend in professional sports in 1997—the selling of stadium naming rights.

The stadium is owned and operated by the city of San Diego, not by the Padres or Chargers. In order to secure the NFL Super Bowl, the city undertook a $78 million expansion and refurbishment of 30-year old Jack Murphy Stadium. The expansion added 10,500 new seats, which brought capacity to 71,500 for football games. Four lounges in the Club Level, 34 suites, two new video screens, and a practice facility for the Chargers were also part of the project.

The city reached an agreement with Qualcomm Incorporated, a local communications firm, to help fund the project. In exchange for naming rights to the stadium for 20 years, Qualcomm contributed $18 million toward the overall project. Despite the usual lawsuits, the expansion proceeded successfully, and San Diego reaped the economic benefits—and bragging rights—of hosting Super Bowl XXXII on January 25, 1998. San Diego will also host Super Bowl XXXVII in January, 2003.

Jack Murphy Stadium was heretofore known as Qualcomm Stadium (or to many, simply the 'Q'). While the name of the stadium changed, the actual *field* is still named in Murphy's honor.

The company certainly got its share of publicity from the deal: In 1998, Qualcomm Stadium became the first facility to host both the Super Bowl *and* the World Series in the same year.

**Gwynn's eighth title** As much as 1996 was a year to remember, 1997 was one to forget. The makeup of the ballclub was virtually unchanged (even upgraded, as a result of the Veras and Hitchcock acquisitions), yet the Padres plummeted from first to worst, finishing below .500 (76-86), 14 games behind the Giants.

The Padres' fall occurred in spite of an incredible season by the 37-year old Gwynn. Tony hit .372, the second-best average of his career, en route to his eighth batting title, which tied the National League record. He stroked a league-high 220 hits, and he achieved personal bests in doubles (49), home runs (17), and RBIs (117). After talking with Ted Williams, Gwynn began to turn on the inside pitch to boost his power numbers. *Sports Illustrated* featured Tony on the cover of its July 28 edition beneath the heading, "The Best Hitter Since Ted Williams".

With the Padres dropping out of sight in 1997, Tony's feats were largely overlooked. Colorado's Larry Walker won the MVP award, his numbers greatly aided by the thin air of Denver. In Tony's three best years ('87, '94, and '97, in which he hit .370, .394, and .372, respectively), he finished no higher than sixth in the MVP voting. Surprisingly, the Padres finished in last place in each of those three seasons. Had Gwynn played for a championship team or a large media market, his achievements would have almost certainly resulted in an MVP award.

In 1997, the SDSU baseball stadium was dedicated in Tony's name. Moores helped fund construction of the new stadium. Tony Gwynn Field was named the fifth-best stadium in college baseball by *Baseball America*.

**Aloha!** The Padres followed their historic series in Mexico with a jaunt to Hawaii for a three-game series in early 1997. The series were part of an ongoing effort by the organization to expand the appeal of major league baseball—and the Padres—beyond the traditional boundaries.

The team lost an estimated $250,000 on the trip, but Lucchino saw the bigger picture: "What we have done in terms of expanding and re-defining our market is significant. What we've done for baseball is show that almost anything is possible. There is a world market that wants to see the national pastime."[82]

In a rematch of the divisional series, the Padres and Cardinals squared off at the Aloha Bowl on April 19 & 20. A doubleheader was scheduled for Saturday, April 19, to be followed by an afternoon game on Sunday.

San Diego didn't fare much better against the Cardinals than they had the previous October, as St. Louis swept the doubleheader. Because of the time difference, the outcome of the second game wasn't reported in San Diego newspapers until the next day. The Padres finally got the Cards back in the third game, 8-2.

Hawaii's governor invited the Padres back on a regular basis. While major league games have since been played in Japan and Puerto Rico, no teams have since returned to Hawaii.

**Odd man out** While Gwynn excelled in virtually every offensive category in 1997, Vaughn's National League struggles continued. Sharing leftfield duties with Rickey Henderson, Vaughn hit just .216 with limited power. The boo birds were out in force at Qualcomm Stadium.

Vaughn was actually traded to the Yankees on July 4 in a deal for pitcher Kenny Rogers, but the deal was voided two days later because Vaughn failed a physical. It turned out to be a blessing in disguise.

At 38, Henderson was still an offensive threat, and had a far more productive year than Vaughn in 1997. Henderson's .422 on-base percentage ranked among the league's best, and he led the team in stolen bases for much of the season. But Vaughn was signed to a three-year contract during the off-season, and the Padres already had a leadoff hitter in Veras. When the Vaughn trade fell through, Rickey became the odd-man out.

On August 14, 1997, Henderson was traded to the Angels for two minor league pitchers and class AAA third baseman George Arias. After the trade, Rivera became the Padres' fourth outfielder.

"I enjoyed you very much," the future Hall of Famer told Padres fans. "You made me feel like I was your family, a part of you."[83]

Though Henderson's clubhouse presence was questioned at different stops in his career, his Padre teammates paid him only the highest compliments. Gwynn praised Henderson as a 'quality person'. Ashby recalled the times that Henderson counseled him, offering the insight and experience of two decades in the major leagues.

**Missing Pieces**  Caminiti and Finley joined Gwynn on the All-Star team, but they both fell off in 1997. Cammy was still regarded as one of the best third basemen in the league, but he didn't come close to matching his sensational MVP campaign. He did capture his third straight Gold Glove award. Finley's average dropped almost 40 points to .261. Joyner had his finest season as a Padre, batting .327, fifth in the league.

The long career of Fernando Valenzuela finally ended in 1997. *El Toro* lost eight of ten decisions, and he was included as part of a six-player trade with St. Louis. The deal brought pitcher Danny Jackson to San Diego.

The season was the last for both veteran lefties: Jackson went just 1-7 with San Diego and retired after the season. Valenzuela never won another game after leaving the Padres.

Hoffman established a team record in 1997 by registering his 109th save as a Padre, breaking the mark previously held by Fingers. Hoffman posted a 2.66 ERA with 37 saves for the last-place club. But besides Trevor, the bullpen was barren: no other reliever had an ERA below 4.77.

Flaherty was a solid starting catcher during his two seasons in San Diego. But the Padres were in need of middle relief, and with Hernandez waiting in the wings, Flaherty was dangled as trade bait. San Diego traded Flaherty to the Tampa Bay Devil Rays on November 18, 1997, in exchange for reliever Brian Boehringer and infielder Andy Sheets (Tampa Bay had selected Boehringer earlier that day from the Yankees in the expansion draft, and he was immediately included in the Flaherty deal). Flaherty's average with the Padres for nearly two seasons was a respectable .284.

After the thrilling pennant race a year earlier, 1997 was a letdown for Padres fans. The team needed a number-one starter and help in the bullpen to become competitive again. That help would come courtesy of a Fire Sale—but this time, the Padres weren't the ones burning.

# 1998

# The Greatest Season

LED BY THE strong right arm of Kevin Brown, the Florida Marlins won the World Series in 1997. Brown established himself as one of baseball's most dominant pitchers over the previous decade. He won 17 games in 1996 with an ERA of just 1.69, then won 16 games in Florida's championship season. While battling the flu, Brown won two games against Atlanta in the '97 NLCS, advancing Florida to the World Series.

Marlins fans had little time to celebrate their championship. Management decreed that payroll had to be slashed, and Brown was one of several veterans on the auction block. The Padres were one of many teams bidding for his services.

The Padres obtained Kevin Brown from the Marlins following the 1997 season. The move put the Padres over the top in '98. (Courtesy, Upper Deck)

On December 15, 1997, the Padres put the finishing touch on their own championship-caliber ballclub. San Diego sent two minor league pitchers (including Rafael Medina, acquired in the Irabu deal) and prized first baseman Derrek Lee to Florida in return for Brown. The Marlins originally wanted pitching prospect Matt Clement, but the Padres refused to part with him. Brown was penciled in as the Padres' number-one starter, assuming the place of Valenzuela/Jackson in the rotation.

After the trade, Medina won just three out of ten decisions with an ERA near 6. He was out of baseball a year later. Lee had mediocre seasons with the Marlins from 1998-99 but he fulfilled his promise in 2000, when he hit .281 with 28 home runs. Still, it was one of the most important moves in San Diego's history. The addition of Brown immediately turned the Padres from also-rans to pennant contenders.

The 33-year old Brown won 18 games against seven defeats with a fine 2.38 ERA for the Padres in 1998. He was second in the league in strikeouts and ERA, and fourth in wins and winning percentage.

Brown's intensity also lit a fire under the other starters. Despite a weak second half in which he suffered tendinitis in his hip, Ashby enjoyed the best year of his career (17-9, 3.34). Hitchcock began the season in the bullpen but joined the rotation later in the year. His record was 9-7 with a 3.93 ERA. Hamilton was the subject of trade rumors all season, including a midseason deal to the Reds for Pete Harnisch that fell through. After a poor start, Hamilton evened his record at 13-13.

To further upgrade the staff, the Padres signed veteran Mark Langston in January. Nearing the end of a fine career that spanned 16 seasons, Langston was initially slated as the Padres' fifth starter. He won just four games, but he was enormously popular with his teammates. His presence in the clubhouse, along with the Padres' need of a left-hander in the bullpen earned him a position on the postseason roster.

Towers set out to further improve the bullpen. In another brilliant move, he sent Worrell to the Tigers, his frequent trading partner, for middle relievers Dan Miceli and Donne Wall.

Miceli went 10-5 as Hoffman's setup man in 1998, leading the team in appearances. Wall's record was 5-4 with a sharp 2.43 ERA. Boehringer rounded out the bullpen with a 5-2 mark.

In addition, the Padres signed a new pitching coach, former All-Star Dave Stewart. It was a move that was as important as any in upgrading the performance of the staff. Like Brown, Stewart was one of the game's fiercest competitors.

The Padres donned three styles of uniforms in 1998: the home pinstripes, the traditional road grays, and the blue softball-style jerseys. The starting pitcher selected the uniform for each game. Whenever the blue tops were chosen, Stewart wore his jacket over a tee shirt. "I don't care if it's a hundred degrees, I'm not wearing those things," he said. Even in the team photo, in which the players wore the blue jerseys, Stewart can be seen in a jacket.

Towers achieved his objectives for the 1998 season: adding a number-one starter, revamping the bullpen, and signing a pitching coach who brought a new attitude to the staff. The changes helped to put the Padres over the top.

**Like a rock**  1998 was the greatest and most memorable season in the history of the San Diego Padres.

Joyner batted .298 with modest power, providing his ever-steady glove at first base. His greatest asset was clutch hitting; Wally finished second in the league in batting with runners in scoring position.

Second baseman Veras hit leadoff and led the team with 24 stolen bases. He also paced the team in walks (84) and on-base percentage (.373). Chris Gomez was solid and steady as Veras' double play partner. In his third year as the Padres shortstop, Gomey hit a career-best .267 with 32 doubles. His fielding percentage was twelve points above the league average for shortstops.

At the hot corner Caminiti continued to fight his aching body. In spite of his ailments, Cammy slugged 29 homers and drove in 82 runs. His average dropped to .252 but his slugging percentage (.509) was similar to that of the previous year. Caminiti's importance couldn't be measured in mere statistics; his leadership on and off the field gave soul to the 1998 Padres. With his rugged good looks and competitive fire, Caminiti is one of the most beloved players to have worn a San Diego uniform.

In rightfield for a seventeenth season was 38-year old Tony Gwynn. Gwynn's .321 average was his lowest in six years, but it was still best on the team and placed him in the league's top ten.

In Finley, the Padres had one of the best defensive centerfielders in the game. One of Finley's finest moments came early in the season against Arizona. With the bases loaded, two out in the bottom of the ninth, and the Padres trailing by two, Finley walloped a dramatic grand slam to give the Padres a 6-4 victory. That at bat seemed to set the tempo for the season.

But as the year progressed, Finley's offensive skills tailed sharply. For the season, he hit just .249 with 14 HRs and a career-worst total of 101 strikeouts. Of the fourteen Padres with at least 100 at bats, Finley's on-base percentage was the lowest. He led the team in games, at bats, doubles, and triples, but his overall decline at the plate was a major reason the Padres elected not to re-sign him after the season.

Leftfielder Greg Vaughn finally mastered National League pitching in 1998. Vaughn's 50 home runs shattered the team record set by Caminiti two years earlier. He struggled during the final month of the season, hitting just five of his homers in September. Vaughn led the team with 119 ribbies, 112 runs, and a .597 slugging percentage. He was the only Padre to have a truly spectacular offensive season.

Behind the plate was Carlos Hernandez, whose wish to play everyday was finally granted in his ninth major league season. The muscular Venezuelan responded with a .262 average and 52 RBIs.

**The "King"**  The Padres swung a trade with Boston on June 21, which would have enormous significance for the postseason. San Diego sent relievers Carlos Reyes and Dario Veras and outfielder Mandy Romero to the Red Sox for backup catcher Jim Leyritz.

The deal was another stroke of genius by the Padres front office. Reyes went won just one game for Boston, and was back San Diego the following season. Veras never won another game after leaving the Padres. Romero played a total of 12 games for the Red Sox before he was out of baseball.

Former teammate Don Mattingly proclaimed Leyritz "The King" after Leyritz bragged he would hit a home run on his next at bat—and did. The nickname stuck, and it suited his personality to a tee. He was known for wearing gaudy fur coats and cowboy hats to hockey games and public events in New York. Leyritz was a postseason hero for the Yankees in 1996, and he'd pump it up one more time in '98.

1998 was not only a grand season for the Padres, but for all of baseball. With the stench of the strike still lingering, it took something special to renew America's love affair with its national pastime. That something was the home run derby between Mark McGwire and Sammy Sosa, who jockeyed all season to surpass Roger Maris' single-season home run record. Vaughn was also in competition until he tailed off somewhat midseason.

The Padres had five representatives in the All-Star game at Coors Field in Denver—Gwynn, Caminiti, Vaughn, Brown, and Ashby.

Brown entered the game in the fourth inning and quelled a four-run uprising by the A.L. Ashby pitched the fifth, allowing a home run to Alex Rodriguez. Hoffman surrendered a homer in the seventh to Roberto Alomar, who was named the game's MVP.

Gwynn gave the Nationals a 2-0 lead with a two-run single in the third. In the eighth inning, Vaughn delivered a pinch single to score two more. Padres hitters drove in half of the N.L.'s runs, but the senior circuit came up short, 13-8.

**Oops**  On August 6, the Padres made the most costly move in their history when they acquired reliever Randy Myers from Toronto. Amidst all of Tower's mastery in assembling the '98 pennant winner, this stood as his one mistake.

At the time, Towers sought a potent lefty-righty punch of Myers and Hoffman in the bullpen. Left-handed relief had been one of the team's weaknesses since 1996, but the Padres GM had other motives. The Braves' Mark Wohlers had become ineffective, and Atlanta was said to be seeking a veteran closer like Myers for the postseason.

Towers thus grabbed the high-rent reliever off waivers, hoping to keep the Padres' potential playoff rival from obtaining his services.

As it turned out, the move backfired. For the remainder of the 1998 season, Myers went 1-3 with no saves and an abysmal 6.28 ERA. He never threw another pitch after the season, but he was under contract through 2000. The Padres were forced to write him a half-million dollar check every month for two years.

In another deal with an eye toward the postseason, San Diego obtained pinch-hitting specialist John Vander Wal from the Rockies. Vander Wal carried a .400 career average against John Smoltz and a .350 mark against Greg Maddux—two pitchers the Padres were likely to see in October. This move turned out considerably better, as Vander Wal made a contribution both down the stretch and in the postseason.

The Vander Wal trade deal stipulated that if the Padres made the World Series, the Rockies could select *two* players from San Diego's minor-league system. Otherwise, they would get only one.

**Bong...** Brown came close to throwing the Padres' first no-hitter on August 16
**Bong...** when he allowed just one hit in a 4-0 whitewashing of the Brewers. On September 10, he broke Clay Kirby's club record of 231 strikeouts. Brown recorded 257 K's on the year, exactly one per inning pitched.

Hoffman turned in one of the greatest seasons ever recorded by a reliever. On July 25, he successfully converted his 41$^{st}$ consecutive save opportunity, tying the major league record held by Rod Beck.

As Hoffman trotted in for his record-breaking save, a tradition was born. From the loudspeakers rang an imposing "Bong...Bong...Bong...", the intro to 'Hell's Bells' by the band AC/DC. From then on, Trevor's entrances into save situations were accompanied by a healthy dose of heavy metal:

> *I'm a rolling thunder, a pouring rain,*
> *I'm comin' on like a hurricane.*
> *My lightning's flashing across the sky,*
> *You're only young but you're gonna die.*

Trevor once remarked that he enjoyed how the song got the fans pumped up, but he'd be embarrassed if his mother heard the actual lyrics.

Hoffman's streak ended that night. He blew his only save opportunity of the season when he surrendered a game-tying home run to Houston's Moises Alou in the ninth inning.

"All good things must come to an end," shrugged Hoffman. "It was fun. It's part of the game."[84]

The record stood for just two months. Boston's Tom Gordon recorded his 42nd consecutive save later that season to establish the new major league mark. The National League record is still held by Hoffman and Beck.

Hoffman finished the 1998 campaign with a league-leading total of 53 saves, which earned him the Fireman of the Year award. Those 53 saves tied the National League record (Randy Myers recorded 53 saves with Cincinnati in 1993). Hoffman's ERA on the season was a scant 1.48.

Trevor's phenomenal season earned him a close second in the Cy Young voting. Hoffman actually received more first-place votes than eventual winner Tom Glavine, but he and teammate Brown split many of the second- and third-place votes, giving the award to Glavine.

Trevor Hoffman finished a close second in the Cy Young voting in 1998, when he saved 53 games in 54 chances. (Courtesy, Hall of Champions)

**Heart and determination**

With the Padres' renewed fortunes came an increase in fan interest. Attendance rose by nearly half a million in 1998. It was the first time the Padres broke the 2.5 million mark in attendance.

For the second time in three years, it was against the Dodgers that the Padres clinched the National League West title. It was Saturday night, September 12, at Qualcomm Stadium. Fittingly, the 60,000 fans on hand were given Tony Gwynn jerseys. The Dodgers routed starter Stan Spencer for seven runs in four innings, and it appeared that fans might have to wait another day.

But the Padres refused to disappoint the capacity crowd. Joyner homered in the fifth to cut the deficit to 7-1. Greg Myers followed with a single and Sheets was safe on an error by third baseman Adrian Beltre. A double by Gomez sliced the Dodgers' lead to 7-3.

Vaughn led off the sixth with a single. With the crowd at fever pitch, Dodgers starter Dave Mlicki was visibly shaken. He walked the next three hitters in order, forcing in another run.

Rookie Sean Maloney was brought on in relief, but he too was rattled. He plunked light-hitting Andy Sheets, the first batter he faced, which brought home another run. Gomez walked to bring the Padres to within one, and Veras lifted a sacrifice fly to knot the score at 7.

After Finley flew out, Sweeney walked to load the bases once more. Vaughn then delivered his second single of the inning, which scored Sheets with the go-ahead run. Gomez was thrown out at the plate, but the Padres had captured a come-from-behind 8-7 lead.

There it stood until the ninth. Then it was Trevor time.

When Hoffman fanned Matt Luke to end the game at 10:12 Pacific time, the Padres were officially champions of the National League West. The final out was followed by fireworks and a five-minute standing ovation. Fans could watch the locker room celebration on the JumboTron.

"That shows the heart and determination we've had all year," said Vaughn. "But it's just the first step. We're not satisfied with just getting here."[85]

"They're going to hate me off the '84 club, but this team is far more talented than that team was," said Gwynn. "The one thing this team doesn't have over the '84 club is speed, but that's about it."[86]

**Congratulations, Sammy?** The Padres were following other races in anticipation of possible playoff match-ups. The preference was to face a wild card team in the first round, rather than a division winner such as Houston or Atlanta. First-round matchups would depend on the teams' relative won-loss records during the season. Also, though they'd clinched the division, the Padres were vying for home field advantage throughout the playoffs, which likewise went to the team with the better record.

Sosa had already surpassed Roger Maris' mark of 61 home runs when the Cubs came to Mission Valley on September 16. Facing Brian Boehringer in a tie ballgame in the top of the eighth, Sosa launched his 63rd home run on the season, a mammoth shot to left. The slam provided the margin of victory and dealt a blow to the Padres' hopes for home field advantage in the playoffs.

The home run derby brought thousands of extra fans to the park. When Sosa's shot cleared the wall, he was given a polite ovation by San Diego fans. But the celebration went way beyond that: The JumboTron flashed "Congratulations Sammy 63" in large letters, followed by celebratory music and even a fireworks display. The Pad Squad blew kisses to Sosa; apparently, the event had been well planned in advance.

The players were understandably upset. Even Moores was angry, calling the display inappropriate.

"This is supposed to be our home. They wanted the guy to beat us with a homer so they could throw their little party," grumbled Vaughn.[87]

**Fifty home runs**  A mini-slump late in the season cost the Padres a chance to win 100 games. Vaughn also went into a funk during September, which nearly cost him a shot at 50 home runs.

Home run number 49 came on September 14, but after that, Vaughn went homerless for his next 38 at bats. Before the last game of the season at Bank One Ballpark, he spent two hours studying video-tapes to detect the flaw in his swing. The homework paid off: in his final regular-season at bat, Vaughn drilled a 1-and-2 pitch from Arizona's Aaron Small just over the leftfield wall for home run number 50.

San Diego was the only team in baseball *not* to have been swept in a series in 1998. For the season they won 98 games against 64 losses, nine and a half games ahead of the second-place Giants. Because of the Padres' late slump, the Braves and Astros ended the season with slightly better records, thus guaranteeing home-field advantage in any series against the Padres.

The Cubs won the National League wild card. Since the Braves had the best all-around record, they faced the Cubs in the first round of the playoffs. The Padres squared off against the central division champion Houston Astros, and the unhittable Randy Johnson.

# A Tall Order

GAMES ONE AND two of the 1998 National League Divisional Series (NLDS) were scheduled for the Astrodome in Houston, with San Diego's Qualcomm Stadium hosting games four and five. The fifth and final game, if necessary, would be played back in Houston, which illustrates the importance of home field advantage.

The Padres were swept in the Divisional Series by the Cardinals in the NLDS two years prior. At that time, the home field advantage rule was not yet in effect. Had it been, that series would have started in San Diego instead of St. Louis, possibly changing the outcome.

The Padres had to face one of baseball's most imposing pitchers, 6'10" strikeout ace Randy Johnson, the tallest player in major league history. At 35, Johnson just seemed to get better with age. Houston obtained Johnson in a midseason trade with Seattle, and the 'Big Unit' went 10-1 with a microscopic 1.28 ERA down the stretch. Thanks to his long left arm, the Astros were heavy favorites over the Padres.

Ironically, the Padres discussed acquiring Johnson during the season. However, Seattle wanted Rivera included in the deal, and San Diego refused to part with him. Had the Padres pulled off the trade, they would have been heavy favorites throughout the postseason.

This was supposed to be 'The Year' for Houston, who'd come close on several occasions but had never reached the World Series. Besides Johnson, the Astros starters included Shane Reynolds (19-8), Jose Lima (16-8), Sean Bergman (12-9), and lefty Mike Hampton (11-7). The team ERA was second in the league.

Out of the bullpen was flame-thrower Billy Wagner, who recorded 30 saves and fanned 97 batters in just 60 innings.

Houston's offense was every bit as strong as their pitching. The Astros led the league in runs in 1998, despite playing in the vast expanses of the Astrodome. The attack was led by former MVP Jeff Bagwell at first base (.304, 34 HRs, 111 RBIs), Moises Alou (.312, 38, 124) in left field, and ex-Padre Derek Bell (.314, 22, 108) in right. Their catalyst was second baseman Craig Biggio, who batted .325 with 210 hits, 20 homers, and 50 stolen bases. Temperamental Carl Everett manned center field, and another ex-Padre, Brad Ausmus, did the catching. The Astros had the whole package—speed, defense, power, pitching.

**Brown dominates** The series began on September 29, 1998. The Padres countered with their own ace, Kevin Brown, for game one. After their September slump, Brown called a players-only meeting to gear the team up for the playoffs.

Brown contributed the greatest pitching performance in Padres history, striking out 16 and throwing shutout ball for eight innings.

The game was scoreless in the sixth when Gwynn doubled down the leftfield line. Vaughn followed with an infield single. The next batter, Caminiti, looped a single just out of the reach of second baseman Biggio. Gwynn stopped at third, which loaded the bases.

Up stepped Leyritz, who carried a career .109 lifetime average against Johnson with 19 strikeouts. Getting the call at first base in place of the left-handed Joyner, Leyritz drove the ball to the warning track in left. Gwynn scored easily and both runners advanced ninety feet. Gwynn aggravated his Achilles' tendon while running the bases and had to leave the game.

Baseball is a game of *what ifs*: Had Biggio gloved Caminiti's soft liner, Leyritz's long fly would have been a routine out, with Gwynn frozen at second. Likewise, had Leyritz's ball carried a few more feet, the Padres would have broken the game open.

With runners on second and third and only one out in the inning, the Padres still had a golden opportunity. But Johnson retired Finley and Hernandez, preventing further damage. San Diego clung to a 1-0 lead.

In his first at bat, Vaughn struck out without swinging the bat. He told himself: "Be aggressive. You can't hit if you don't swing…"[88]

Vaughn followed his own advice, delivering a single in the fourth before his critical infield hit in the sixth. And then came the eighth, with Johnson still serving heat and the Padres up by a precious run. They needed insurance, and Vaughn provided it.

On a two-ball count, Vaughn crushed a breaking pitch over the leftfield wall. He was one of the league's few hitters who seemed to solve the mystery of Randy Johnson: It was Vaughn's fifth hit in eight at bats against the Unit on the year. The two runs given up by Johnson were as many as he'd allowed in 44 innings at the Astrodome during the regular season.

The Padres were up 2-0, which seemed safe with Brown on the mound and Hoffman waiting in the wings. But the Astros wouldn't give up.

Brown concluded his dominating performance by retiring the Astros in the eighth, but after 118 pitches, Bochy feared that his ace was tiring. Hoffman was summoned to protect the lead in the ninth.

Third baseman Bill Spiers greeted the Padres closer with a leadoff double past Caminiti. Hoffman then retired Bell and Bagwell, which brought up the dangerous Alou. One couldn't help but remember Alou's home run, which ended Hoffman's save streak two months earlier.

Alou drove a shot down the third base line. Caminiti made a spectacular diving stop but threw wide to first, which allowed Spiers to score. The potential winning run stepped to the plate in the person of Carl Everett, who was 3-for-6 against Hoffman on the year.

Everett lifted a high fly to center field…into the waiting glove of Finley. The Padres prevailed by a score of 2-1.

The line on Brown was 8 innings, two hits, two walks, no runs, and 16 strikeouts. Only Bob Gibson, who fanned 17 in the 1968 World Series, had more strikeouts in a postseason game.

"I don't think I've ever seen a playoff performance like that by a pitcher, ever," said Stewart, himself a former playoff and World Series MVP.[88]

**Heat**  The unusual scheduling of the new postseason format gave the teams a day off before game two. Ashby, who was dominating for much of the season but struggled down the stretch, was to start for the Padres. 19-game winner Shane Reynolds got the call for the Astros.

Throughout the season, Brown and Stewart mentored Ashby, helping to focus his competitive edge and channel his natural talents. The highlight of Ash's year came on a sensational 75-pitch shutout of Colorado on July 5.

Houston reached Ashby for a run in the first inning and two more in the third. With the Padres trailing 3-0, Ashby was relieved by Hamilton in the fifth. For now, Hamilton held the job of long relief, with the lefty Hitchcock given the nod in the three-man playoff rotation. Hamilton turned in a brilliant outing, yielding just one hit and no walks through three scoreless frames.

"Throwing out of the bullpen is a lot different than starting," he said. "I'm pumped when I come out of the bullpen."[89]

Veras, hitless in his last 20 at bats, led off the sixth with a single. He scored the Padres' first run on a double by Steve Finley. Gwynn followed with a single to knock in San Diego's second run. The Padres had a man on with nobody out and the heavy hitters due up.

But Caminiti promptly bounced into a double play. Vaughn, the hero of game one, fanned to end the inning. The Astros were still leading, 3-2.

Houston got one of those runs back when Derek Bell greeted Donne Wall, on in relief of Hamilton, with a home run to lead off the eighth. The Padres went into the ninth with the formidable task of facing closer Billy Wagner with a two-run deficit.

With Caminiti at first base and two out, Leyritz was called on to pinch-hit for Joyner. Throwing smoke 97 to 99 mph, Wagner looked unhittable. As it turned out, it was Wagner's only appearance of the series.

Before his at bat, Leyritz asked his teammates what Wagner threw. "Heat" was the reply.

The count ran full. With the Padres down to their last strike, Leyritz, an ordinary performer who always seemed to turn in extraordinary performances in the postseason, kept the game alive. He lifted Wagner's eighth pitch high and deep toward the rightfield line. Both sides held their breath…Would it stay fair or hook foul? The ball finally landed just inside the foul pole for a two-run homer, tying the game in dramatic fashion, 4-4.

"I was trying to see how many pitches I could see from him so I could catch up to his fastball," said Leyritz.

"I've never seen a ball off a right-handed hitter do that here," said Ausmus. "To be honest, I don't know how it stayed fair."[90]

In the bottom of the ninth, Bochy had to decide whether to summon Hoffman or Miceli. The Padres manager usually saved Hoffman for save situations and with the score tied, he went with Miceli. Had the Padres been the home team, Bochy said he would have brought in Hoffman.

Former Padre Ricky Gutierrez led off with a grounder to short. Gomez gloved it but threw wide to first. Leyritz stretched but couldn't keep his foot on the bag. After pinch-hitting for Joyner, Leyritz stayed in the game at first base, which cost the Padres defensively.

Ausmus was called on to bunt. On his first attempt, he popped the ball toward first base in foul territory. Leyritz made a diving stab, but his timing was off and the ball kicked off his glove. It was the second play on which the Padres missed the sure-handed Joyner.

Ausmus successfully executed a sacrifice on his second attempt. The winning run now stood at second base.

Bochy finally summoned Hoffman into the game to face Biggio. Hoffman was using his high leg kick, and on the first pitch Gutierrez broke for third. He stole the base without a throw.

"The steal was my fault. I didn't go into the slide-step," said Hoffman. "Letting him get to third changed everything."[91]

Biggio was intentionally walked, which brought up Spiers, who had three doubles in his last five at bats. On a 2-and-1 count, the Astros third baseman served a soft single into right field, scoring Gutierrez and giving Houston a 5-4 victory. The series shifted to San Diego, with the Padres and Astros tied at one game apiece.

**Long live the King!** Forgoing the three-man rotation, Bochy turned to Kevin Brown for game three, reasoning that the series was now a best two-out-of-three.

"Outstanding," said Bagwell, hearing that Brown was moved up in the rotation. "They're playing their trump card early."[92]

Brown was starting on three days rest for only the third time in his career. Sticking with his set rotation, Houston manager Larry Dierker went with lefty Mike Hampton. Facing a left-hander meant that the red-hot Leyritz got another start at first base, which proved extremely significant.

Both Brown and Hampton turned in masterpieces for six innings. The Padres' first hit of the game came on a single by Gomez to lead off the sixth. Brown sacrificed him to second, and Veras followed with a single. That brought up Gwynn with runners at first and third and one out.

Gwynn tapped what looked like an inning-ending double play ball, but he barely beat the relay throw to first, which kept the inning alive and allowed Gomez to score. The Padres earned this run: Veras slid hard into second base to break up the double play, and Gwynn hustled down the line to beat Biggio's throw by a foot. The Padres took a 1-0 lead.

Brown finally tired in the seventh. He allowed a single to Alou to start the inning, and Everett followed with a hit to right. On the play, Alou rounded second and headed for third. Gwynn gloved the ball and made a game-saving throw to nail Alou at third base. Instead of the Astros having runners at first and third with nobody out, they had a man on first with one out.

Brown hit Gutierrez, the next batter, which stirred the bullpen—possibly a batter too late. Ausmus flied out, but Brown walked the pinch-hitter for Hampton to load the bases. With two out, Bochy stuck with his ace, hoping he could retire one more batter. On pitch number 100 of the night, with only three days rest after throwing 118 pitches his last outing, the ultimate competitor was simply out of gas. Brown walked Biggio to force in the Astros' first run and tie the game.

Brown was given a standing ovation from the crowd of 65,325 as he made his way off the field. In contrast to the remarkably silent crowds in Houston, San Diego fans packed the 'Q' and ran the decibel level to fever pitch. The usually stoic Brown acknowledged the fans with a tip of the cap.

Miceli relieved with two out and the bases still loaded. He atoned for his game two loss by fanning Spiers on a forkball, preserving the 1-1 tie.

With Hampton out of the game, Scott Elarton entered in relief in the bottom of the seventh. Leyritz was due to bat second in the inning. Ordinarily, he would have been removed against the right-handed Elarton—Joyner was still on the bench—but Bochy couldn't take out the offensive hero of the series to date.

'The King' didn't disappoint. With one out, he drove Elarton's second pitch into the leftfield seats to give the Padres a 2-1 advantage.

"I was really thinking Wally was going to be hitting for me there," said Leyritz.

Said Bochy, "It would've been tough to keep Leyritz out of there, the way he's been swinging the bat. You can't say enough about how he performs under pressure."[93]

Leyritz's home run proved to be the decisive blow. In the top of the ninth, fans heard the now-familiar "Bong…Bong…" Hoffman fanned all three batters he faced for the save, and San Diego hung on to win game three by a score of 2-1. Miceli was credited with the win, as the Padres took a two-games-to-one series lead.

**A Sterling performance** The Astros went with the well-rested Johnson for game four. If their ace could come through with a win, the series would return to Houston for the fifth and final game.

The Padres countered with Hitchcock. At first glance it was a mismatch: Johnson, Cy Young winner and future Hall of Famer, against a man who won nine games and started the year in the bullpen. As they had the entire series, the media proclaimed San Diego as the underdogs. But the Padres didn't see it that way.

As was his habit during the season, Hitchcock chose Leyritz, his former teammate with the Yankees, as his catcher. Hitchcock's decision looked like a smart one: Leyritz was the series' leading hitter to that point, batting at a sizzling .429 clip.

The move definitely paid off. In the second inning, Leyritz deposited a Johnson fastball into the leftfield seats for a solo home run, giving the Padres a 1-0 lead. It was Leyritz's third home run in his last five at bats, and he'd knocked in five of the Padres' last nine runs.

Houston tied the game with a run in the fourth. After Leyritz's homer, Johnson mowed down 12 of the next 13 batters he faced.

An unraveling of the Astros defense allowed the Padres to take the lead for good. With two out in the sixth, Vaughn lofted a routine pop into short left field. Alou charged in on the play as shortstop Gutierrez ran out. Alou took his eye off the ball to look for Gutierrez, and it cost him. He lost sight of the ball, and Vaughn ended up at second.

Caminiti grounded to third baseman Sean Berry, who was playing in place of Spiers against the left-hander Hitchcock. Berry bounced a low throw that kicked under the glove of first baseman Bagwell. Vaughn scored and the Padres were on top, 2-1.

Hitchcock was removed after six dominant innings. He fanned 11 and allowed just one run. He retired the side in order in each of the first three innings.

Hamilton came on in relief, and he allowed the Astros to load the bases with one out in the seventh. Behind the plate, Hernandez saved at least one run when he blocked two pitches in the dirt. But on came Miceli, who had quietly turned in a sensational series. He retired Ausmus on a called third strike, then got pinch-hitter Everett to pop to third. The Padres clung to their tenuous 2-1 lead.

Miceli also retired the Astros in order in the eighth, and it looked like yet another game would be decided by one run. That is, until the bottom of the eighth, when the Padres broke it open…

Fittingly, it was Gwynn who started the Padres' rally with a double off reliever Doug Henry. Finley pinch ran, and the fans rewarded Tony with a standing ovation as he left the field. A fly ball by Vaughn advanced Finley to third. Dierker summoned Jay Powell from the bullpen.

Caminiti was intentionally walked. With the pitcher's spot due up, Vander Wal was called on to hit against the right-handed Powell.

The pinch-hitting specialist responded with a two-run triple, putting the Padres up, 4-1. The next batter was Joyner, who was hitless in just five at bats in the series to that point. But his next at bat would be the biggest of his long career.

Wally hammered a 1-and-0 pitch into the rightfield seats to put the game on ice. The Padres led, 6-1. Along with Garvey's home run in the '84 NLCS, this may have been the loudest moment in the history of Padres baseball.

"Hell's Bells" never sounded so imposing as Hoffman came on in the ninth. He promptly retired the Astros in order, giving the underdog

Padres the game and the series. Champagne flowed freely in the Padres clubhouse.

Leyritz, Brown, and Hitchcock are remembered as the heroes of the series. Leyritz's slugging percentage was a stratospheric 1.300. Brown's ERA was 0.61 in his two starts. Hitchcock outpitched Johnson in game four; if not for his clutch performance, the series would have returned to Houston for a fifth game. Miceli, who was Lopes' choice for MVP of the series, pitched the Padres out of two major jams.

Hernandez actually led both teams in batting with a .417 average. Vaughn and Gwynn provided timely hits, the latter contributing directly to Padres scoring in all four games.

The two teams combined for 81 strikeouts, which set the record for a four-game postseason series. The Padres' big bats were silent for most of the series: Veras, Caminiti, Finley, and Joyner combined to hit just .133 against Houston pitching. But in the end, that mattered not. The Padres got the timely hits when they needed them, and their pitching shut down the dangerous Houston bats. And best of all, the celebration took place before the home fans.

"A big part of the night was the crowd," said Hitchcock. "Every time I got two strikes on someone, the whole place stood up. That pumps you even higher…It had to affect the Astros."[94]

# Home of the Braves

IT WAS ON to Dixie for the next round of the playoffs. Atlanta, winners of 106 games during the regular season, dusted off the Cubs in three straight to win their divisional series.

The National League Championship Series (NLCS) was now a best-of seven contest. (The NLCS between the Padres and Cubs in 1984 was only best-of-five.) With the better record, the Braves were entitled to home-field advantage. The first two games were to be played in Atlanta, followed by three in San Diego. The last two games of the series, if necessary, would take place back in Atlanta.

"I'm so pumped I don't know what I'm doing," said Gwynn. "This really means something. The first round of the playoffs was nice, but that's the first round. I'm really happy that we defeated Houston. But I'm not satisfied. There's a lot more to accomplish…I want more.

"I've been trying to get back here (the NLCS) for 14 seasons. Who knows? Averages say this could be my last shot. You don't want to end a rung short.

"The one thing that struck me from 1984 was the deafening roar of the crowd when we got back home to San Diego down 2-0 to the Cubs. The electricity shot right through you. And there it was again last weekend. Bam!

"We're one of those teams that just gets it done…Veteran teams find a way, and that's what we are. Wear them down, and punch a few across."[95]

Hot-lanta For their perennial successes, the Braves were regarded as the "Team of the 90s". Billionaire owner Ted Turner wasn't afraid to spend lavishly on player salaries, and the club's revenues were also augmented by the team's national super-station. Atlanta appeared in a total of five World Series during the decade, but had just one world championship (1995) to show for it. This was their record seventh consecutive NLCS appearance.

Atlanta boasted baseball's best starting staff in a generation. With a three-man rotation of Smoltz (1996 Cy Young winner), Glavine (1991 & 1998 Cy Young winner), and Greg Maddux (winner of four straight Cy Young awards, 1992-95), the Braves were extremely formidable in a short series. Kevin Millwood (17-8) and Denny Neagle (16-11) were no slouches as the fourth and fifth starters.

The Atlanta staff may have had one weakness: the bullpen. Mark Wohlers, the Braves star closer for much of the decade, tore a muscle in his side and went on the disabled list. When he returned, he developed an apparent inability to throw strikes. He was replaced by John Rocker and Kerry Ligtenberg.

Like Houston, the Braves boasted a tremendous offense. First baseman Andres Galarraga (.305, 44 HRs, 121 RBIs) proved he could hit outside the high altitude of Denver. Third baseman Chipper Jones (.313, 34, 107), catcher Javy Lopez (.284, 34, 106), centerfielder Andruw Jones (.271, 31, 90), and leftfielder Ryan Klesko (.274, 18, 70) made for an awesome middle lineup. Shortstop Walt Weiss (.280) made the All-Star team. Atlanta set team records for wins, home runs, and runs scored in 1998.

The Braves, veterans of numerous playoff situations, were overwhelming favorites over the Padres. But then, so was Houston.

**"My eyes got big"** Game one of the NLCS was scheduled for Tuesday, October 7, 1998, at Turner Field. After a two-hour rain delay, Andy Ashby took the hill.

At one time Ash looked like a cinch to win 20, but he struggled late in the season when he suffered tendinitis in his hip.

"Subconsciously, I did things to compensate (for the tendinitis) and it snowballed. I started getting my pitches back a couple weeks ago," he said. Before the playoffs, Ashby worked with Stewart to correct a flaw in his mechanics.[96]

In game one he was the Ashby of old, tossing a gem for seven innings. The only time he looked hittable was in the third inning, when Andruw Jones tagged him for a home run and Michael Tucker followed with a double off the wall. But Ashby avoided further damage when he caught Weiss' bunt and doubled Tucker off of second base.

The Padres suffered a misfortunate in the fourth inning when Vaughn slipped on the wet outfield grass while charging a soft liner. He suffered a strained quadriceps muscle above the left knee. Vaughn tried to bat in the next inning, but he had a noticeable limp. The

Padres' leading run producer was forced to leave the game, and trainers had no idea how many games he would miss.

Ashby's opposite number was Smoltz, who led the league in winning percentage with 17 victories against just three defeats. The strong right-hander shut down the Padres until the fifth, when Hernandez led off with a single. Ashby sacrificed him to second and Gwynn drove an RBI single to center tie the game, 1-1.

Rivera took the place of the injured Vaughn in the lineup, and he emerged as an unlikely hero in the top of the eighth. Rivera hit just .133 during the season against right-handers, but he led off the inning with a sharp double off of Smoltz. Cox quickly summoned temperamental reliever John Rocker.

Caminiti followed with a liner that was speared by Andruw Jones. Rivera dared to test the cannon-armed rightfielder, tagging from second and narrowly beating the throw to third. Rivera actually overslid the bag and could have been tagged out, but third baseman Chipper Jones didn't see that when he turned to argue the call. The play set up the finest moment of Rivera's career.

Leyritz hit for Joyner, which prompted a call to the bullpen. Into the game came 43-year old right-hander Dennis Martinez; 'El Presidente' faced 'The King'.

Leyritz topped the ball back to Martinez, who took a look at Rivera and lobbed a soft toss to first base. The moment he released the ball, Rivera broke for home. First baseman Galarraga made a desperate throw home, but Rivera slid safely across the plate. It was one of the boldest plays of the season.

"When Martinez caught the ball he checked me once," said Rivera. "But he didn't really check me good because I was still leaning a bit toward the plate. When he turned, I could see he was throwing so I took off."

"It was unbelievable, just great instincts," said third base coach Flannery. "Those two sprints are plays you can talk about all winter."[97]

The Padres' 2-1 lead held until the bottom of the ninth. The game was given over to Hoffman, who'd blown just one save all season. This was to be his second.

Hoffman gave up a walk to Klesko and a single to Javy Lopez. On Lopez's hit, Klesko made a daring dash from first to third. Rivera's throw came in first, but Klesko slid safely around the tag—bloodying his nose when he slammed into Caminiti's shoulder. Klesko's hustle paid off; he scored the tying run when Andruw Jones delivered a sacrifice fly. The game went into extra innings.

Cox brought on Kerry Ligtenberg for the tenth. With one out, Ligtenberg fell behind Caminiti, who hadn't homered in nearly a month. Caminiti knew the Braves didn't want to walk him—he was in the midst of an offensive slump—and with the count three balls and a strike, he guessed fastball.

He guessed right. Caminiti deposited Ligtenberg's pitch just over the wall in centerfield to give the Padres a 3-2 advantage.

Hoffman stayed on the mound for the tenth as the Padres clung to their tenuous lead. He retired the first two batters in the inning, and with the pitcher's spot due up, the Braves actually ran out of position players. Cox was forced to use pitcher Tom Glavine as a pinch-hitter against the Padres closer.

Hoffman needed only to retire Glavine to end the ballgame. But the exhausted closer, working one of his longest outings ever, walked Glavine to keep the inning alive.

Bochy had to summon Donne Wall, normally a setup man, to retire the final hitter. Wall walked the first man he faced, which brought up the Big Cat, Andres Galarraga, who clouted 44 home runs during the season.

With the tying and winning runs on base, Wall grooved a pitch down the heart of the plate. Galarraga hammered the ball to the deepest part of Turner Field, nearly 400 feet away. Finley camped under it on the warning track and gloved it for the final out.

"As soon as Donne let that pitch go my eyes got big," said Finley. "As soon as he hit it though, I had a good track on it."[97]

The final out was recorded at 1:43 a.m. eastern time. The crowd was the smallest in Atlanta's postseason history, and still fewer hung around the rain-soaked ballpark to see the dramatic finish.

The game one win was huge: The Padres had beaten the Braves on their home turf, and ace Kevin Brown was rested and ready for game two.

**Kevin Brown, man of the hour** Brown was opposed by Glavine, the league's only 20-game winner in 1998. The playoffs must have seemed like old hat to Braves' fans: 7,000 seats were empty for the series' second game.

Still nursing his strained quadriceps, Vaughn had to sit out again: "I'm very disappointed...With all we've accomplished this year...You wait to get to this point, and now I can't play."[98]

Glavine held the Padres scoreless until the sixth, when Gomez and Brown smacked two-out singles. Veras followed with the Padres' third straight single, which scored Gomez from second. When Andruw Jones' throw bounced past the catcher, Brown attempted to advance to third, not realizing that Glavine was backing up the play. Brown slid headfirst into third and was easily thrown out. The Padres gasped as they watched the play, but Brown emerged unscathed, save the dirt streaked across his uniform.

The Padres added two insurance runs in the top of the ninth. Brown, who bedeviled the Braves as a member of the Marlins in the NLCS the year before, picked right up where he left off. He went the distance with a masterful 3-0 shutout, giving the Padres a two-zip edge in the series.

**Three-zip** The scene shifted to San Diego for game three on Saturday, October 10. The momentum was clearly with the Padres; they needed only two more victories to earn a trip to the World Series for the second time.

Hitchcock, who stunned the baseball world with his triumph over Randy Johnson the week before, got the call for game three. Hitchcock's task was no easier than it'd been in the divisional series: He was opposed by Maddux, a four-time Cy Young winner and, like Johnson, a certain Hall of Famer.

Compared to damp, dark Turner Field, the atmosphere in San Diego was electric. Qualcomm Stadium was overflowing; Padres fans were delirious with pennant fever. "Welcome to the Jungle" by Guns 'N Roses accompanied Hitchcock's warm-ups.

Atlanta jumped out to a 1-0 lead in the third, and they almost plated a second run. Vander Wal, playing leftfield in place of the injured Vaughn, gunned down Weiss with a beautiful throw to the plate. Weiss rammed into Leyritz with a hard shoulder tackle, but the Padres catcher managed to hold onto the ball. It was just Vander Wal's sixth start in left all season.

In the fourth inning, Maddux, baseball's preeminent control-artist, drilled Leyritz in the hip with a fastball. Leyritz glared back at the mound before taking first base. Maddux denied hitting Leyritz intentionally: "It got away," was his only comment.

Said Caminiti, "He fired the entire team up. Heck, he fired 60,000 people up."[99]

(The following season, Hitchcock returned the favor by plunking Maddux with a pitch. He also explained that the ball "got away".)

Padres pitchers continued to contribute at the plate as well. The light-hitting Hitchcock poked a one-out single in the fifth, and he scored on a double by Finley. With first base open, the Braves elected to walk Gwynn, who carried a lifetime .443 lifetime average against the great Maddux. Caminiti made them pay, driving home Finley with a single. The Padres went up, 2-1.

The Braves tried to climb back, loading the bases with one out in the eighth. Myers made perhaps his only contribution since rejoining the Padres when he retired lefty Keith Lockhart on a popup for the second out.

Hoffman then came on and threw three bullets past Javy Lopez to end the inning, stranding all three runners. For all practical purposes, the game—and perhaps the series—were over.

The Padres added two insurance runs in the eighth, aided partly by the field conditions. Joyner drew a walk with two out, and Hernandez doubled to left. While chasing Hernandez's drive, Klesko stumbled on a divot—the field was badly ripped up from the football games—which allowed Joyner to score and Hernandez to go to third. The Padres took a 4-1 edge when a passed ball brought in Hernandez.

Hoffman retired the side in the ninth, giving San Diego a three-games-to-none lead. The Atlanta offense had combined for exactly three runs in the first three games of the series. The Padres were just one win away from the World Series, and the Braves' prospects didn't look promising: No team had ever won a postseason series after losing the first three games.

**"Sweep!"** Joey Hamilton, the forgotten man in the Padres rotation, made his only postseason start in game four. Southpaw Denny Neagle was trying to avoid the sweep for Atlanta.

The Padres took a 2-0 lead off Neagle in the third inning when Veras walked and scored on a double by Gwynn. Leyritz singled to bring home Gwynn.

Hamilton held his own, but the Braves chipped away, tying the game with a run in the fourth and another in the sixth.

Leyritz continued his postseason heroics with a home run in the bottom of the sixth, which barely cleared the wall in right. 'The King' gave the Padres a 3-2 lead.

A chant of "Sweep! Sweep!" engulfed Qualcomm Stadium. Many fans brought brooms in anticipation of a four-game whitewash.

But as it happened, the lead didn't last long. Lopez tied the game with a home run to center on Hamilton's first pitch of the seventh inning. Viewers at home didn't see the pitch: Fox came back late from commercial break, just in time to show the ball clear the fence. The score was tied, 3-3.

Hamilton then allowed an infield single to Andruw Jones, the final batter he'd face on the evening. Myers entered in relief, but the pricey left-hander turned in an abysmal outing.

Myers wild-pitched Jones to second base, before he retired pinch-hitters Gerald Williams and Greg Colbrunn. Were it not for the wild pitch, Colbrunn's grounder would have been an inning-ending double play. As it was, the inning was still alive, and Myers was unable to record the third out.

The next batter, Ozzie Guillen, drove in Jones with a single, which gave the Braves a lead they'd never relinquish. Light-hitting Keith Lockhart followed with another single, then Myers walked Chipper Jones to load the bases. Bochy had seen enough: With the right-handed Galarraga due up, Myers' evening was over.

In came Miceli, one of the heroes of the Houston series, but he'd fare no better than Myers. Galarraga, who narrowly missed winning the first game of the series on his last at bat, didn't miss this time. The Big Cat deposited the ball 450 away for a grand slam, cementing the game and keeping Atlanta's faint hopes alive.

The final score was 8-3. The mighty Braves wouldn't be swept after all. To win the series at home and avoid another trip to Atlanta, the Padres would have to win game five.

**Midnight train to Georgia** There was talk that the Padres might go for the kill by using Brown to start game five, but Bochy and Stewart dismissed that as an act of panic. Instead, the game featured a rematch between Ashby and Smoltz, the starters in the series opener.

Caminiti wasted no time going after Smoltz, swatting an opposite-field two-run homer in the first inning. The Braves tied the game with runs in the fourth and sixth innings off of Ashby, who turned in his second strong outing of the series.

The Padres were still without Vaughn. Vander Wal, a career .438 hitter against Smoltz, got another start in his place.

San Diego broke the tie in the bottom of the sixth. With two out and a man on, Vander Wal continued his mastery of Smoltz, drilling an 0-and-2 pitch over the leftfield wall for a two-run home run. On the strength of the long ball, the Padres took a 4-2 lead.

Langston made the first postseason appearance of his 15-year career when he entered in relief to start the seventh. The veteran allowed a hit to the only batter he faced, which brought Bochy to the mound. What happened next sent the capacity crowd at Qualcomm Stadium into a frenzy. In from the bullpen came none other than ace Kevin Brown, making just the second relief appearance of his career, to protect the precarious two-run lead.

As if on cue, Brown retired the side in order. The World Series was just six outs away.

Leading off the eighth inning, Klesko worked Brown to a full count. The next pitch was close, but it was called ball four.

Lopez then bounced to the hole in short. Gomez fielded the ball and threw to second, a split-second too late to force Klesko, whose hustle again proved critical to the outcome of the game.

Andruw Jones fouled out, which left two men on base with one out. To the plate stepped Michael Tucker, who'd driven in both Braves runs on the night. Tucker hit just .244 with 13 homers during the season. He battled Brown at the plate, fouling off three full-count pitches. Then came the biggest swing of his otherwise-nondescript career.

Tucker stunned the Padres when he deposited Brown's next pitch over the wall in rightfield to give the Braves an impossible 5-4 lead. 60,000 fans sat in disbelief.

With Brown coming out of the bullpen, the series was supposed to have been over…But Bochy's gamble failed, and having failed to hold the lead, Brown's evening was over. He surrendered a total of three big runs in just an inning and a third, and he left the ballgame as the pitcher of record.

Donne Wall was the next victim of the Braves attack. Called on to prevent further damage, he just threw gas on the fire. Wall proceeded to walk pitcher John Rocker, who had never previously batted in the major leagues. The next batter struck out. Had Rocker been retired, the inning would have been over.

Next up was utilityman Tony Graffanino, a .211 hitter during the season, who further stunned the Padres with a two-out double to left. Rocker stormed around the bases and scored all the way around from first, upending Hernandez at the plate to score the first run of his career. On the play, Gomez's throw home ended up in the seats, which allowed Graffanino to score. It was the Padres' first error of the series and a costly one: the Braves extended their lead to 7-4.

The Padres went down in order in the eighth. Three more outs, and the series would return to Atlanta.

The home team made a valiant attempt to rebound in the bottom of the ninth. Sweeney walked on four pitches, and pinch-hitter Greg Myers slammed the Padres' third two-run homer of the game, slicing Atlanta's lead to 7-6. Were it not for the walk to Rocker in the eighth, the game—and the series—would have ended on Myers' home run, allowing fans to begin the celebration at home.

Cox then called on Maddux to make a rare relief appearance, hoping that the Braves ace would halt the emotional roller coaster. With the tying run at first base and two out, Maddux retired Gwynn on a ground ball to end the game. The final score remained 7-6, and the teams made travel plans for Atlanta.

Said Vaughn, "It's tough to lose. But both teams pushed it to the limit tonight."

Vander Wal, the game's hero for a short while, added: "We wanted to win in San Diego, but we're going back to Atlanta and we're going to do all we can to take it to them."

"It was like a chess match out there," said Joyner. "When you go back and start looking for one play, you find about 20 of them.

"From start to finish, that might have been the best game I've ever participated in."[100]

**Hitch comes through** While no one was panicking just yet, the next 48 hours were unbearable for San Diego fans. The Padres' once-invincible 3-0 series lead was down to 3-2, and the Braves needed only to win the next two in their home ballpark.

The next day was a travel day, with game six slated for Wednesday, October 14. Game seven, if necessary, would be played on Thursday.

The Braves' rotation was cast in stone, and it was Glavine's turn for game six. Bochy considered moving Brown up in the rotation, as in the Houston series, but he finally made the decision to stick with Hitchcock. If the Padres won, Bochy reasoned, Brown would be ready for the first game of the World Series. If they lost, Brown could still get the call for a game seven.

This time, Bochy's gamble paid off—big time.

Hitchcock and Glavine matched scoreless frames until the sixth. Vaughn returned to the lineup and ignited the rally against the Cy Young winner with a one-out single in the sixth. After receiving assurances that Vaughn was well enough to put in motion, Bochy called for a hit-and-run. The play was successful; Caminiti bounced a weak dribbler into the hole vacated by second baseman Graffanino, who broke to cover on the stolen base attempt. Bad leg and all, Vaughn dashed all the way to third.

Leyritz, Hitchcock's designated catcher, then hit a slow chopper to third. Jones' only play was to first, which allowed Vaughn to score the game's first run. Caminiti came around to score on a single by Joyner to extend the lead to 2-0. Finley followed with a single and Gomez walked, loading the bases with two out for Hitchcock.

Though it might have seemed like a prime pinch-hitting situation, Bochy left Hitchcock in to hit for himself. Who would have expected that the light-hitting pitcher, who ignited the rally against Maddux in game three, would come through at the plate once more?

Glavine got two quick strikes on his opposite number. But Hitchcock swung softly on Glavine's next offering and looped a dying quail into shallow left. Danny Bautista, who was playing surprisingly deep in left field, hesitated at first, then raced in and made an awkward diving stab. It should have been an easy third out, but the ball caromed off his glove for an error. Joyner and Finley came around to score.

With a left-hander on the mound, Bautista was playing in place of Klesko. Bautista had committed just two errors all season, and he said he lost the ball in the lights. He also claimed that the coaches positioned him too deep against Hitchcock.

Rocker came on in relief, but the assault continued. Veras laced a single to score Gomez for San Diego's fifth unanswered run.

During the long visitors' sixth, Hitchcock's arm stiffened, and he walked the first two batters in the bottom of the inning. Bochy summoned the right-handed Boehringer, who retired all three batters in order. Braves fans sat in stunned silence as the clock ticked on yet another squandered postseason opportunity.

Boehringer, Langston, and Hamilton each contributed scoreless frames, and then it was Trevor time. With two out in the ninth and the Padres still up 5-0, Jerry Coleman made the call:

*"Drive to center—Finley, Finley, Finley, he's under it, he's got it.
And the Padres drape the National League flag around their
shoulders for 1998! Ohhh, doctor!"*

**Cy Young who?** After two spectacular upsets, the Padres were headed to the World Series for the first time in 14 years, and the second time in their existence!

Atlanta won 106 games on the season, more than any team in history that failed to make the World Series. The Braves tied an NLCS record with eight errors. Glavine also set a record with the seventh NLCS defeat of his career.

Hitchcock was named MVP of the series. He'd had an awesome postseason, trumping Cy Young winners Johnson, Maddux, and Glavine. Though he never went past the sixth inning, it was one of the gutsiest performances in memory—and all by a starter/reliever who'd been cut loose by two other contenders in the last four seasons.

"Sterling has a big heart," said Vaughn. "As long as you have a heart that size and believe in yourself, you're pretty hard to beat."

"Hitch was amazing today. His stuff, his attitude," said Ashby. "They weren't going to score first. Ever."

"There's a lot of MVPs on this team. Everyone contributed a lot," said Veras.

"I don't know whether to cry or laugh," said Hernandez. "When the last out was in the air, I just fell over and kissed home plate. We have worked so hard!"[101]

# 1998

# The Big Apple

"NO ONE EVER thinks about San Diego when they think of Southern California sports," said Gwynn. "We're the 'other' team…But now San Diego is in the World Series. And we've earned that right."[102]

Gwynn was making his first trip to Yankee Stadium. He'd always looked forward to touring the famed Monument Park and hearing legendary announcer Bob Shepard introduce him.

"To me, this is sacred ground. And when I was looking around at the stands and the monuments, it's everything I dreamed it would be. You can feel the tradition."[103]

Since the '84 Series, Gwynn collected 2,566 base hits—the most by any player between World Series appearances.

**Bottomless pockets** Like the Braves' Turner, Yankees owner George Steinbrenner wasn't afraid to dig into his bottomless pockets to build a winning team. Playing in the world's top media market, with a television contract to rival the GNP of small nations, the Yankees could throw money at one star after another.

Someone once remarked, "Rooting for the Yankees to win another World Series is like rooting for Bill Gates to win the lottery."

The '98 Yankees won an American League record 114 games (since topped by the '01 Mariners), which earned comparisons with the greatest teams in history. Like the Astros and Braves, the Bronx Bombers were heavy favorites.

The Yankees' starting rotation was led by Point Loma alumnus David Wells. The stocky San Diego native pitched a perfect game in April and started the All-Star game for the American League. Wells won 18 of 22 decisions on the year.

The rest of the staff was just as imposing. Veteran David Cone (20-7), Andy Pettitte (16-11), Orlando 'El Duque' Hernandez (12-4), and Irabu (13-9) completed the rotation. The virtually unhittable Mariano Rivera emerged as the best closer in the American League.

New York's infield featured Tino Martinez (.281, 28 HRs, 123 RBIs) at first base, Chuck Knobluch (.265, 17, 64, with 31 steals) at second, budding superstar Derek Jeter (.323, 19, 84, with 30 steals) at shortstop, and Scott Brosius (.300, 19, 98) at third. Jorge Posada and Joe Girardi split time behind the dish.

The outfield consisted of Paul O'Neill (.317, 24, 116), Bernie Williams (.339, 26, 97), and Chad Curtis, with veterans Chili Davis and Tim Raines in reserve. Ricky Ledee replaced outfielder Darryl Strawberry (24 HRs), who was diagnosed with colon cancer and missed the series.

**"You gotta be (bleeping) me"** Caminiti's health was a significant concern throughout the postseason. The Padres would need Caminiti, Vaughn, and the rest of their banged-up vets to come up huge against the American League champions.

For the third straight time in the postseason, the Padres were starting a series on the road. Brown and Wells were ready to lock horns in game one on Saturday, October 17, 1998. Back in San Diego, over 20,000 fans came to the stadium to watch the game on the JumboTron.

Brown was suffering from a case of sinusitis, which he hadn't revealed beforehand. He later confessed that he felt weak and congested prior to the game.

Brown was ailing for another reason, as well. In the second inning, Yankees DH Chili Davis ripped a shot back to the mound that struck him on the left shin, causing a deep bruise. Davis was safe at first, and Brown's delivery was affected for the rest of the game. He subsequently walked Martinez and Posada to load the bases. Up came number-nine hitter Ricky Ledee, toting a .241 average in just 79 career at bats. If any proof was needed that Brown was not one hundred percent, the next at bat provided it.

Ledee, whom the Padres originally sought in the Irabu deal, worked Brown to a full count. He then knocked a double to right—something he'd accomplished just five times all year—driving in the first two runs of the series. The Yankees led, 2-0.

"I was struggling out there. I was very tired. This was one of my worst nights in a long time," said Brown, who bore down and fanned Knobluch, stranding two runners in scoring position.[104]

The Padres got the two runs back the third inning. With Gomez at first base and two out, Vaughn hammered an 0-and-2 offering to right-center for a two-run home run.

The Padres appeared to break the game open in the fifth. With two out, Veras singled to center. On Wells' next pitch, Gwynn, whose bat caught fire in the World Series, blasted a two-run home run high off the façade of the third deck in right field. Gwynn called it one of the most memorable at bats of his career.

Lightning struck twice for Vaughn, who deposited the next offering from Wells just inside the leftfield foul pole for another home run. The Padres took a 5-2 lead, and a big road win to open the series appeared imminent.

With a healthy Kevin Brown, the game was a lock. Indeed, the Padres ace regrouped and shut down the Yankees until the seventh. But by then, the effects of the sinusitis and the bruise on his leg finally took their toll.

With one out, Brown allowed a single to Posada and walked the rookie Ledee on four straight pitches. With two men on base and the tying run coming to the plate, Bochy summoned Wall in relief. It was another decision that would subject the Padres manager to endless second-guessing.

Wall was just two games removed from his game five shelling at the hands of the Braves. Miceli, who pitched so brilliantly in the Houston series, was passed over; Bochy was concerned that his arm was fatigued. Boehringer, who had also pitched impressively in the postseason, was bypassed as well.

Wall immediately fell behind Knobluch, and the New York second baseman made him pay. Knobluch clubbed a three-run home run, which tied the score at 5.

Jeter then smoked a single to center, thus ending another forgettable evening for Wall. With the lefty-dominated heart of the order due up, the call went to Langston. Other than Myers, the veteran Langston was the only left-hander available.

Langston did his job on the first batter, inducing Paul O'Neill to fly to rightfield for the second out. Langston then wild-pitched Jeter to second. With first base open, the next batter was intentionally passed. Chili Davis stepped to the plate.

Davis worked the count to 3-and-2 before Langston threw ball four, which set the game's moment of drama. The bases were loaded with two out and the score tied. Up stepped Tino Martinez, mired in a deep postseason slump.

Langston ran the count to 2-and-2. Then the Padres southpaw delivered a curveball that appeared to split the plate just above the knees. Strike three, inning over, score still tied—right?

Wrong. Umpire Richie Garcia called it ball three. In the dugout, lip readers could see Bochy say, "You gotta be (bleeping) me."

The *New York Post* wrote, "Langston looked as if he had struck out Martinez looking with a pitch over the heart of the plate at the knees. But Richie Garcia…ruled ball three."

What followed is forever etched in the minds of Padres fans. Langston's next pitch was a fastball right down the middle, which Martinez turned on for a devastating grand slam. With one swing of the bat, the Yankees took a 9-5 lead.

The Padres scored an unearned run in the eighth to pull to within 9-6, but Mariano Rivera easily closed out the game. With a little luck, the Bombers jumped out to a 1-0 series lead.

**The wind knocked out** Orlando Hernandez, a.k.a. "El Duque", got the nod for game two. Bochy countered with his number-two man, Andy Ashby. But like Brown the day before, Ashby was less than one hundred percent. Several players on the team, especially the pitchers, were hit by a flu bug. It couldn't have come at a worse time.

The Padres came close to taking a comfortable lead in the top of the first. Gwynn singled and Vaughn walked, which brought Joyner to the plate with two out. Wally hammered the ball toward Yankee Stadium's shallow rightfield wall. It looked like a three-run homer off the bat, but O'Neill made a running catch high off the wall to end the inning. Joyner was robbed of a certain double, and the catch saved at least two runs.

"When I hit it, I thought it had a chance," said Joyner. "But the ball had some topspin on it and it came back down. O'Neill climbed the wall and made a great catch."[105]

The wind knocked out of their sails, the Padres then succumbed to the Yankee attack. The Bombers scored three in the first and three more in the second. Ashby's night was over after the Yankees added their seventh run in the third inning. Boehringer was summoned to stop the bleeding; Ashby lasted just 2 2/3 innings, the shortest outing of any Padres starter all year.

Ashby was also victimized by poor defense. Myers dropped a popup off the bat of leadoff hitter Knobluch, and Caminiti sent a throw sailing over the head of first baseman Joyner. The latter error led to three unearned runs in the first inning.

The final score was 9-3. The Padres were suddenly down, two-zip.

"It's a four-of-seven series and we lost the first two," said Gwynn. "Now, you have to win four of the next five, which won't be easy. But this is the time of year that miracles happen."[106]

**To the cow pasture**  The Padres were more than happy to leave New York. San Diego fans reported being verbally and physically abused at Yankee Stadium. Fans in rightfield shouted personal insults at Gwynn.

The Padres limped back to San Diego. The team was ailing physically, and they had to deal with the frustration of two painful losses. The Padres hoped the blue skies of southern California and the 'tenth man'—the energetic, enthusiastic home crowds that packed the Q throughout the postseason—were the tonic for their ailments. Even for a veteran team, the psychological aspect of their ordeal in New York took its toll.

These same Yankees were down two-games-to-none against Atlanta in the World Series two years earlier, and they came back to win the next four games, proving that it can be done. But this year, such a comeback against one of the century's best teams would take a minor miracle. Some Vegas sports books even stopped taking World Series bets.

The Padres had reason for optimism, however: Sterling Hitchcock, with a record of 3-0 and a 1.13 ERA in the postseason, was on the hill in game three before a welcoming home crowd. For television purposes, postseason games on the west coast started three hours earlier than usual. Thus, Hitch's split-finger was especially devastating in the late-afternoon shadows, which partly explained his postseason successes.

Hideki Irabu, in San Diego for the first time since spurning the Padres, was roundly booed during pre-game introductions.

The Chargers had played a home game just two days earlier, and as was always the case during football season, the field was a wreck. The stadium crew did its best to get it ready for its prime time audience, but divots and bare spots were apparent everywhere. Steinbrenner got in his licks before the game: "That thing is like a cow pasture," he complained on national television, making one of the arguments for a new baseball-only park.

**Brosius strikes again**  The World Series returned to San Diego for the first time in 14 years on Tuesday, October 20. Hitchcock's counterpart was 20-game winner David Cone. The two battled to a scoreless tie through five innings—Cone, in fact, had a no-hitter into the sixth.

The Padres struck first, thanks once again to Hitchcock's bat (in the National League park, the DH rule was no longer in effect). Hitchcock led off the sixth with a single to center for the Padres' first hit. Veras walked and Gwynn followed with a sharp single to right.

Rightfielder O'Neill gloved Gwynn's hit and threw wildly, which allowed both Hitchcock and Veras to score. Gwynn advanced to third on the play. Caminiti followed with a 400-foot drive to deep center field. To any other part of the park, it would have been a two-run home run, but Caminiti had to settle for a long sacrifice fly. The Padres took a 3-0 lead.

Hitchcock finally wore down in the seventh. The afternoon shadows were also gone, removing some of the advantage on his split-finger pitch. Hitchcock got ahead of Scott Brosius 0-and-2, but Yankees third baseman worked him to a full count. Brosius hammered his next pitch, a high fastball, over the leftfield wall. The lead was down to 3-1, and the bullpen quickly got to work.

The Padres starter's night ended when the next batter, Granite Hills alumnus Shane Spencer, doubled. Hitchcock departed to a standing ovation—except for the last two batters he faced, he'd turned in another clutch performance.

Hamilton entered in relief and struck out Jorge Posada. Pinch-hitter Chili Davis then hit a routine grounder to Caminiti that looked like an easy out. Indeed, the Caminiti of old would have made an easy play of it, but the aching, battered Caminiti of 1998 couldn't make the play. The ball bounced right through him, and Spencer crossed the plate with the Yankees' second run.

Hamilton eventually got out of the seventh with the Padres still up, 3-2. San Diego was six outs away from their first series win.

The left-handed O'Neill was due to start the visitors' eighth, so the southpaw Myers came on to start the inning. It was precisely the situation for which the Padres acquired the veteran left-hander, but once again he failed to come through. Myers issued a walk to O'Neill, and Bochy wasted no time giving him the hook (it was actually Myers' final major league appearance). In came Hoffman, an inning earlier than he was accustomed, in as clutch a situation as ever.

After the game, Stewart remarked that he thought Hoffman might have been fatigued. During his outing, Hoffman's pitches were clocked several miles per hour slower than usual.

"Hoffy was ready," said Bochy. "I don't want him sitting there with a runner on and not use him with a lead."[107]

Williams flew out to the warning track in right, but Hoffman walked Martinez, putting two men on. The next batter was Brosius, who homered just the previous inning. With the count 2-and-1, Stewart paid a visit to the mound. He told Trevor to be aggressive and establish the fastball.

Brosius fouled off the next offering, evening the count at 2-and-2. The following pitch was the most devastating of the season for the Padres. Trevor delivered a 91 mph fastball out over the plate, which

Brosius tomahawked over the centerfield wall for a three-run home run. The Yankees took a 5-3 come-from-behind lead.

The crowd sat in stunned silence. It was at that moment that a series victory was all but inevitable for New York.

The Padres had two innings to score at least two runs against the dominant Yankees bullpen, and to their credit, they didn't surrender. Veras doubled to left with one out in the bottom of the eighth. On came closer Mariano Rivera, cousin of the Padres' Ruben. Gwynn singled, bringing up the powerful Vaughn as the potential go-ahead run. Vaughn just missed a home run, settling for a deep sacrifice fly that scored Veras. That one at bat embodied the frustrations and near-misses of the entire series.

With the tying run at first, Caminiti fell to the ground as he swung and missed at a pitch from Rivera. He gamely picked himself up, but on strike three he hit the ground a second time. His legs could no longer handle the strain.

Hoffman pitched a scoreless ninth, keeping the Yankees' lead at 5-4. In the bottom of the ninth, Hernandez and Sweeney kept the Padres' hopes alive with two-out singles. Andy Sheets, who entered the game at shortstop on an earlier double switch, stepped to the plate. The Padres were one hit away from tying the game.

Against the right-handed Rivera, Bochy could have gone to the left-handed Vander Wal to bat for Sheets. But Vander Wal pinch-ran for Hernandez at second base, and Sheets hit for himself.

Sheets managed to foul off three tough fastballs, but he was finally overmatched by Rivera. The Yankees closer blew the utilityman away with high heat, and the ballgame was over. The final score was New York 5, San Diego 4.

"Even though we haven't played that bad, we haven't done enough," said Gwynn.

"What it flat-out comes down to is the Yankees have a good ballclub," said Stewart. "They keep battling until they get an advantage on you."

"If we win this year, it marks us as one of the best," crowed Steinbrenner. "Everyone talks about Ruth and Gehrig. Who knows how great they'd be stacked up against these guys?"[107]

**Lady Luck** The Yankees pulled out to a seemingly invincible three-games-to-none lead. Could the Padres somehow reel off four straight wins? The burden of prolonging the series fell to Kevin Brown, tired but healthy again.

Torre countered with left-hander Andy Pettitte, who appeared to be the most beatable member of the Yankees starting rotation. Pettitte was roughed up by Cleveland in the ALCS, and it looked like the Padres' best opportunity of the series.

Caminiti fell once more while striking out in the fourth inning. The strikeout was his seventh, tying the record for a four-game World Series.

Brown was his dominant self for five innings, retiring 12 of the first 13 batters he faced. But the Yankees—aided by lady luck, again—plated the game's first run in the sixth. With Jeter on third, Williams hit a high chop back to the mound. By the time the ball came down, it was too late to get Jeter at the plate. Brown had to settle for the out at first, as New York took a 1-0 lead.

With a left-hander on the mound and Finley in the midst of a slump, Rivera got the start in center field. In the bottom of the seventh, the youngster nearly started a Padres rally, but his inexperience cost them a chance to score.

Rivera uncorked a double against Pettitte. Hernandez followed with a comebacker to the mound, but Ruben broke for third base too soon. Pettitte wheeled and threw to second, and Rivera was a sitting duck. It was the closest the Padres came to scoring against Pettitte, who dominated throughout the game. The Yankees held their 1-0 lead.

With the left-hander on the mound, Bochy opted to sacrifice defense by starting the right-handed Leyritz to start at first base in place of Joyner. Missing their slick-fielding regular first baseman proved costly. Brown walked Jeter to open the eighth, and O'Neill chopped a ground ball wide of first. Leyritz gloved it as Brown raced to cover the bag. It's a play pitchers and first basemen work on countless times in spring training; all Leyritz had to do was flip the ball to Brown for the out.

But Leyritz, a catcher by trade, badly misjudged the play. He charged the base to make the force himself. Replays from every angle appeared to show that Leyritz's foot hit the base at virtually the same moment as O'Neill's.

But the Yankees got the call. In this series, they always seemed to get the calls…

The Yankees went on to load the bases for (who else?) Brosius, who drove home Jeter with a single. With the bases still loaded, a sacrifice fly by Ledee produced another run. New York grabbed a haunting 3-0 lead.

The Padres tried desperately to come back, but once again they were rebuffed by the mighty Yankee bullpen. With two men on in the eighth, Vaughn, the Padres' fifty-homer man, stepped to the plate. Torre made the decision to pull Pettitte in favor of right-hander Jeff

Nelson. One swing of the bat could have tied the game, but instead, Vaughn went down on strikes.

He couldn't have known that it would be his final at-bat as a Padre.

Torre then made the call to Rivera, who'd logged 12 scoreless innings in the postseason.

Caminiti, also in his final plate appearance in a Padres uniform, was the next hitter. He singled to load the bases, thus setting the stage for Leyritz. Hitless in nine at bats in the series so far, could 'The King' repeat his earlier postseason heroics?

No. Leyritz flied out to end the inning.

Not all of his ex-Yankee teammates were so enamored of Leyritz, who went 0-for-10 for the World Series. Said New York coach Willie Randolph, "He's a fine player and I wouldn't mind having him on our team. But he sure does love himself."[102]

Ruben Rivera led off the bottom of the ninth with a single off of his cousin, Mariano. It was his third hit of the game. Unfortunately, he was erased when Hernandez grounded into a double play. The Padres' last batter was Sweeney, who was pinch-hitting for Gomez.

Sweeney hit it hard, but right at Brosius. The Padres' nemesis made the easy throw across the diamond, and the season was over.

The Yankees won the final game by a score of 3-0, sweeping the series four-games-to-none. San Diego fans could only watch as the Bombers celebrated on the Padres' battered home turf.

**Curtain call** Afterwards, Brown could barely hide his frustration: "I can't, for the life of me, think of one good break that we had in the whole series. It's tough to beat a team that's that good, that solid from top to bottom, without something going your way."[108]

After the final out, most of the 65,427 fans in attendance stayed to bid farewell to their beloved Padres. There was a sense of sadness: as the curtain closed on the storybook season, fans knew that many of their old favorites wouldn't be back. The players took a few minutes to regroup in the clubhouse before returning to the field for one final, emotional farewell.

It was, as we said earlier, the greatest moment in the history of the San Diego Padres.

Said Gwynn, "I don't know what we could have done differently to change the outcome of the series. They beat us. This Yankees team was one of the best I've ever seen."

"This was one of the best moments I've ever had as a player," said Hoffman, fighting back tears. "It's an honor to play before people like this. It makes you proud to be an athlete."

"When I got out there and looked up and saw everyone, I almost wanted to apologize," said Finley. "This was fantastic. I remember last year, when we were terrible, and on the last day of the season all those fans stuck around after the game. That was special…But this…"

Added Joyner, "There were more than a few wonderful moments and times. It's been the best team and the best season I've ever been around. It's a special group. A lot of chemistry. A lot of friendships. I don't think I have one bad memory.

"What a great tribute," said Vander Wal. "We don't win and they're there for us…That was beautiful."

"I love these guys," said Moores, who was visibly choked up. "It's going to be hard to see some of them not come back."[108]

**Sweep the faith** It was the sixteenth sweep in World Series history, seven of which have been won by the Yankees. Because the series ended in four games, the Fox network lost an estimated $15 million in advertising.

Brosius, who hit .471 and single-handedly won game three, was named World Series MVP.

The Yankees won 114 games during the regular season and eleven more in the postseason for an incredible total of 125 wins overall. The last time San Diego was in the World Series, they ran into the best team of the decade, the '84 Tigers. This time, the Padres ran into not only the best team of the decade, but arguably of all time.

Gwynn was the offensive star of the series for the Padres, batting 8-for-16 (.500). He was the only Padre to hit safely in all four games, and his average was the highest among regulars on either team. Rivera went four-for-five. The veterans failed to produce, however. Joyner, Finley, Caminiti, and Leyritz combined for just three hits in 44 at bats—a .068 average. Vaughn's two home runs in game one were his only hits of the series.

As a team, the Padres hit .239 for the series, seventy points lower than the Yankees' .309. San Diego's team ERA was 5.82, more than twice New York's 2.75. Overall, the Yankees outscored the Padres, 26-13.

Still, other than game two, any of the games could have gone either way. The Padres had every reason to hold their heads high. The big question was: What next?

# The Aftermath

SO THEN, WHAT happened to the 1998 San Diego Padres? After the World Series, it was time to consider the team's direction.

The top priority was the long-term financial stability of the club, which centered around development of a new baseball-only park. At Qualcomm Stadium, the Padres were in a situation where the ballclub was losing millions each year—even when they went to the World Series—and the present arrangement had become simply unworkable.

The first step toward securing the future of the Padres came on November 3, 1998. By a 60%-40% margin, San Diego voters passed Proposition C, a referendum authorizing a public-private partnership for a downtown redevelopment project. The centerpiece of the project was a beautiful baseball-only ballpark. The community clearly understood the park's importance to the viability of major league baseball in San Diego.

So it was decided! On opening day 2002, the Padres would move into their own ballpark in the heart of a revitalized East Village. Qualcomm Stadium served a useful purpose in its time; the structure was designed in the 60s, an era when many baseball and football teams moved into multi-purpose "cookie cutter" facilities. With the opening of Baltimore's Camden Yards in the early-90s, the trend returned to intimate, fan-friendly, baseball-only parks.

The economics of baseball have changed dramatically in the last thirty years, and the Padres could simply not compete under the terms of the stadium contract at Qualcomm. The Padres have an unfavorable split of income with the Chargers from advertising, parking, luxury box sales, and other stadium-generated revenue. (It also costs roughly $60,000 to make stadium conversions from baseball to football, and vice-versa).

Additionally, the stadium was built primarily to accommodate football, and the seating configuration for baseball games has always been awkward. With the new park, more seats will be available that will bring fans much closer to the action.

The Padres are the only team in N.L. West (and one of the few left in baseball) that must share a stadium, and the revenue-split puts them at a significant disadvantage. By way of comparison, the Dodgers, who own their own stadium free and clear, enjoy 100% of all income from parking, concessions, advertising, and other revenue.

Not only would the Padres afford a payroll more in line with the rest of the league with their own ballpark, but the city would reap the benefits of the expanded downtown business district. The ballpark is to be part of a comprehensive redevelopment effort for the dilapidated East Village area, similar to the Horton Plaza / Gaslamp renewal.

As if more arguments were needed for a new ballpark, Qualcomm Stadium is showing its age: In July 2001, a transformer exploded in leftfield, which caused an electrical outage and forced the postponement of a game. Stadium officials blamed the incident on 35-year old equipment.

Would the Padres have remained in San Diego had Proposition C been rejected, or if opponents had prevailed in court? No one can answer for certain. Though other cities have expressed interest (including Washington D.C., which nearly claimed the Padres three decades earlier), the Moores group has made every effort to keep the Padres in San Diego, despite the team's financial losses. Management has also striven to keep the team competitive, even while rebuilding in anticipation of moving to the new park.

Despite the clear outcome of the election, opponents of the ballpark wouldn't quit. The project became bogged down in a myriad of lawsuits that delayed the opening of the new park by at least two years.

**Goodbye, Cammy** Even with approval of Proposition C, it would be difficult to keep the 1998 Padres together. The team was aging, and several players were in the final year of their contracts.

Under the best of circumstances, it would require millions more in payroll to retain the team's top players. A number of promising youngsters and minor leaguers were auditioning to play in the major leagues. So the Padres were at a crossroad: Do they risk losing even more money by re-signing their veterans, hoping they still have a few quality years left, or do they rebuild, with the goal of making the team younger?

The Padres chose something of a middle ground. The decision, much criticized at the time, has proven to be the sensible course.

The first to leave was Caminiti. Of all the postseason moves, this was the most difficult and emotional. Caminiti was clearly not his old self, which was painfully evident during the World Series. Cammy was a true favorite of Padres fans, and the front office insisted that it was acting with its head, not its heart.

Detroit offered Caminiti a huge contract worth $21.5 million, but he turned it down. Cammy stating his preference to either remain with the Padres or return to the Astros, his first professional team. Minor league phenom George Arias was coming through the ranks, and the Padres deemed Caminiti, who'd turn 36 the next season, expendable.

Arias put together a mammoth season at AAA Las Vegas (36 HRs, 119 RBIs) which earned him the Padres minor league player of the year award. Caminiti realized he didn't fit into San Diego's plans for 1999. On November 15, he signed a two-year $9.5 million contract which returned him to the Houston Astros.

"I'm just looking forward so much to being healthy again," he said. "I want to be clean-headed, sure-footed, so I can play my style. It's hard to be yourself when you're hurting."[109]

As it turned out, Caminiti never played another full season after leaving San Diego. In 1999 he tore a calf muscle on a stolen base attempt and spent most of the season on the disabled list. In June 2000, he ruptured a tendon in his wrist, which sidelined him for the year.

During the 2000 off-season, the former MVP had a relapse with alcohol that ended his marriage and landed him in a treatment program. Back in 1993, Caminiti spent 16 days in a rehabilitation program. He managed to stay sober for three years, but he started drinking again in 1997. He hit the bottom after his injury in 2000.

"I sat in the hospital for nearly 30 days and looked at myself, and everything runs through your mind," Caminiti told *The Dallas Morning News* before spring training. "You think of everything negative and then, eventually, everything positive. What I finally realized was that I had a second chance and I didn't want to go out like a sucker."

At age 38, Cammy signed with Texas in 2001. He was released during the season, and the Braves picked him up as a backup third baseman. Unfortunately, Caminiti was arrested in November on drug possession charges after authorities said he was found in a Houston hotel room with crack cocaine.

**The next to go...** The next member of the 1998 Padres to depart was Steve Finley, who'd suffered through a dreadful season. With Ruben Rivera waiting in the wings, the Padres had no intention of re-signing Finley.

On December 7, Finley, who'd turn 34 the next season, inked a four-year deal for $23.6 million with the Arizona Diamondbacks. The amount was double what the Padres offered.

"I would expect our fans to be disappointed," said Moores, who was also a close friend of Finley. "But we have to get younger."[110]

Unlike Caminiti, Finley stayed healthy and revitalized his career with three sensational years in Arizona. While Rivera struggled mightily as his replacement, Finley thrived in his new environment. He averaged 35 HRs, 100 RBIs, and 100 runs in his first two seasons with the Diamondbacks, making the All-Star team in 2000 and helping Arizona to a world championship in '01.

**"It's not about the money"** Kevin Brown, named *The Sporting News* pitcher of the year, was the most prized free agent of all. The Padres offered him the highest salary in team history: $40 million for four years—an incomprehensible figure for the average fan. Moores even suggested extending the offer to six years for $60 million—an incredible sum of *$10 million* per year.

But Brown turned down the deal, reiterating his oft-stated desire to move closer to his family in Georgia. He then signed a seven year, $105 million contract with the Los Angeles Dodgers on December 12.

"It's not about the money," he insisted.

The deal was a record in major league baseball at the time, and the Padres could not possibly have offered such a massive contract. The Fox-owned Dodgers had bottomless pockets, and new GM Kevin Malone wasn't afraid to spend.

"I'm the new sheriff in town," declared Malone.

Brown's average annual salary of $15 million over the next seven years was more than triple what he'd earned with the Padres. For their part, Padres officials expressed serious concerns about the impact of such salaries, which have the potential of pricing the average fan out of the game. They also expressed the concern—echoed by several other ballclubs and the commissioner's office—that free-spending teams like the Dodgers, Yankees, Mets, Braves, and Rangers could permanently upset baseball's competitive balance, allowing only a handful of teams to compete.

"These shocking numbers ought to offend the consciousness of every owner, player, and fan," lamented Moores.

"It's lunacy…It's crazy," said Towers. "I'm scared where some of these salaries are going and where they're going to take the game."[111]

**Rebuild** The Padres gave it their best shot, but losing Caminiti, Finley, and Brown seemed to answer the question. The only sensible approach now was to rebuild and stock the team with younger players in anticipation moving into the new ballpark.

Also lost during the off-season was pitching coach Dave Stewart, who accepted a job as assistant general manager of the Toronto Blue Jays. The Padres hired longtime Astros reliever Dave Smith to fill his large shoes. Stewart made no secret of his desire to move to a front office position, so his departure was expected. When he arrived in Toronto, one of Stewart's first moves was to recommend a trade for Joey Hamilton.

Just two days after the Brown signing, the Padres dealt Hamilton to Toronto for starting pitcher Woody Williams, reliever Carlos Almanzar, and outfielder Pete Tucci. The trade surprised many of the Padres, who didn't think the team would trade Hamilton after losing Brown.

The key to the deal was Williams, who went 10-9 for the Blue Jays in 1998. "I see Woody as being like Sterling Hitchcock," said Towers. "I think his style is more suited to the National League than the American League."[112]

The Hamilton swap turned out well for San Diego. Williams—who also had a lower salary than Hamilton—became the ace of the staff, and he got the call to start on opening day, 2001. Hamilton would not fare as well. He battled injuries, and his ERA over the next two seasons was near six. Hamilton was finally released by Toronto in August 2001.

**One more goodbye** Vaughn was the last of the Padres regulars to go. The team's top slugger was entering the final year of his contract in 1999, and the Padres felt they had little chance of resigning him after the season. He was nearly traded to the Angels for centerfielder Jim Edmonds, but the teams couldn't agree on final terms. On February 2, Vaughn and Sweeney were sent to Cincinnati for outfielder Reggie Sanders and second baseman Damian Jackson.

Vaughn's average dipped the next season but he still produced 45 round-trippers for the Reds. He signed with Tampa Bay in 2000 and was named to the '01 All-Star team. Though he continued to enjoy solid seasons after leaving San Diego, Vaughn never came close to matching his spectacular 1998 campaign.

The oft-injured Sanders spent the previous seven seasons in Cincinnati. He enjoyed his finest year in 1995 when he placed fifth in the league MVP voting. Sanders brought a combination of speed and power to the Padres, and he was younger—and cheaper—than Vaughn. But despite his talents Sanders was brittle, having never played more than 135 games in a full season. Jackson was a fleet-footed middle infielder who was expected to back up Gomez at shortstop.

Towers tried mightily to unload expensive reliever Randy Myers during the off-season, but without success. Although still under contract for two more years, Myers remained sidelined with a left rotator cuff injury, his professional career effectively over.

Sensing fan discontentment with the rash of off-season moves, Padres management moved to secure the services of one of its most popular players well into the next century. Prior to the '99 season, Trevor Hoffman signed a 4-year, $32 million contract, making him the highest paid reliever—and the highest-paid Padre—in history. The move ended speculation that Hoffman might also be on the trading block, and it reassured fans that the front office was still committed to fielding a competitive team. Management also tried to soften the blow by re-signing less expensive veterans Joyner, Hernandez, and Gomez.

But everyone knew that 1998 was a very special season, and it was hard to say goodbye.

# More Rebuilding

COUNTRY SINGER GARTH Brooks joined the Padres as a non-roster invitee to spring training. Brooks' lifelong dream was to suit up and play major league ball, even if only for exhibition games. He actually participated in two days of workouts during the previous spring, and the Padres invited him back to Peoria in 1999. Brooks donated his entire spring training salary to the Touch'em All Foundation, a charity benefiting underprivileged children.

Brooks was enormously popular with teammates and fans; he patiently signed autographs for the capacity crowds that came to see him. His only hit of the spring was a single up the middle off the White Sox' Mike Sirotka.

**Phil Nevin** Could the Padres strike a balance between rebuilding, while also remaining competitive? 1999 would provide a strong indication.

The team's fortunes appeared to take a major hit during spring training when Hernandez, who'd just signed a three-year, $6.5 million contract, ruptured his left Achilles' tendon. He was lost for the entire season, but the dark cloud actually had a silver lining.

The Padres planned to carry three catchers, with Leyritz and Myers slated to back up Hernandez. Now short a catcher due to Hernandez's injury, they agreed to a trade with the Angels, who needed a middle infielder to backup the oft-injured Gary DiScarcina. On March 29, the Padres sent shortstop Andy Sheets to Anaheim for catcher Phil Nevin, who could also play the infield.

It was the most lopsided trade in Padres history.

Houston selected Nevin as the number one overall pick in the 1992 draft (among those picked *after* him were Derek Jeter and Jason Giambi). Playing third base for Cal State Fullerton, Nevin was named

Most Outstanding Player of the '92 College World Series, the same award Dave Winfield won almost twenty years earlier.

Future Padres star Phil Nevin was the third baseman on the U.S. Olympic team in 1992 (Courtesy, Topps)

Nevin always dreamed of becoming a major leaguer: "It's all I ever thought about doing. I remember having to write an autobiography for a class assignment in sixth grade and writing that I was going to be a major leaguer. There was another school assignment to write a poem about one of your heroes and I wrote a poem about Alan Trammel."[113]

Nevin decided against signing with the Dodgers out of high school, choosing to attend college at CSF. In his senior year, he hit .402 with 22 homers and 86 RBIs. He was the starting third baseman for the U.S. Olympic team that summer.

After a taste of the majors with Houston, Nevin was dealt to the Tigers in 1995. It was in Detroit that he taught himself to play catcher. He was traded to the Angels in '98, then to the Padres a year later.

Sheets hit .189 after the trade, and he was practically out of baseball by the following year. Nevin shifted from behind the plate to third base midway through the 1999 season, and was voted MVP of the Padres three straight times. His fiery competitiveness inspired memories of Caminiti at the hot corner. And all because of a fluke spring training injury.

**Winning streak** The Padres outfield in 1999 was to consist of Gwynn, Rivera, and Sanders—the latter two taking the places of Finley and Vaughn. But an unexpected phenom fought his way onto the roster in spring training: Eric Owens.

'Ebo' (so nicknamed for his initials) played sparingly with Cincinnati and Milwaukee for four seasons before making the Padres after a sensational spring training. Owens' gutsy style and all-out hustle quickly endeared him to Padres fans. He ended up leading the team in games played in 1999, splitting his time between all outfield positions and even trying his hand at first and third base. He hit .266 with 33 stolen bases for the season.

With Brown's departure, Ashby became the leader of the staff and was called on to start opening day. The other spots in the rotation went to Hitchcock, the newly acquired Williams, and rookies Matt Clement and Stan Spencer.

Opening day was played in Monterrey, Mexico, so fans back in San Diego had to wait an extra day to welcome home their defending National League champs. The Padres' one-game return south of the border was not as glorious as their dramatic series three years prior. Although the Padres were officially the home team, the crowd was clearly behind native son Vinnie Castilla and his Colorado Rockies. Ashby began the new season as he'd ended the last, getting hit early and often as Colorado prevailed, 8-2.

The Padres' 1999 season is remembered for two major events: the 14-game winning streak and Tony Gwynn's 3,000[th] hit.

The winning streak, the longest in the majors in five years, lasted from June 18 through July 2. Along the way the Padres took three from Pittsburgh, swept a pair of three-game series from the Dodgers, and took five straight from Colorado.

The streak came to an end on July 3 at Coors Field. In the first game of a doubleheader, the Rockies jumped out to an early 7-0 lead. The Padres rallied but lost, 12-10. Ironically, the Rockies had *lost* nine straight coming into the game.

Said Owens: "We knew we weren't going to win every game the rest of the year."

"It just kind of snowballed," said Williams. "Everyone played with confidence and every move Bochy made was the right move."[114]

**March toward 3,000** When the season began, Gwynn was only 72 hits shy of 3,000. His march toward 3,000 was slowed when he went on the disabled list in May with a strained left calf. The fans elected Gwynn to start the '99 All-Star game, but still not fully recovered, he made the decision not to play.

"There's a right way to do things and a wrong way to do things, and the wrong way would be to be on the DL going right into the break and then playing in the All-Star game", said Gwynn, who missed all but two of the team's 14 straight wins.

"Once again, you're honored to be able to go and be voted in by the fans, but this time I can't. I'd rather see someone else get the opportunity to play."[115]

Tony still attended the All-Star game at Fenway Park, which was highlighted by Ted Williams' ceremonial first pitch. Gwynn helped to steady Williams on the mound as the 80-year old legend hobnobbed with today's stars at his old ball yard. Gwynn called it one of the most memorable moments of his career.

Ashby and Hoffman were also named to the '99 All-Star game, and each threw a perfect third of an inning. As the Padres were defending National League champs, Bochy had the distinction of managing the N.L. squad. He brought along most of his coaching staff.

On July 31, the Padres traded Leyritz to the Yankees, his former team. Unfortunately, he couldn't resist taking potshots as he departed, alleging that Gwynn was 'selfish' and not a 'team player'. The comments were made at a time when the media were smothering Gwynn as he approached 3,000 hits.

"Mediocrity will always have difficulty evaluating greatness," was the reaction of Expos manager Felipe Alou to the comments.

"Good riddance" was the near-universal reaction of players and fans to Leyritz's departure. Fans appreciate Tony Gwynn's commitment to his team and his community, and no backhanded remarks by a journeyman utility player could ever change that.

**Pride of the Padres** As the season progressed, attention focused on whether Gwynn's 3,000th hit would come at home or on the road. As expected, the event was heavily anticipated in San Diego. Banners were posted around the light ring atop Qualcomm Stadium in tribute to those who'd previously achieved the milestone. Gwynn's banner was to remain covered until he recorded his 3,000th. He desperately wanted the hit to come at home, before a full crowd of Padres fans, to be followed by the ceremonial unveiling of his banner.

But the schedule wouldn't cooperate: Tony neared #3,000 as the team embarked on a lengthy road trip in early August.

The Padres were scheduled to face the Cardinals at Busch Stadium. Gwynn stated that if he couldn't achieve the milestone in San Diego, he preferred St. Louis, a strong baseball town that drew large, enthusiastic crowds, as his second choice.

Fans were almost treated to a 2-for-1, as the Cardinals' McGwire recorded his 500th career home run during the series. There was a chance that Gwynn might record his 3,000th hit the same game, but Tony left St. Louis stuck at 2,999 hits.

The Padres' next stop was Olympic Stadium in Montreal.

Through the years, Gwynn expressed his distaste for this ballpark, which is widely regarded as the worst venue in the major leagues. But unless Tony went hitless in the series, it was inevitable that the big event would happen here, against the vast expanse of empty seats.

Someone likened getting your 3,000th hit at Montreal to getting married in your in-laws' basement.

Dan Smith was the starting pitcher for the Expos on August 6. Despite the momentous occasion, *Le Stade Olympique* (a.k.a., the "Big O") was nearly empty, which was standard for home games in Montreal. Only 13,450 people showed up, about one-fourth the stadium's capacity. In San Diego, 5,000 fans watched the game on the JumboTron at Qualcomm Stadium.

Veras singled to start the game. Batting second, Gwynn strolled to the plate. He'd never faced the rookie Smith before.

It was 7:08 local time; 4:08 in San Diego. Jerry Coleman made the call on KFMB radio:

> *"One ball, two strikes. Tony Gwynn will be the 22nd man in baseball history to get to 3,000 with his next base hit. Smith is ready, Gwynn waiting, the pitch…There's a drive, right center field, base hit. And there it is! Ohhhhh doctor!! You can hang a star on that baby! A star for the ages for Tony Gwynn. Number 3,000! Well the entire Padre ballclub is heading to first base to congratulate Tony. The entire team is out there…And a very wise Reggie Sanders goes over and retrieves the ball from Mike Mordecai to give to Tony Gwynn. Number 3,000. Incredible!"*

"I was saying, 'Dang it, that's a hit, it's over'," said Gwynn, who'd relinquished most of his privacy for several days. "There was always a camera on me. After [number 3,000], that was the first really deep breath I've been able to take in a week."

Tony's family also came out to greet him. He whispered "Happy birthday" to his mother, Vendella, who was celebrating her 64th birthday.

"My parents raised me right. I got my behind whupped when I needed it, and I got taught some values I believe in. I owe a lot to my mom and dad."

Tony recalled how his father urged him to move to another team during the Fire Sale. But Tony stood firm: "He would understand now. Being in San Diego is where I'm supposed to be. Here I am, still here. So to do this in a Padre uniform, being in the National League for my whole career, that really means a lot to me."

Tony's father had since passed away, but his son still felt his presence: "In the tunnel I did…Because all last week, I kept hearing his voice: 'You can get three thousand.'"[116]

Only Ty Cobb and Nap Lajoie reached 3,000 hits in fewer games. Tony Gwynn became the 22nd member of baseball's 3,000-hit club, and only the seventh to spend his entire career with one team.

The Padres returned home one week later. In an elaborate ceremony on August 13, Gwynn's banner at Qualcomm Stadium was finally unveiled. The moment was perhaps the culmination of all of his incredible accomplishments as a ballplayer. August 13 through September 12 was proclaimed 'Tony Gwynn Month' in San Diego.

"I have to apologize for not getting the hit at home," Gwynn told fans during the ceremony. "I feel bad about that. Being in Montreal, I think we all felt your presence. You people are amazing."

**Plusses and minusses** The Padres' experiment with George Arias at third base turned out to be a failure. Arias consistently provided impressive numbers in the minors, but he could never translate that success to the big league level. He especially fell short when tapped as the replacement for the popular Caminiti. Arias came to bat just 164 times in 1999. He hit .244 with 7 home runs, and he drew just six walks against 54 strikeouts—an average of one whiff for every three at bats.

Bochy searched for an answer, trying Owens, veteran Dave Magadan, and a host of others at third base. Finally Nevin, who played third base in college, asked Bochy to let him try his hand at the hot corner. Nevin responded with 24 HRs with 83 RBIs in just 383 at bats for the rest of the 1999 season. He provided a potent power bat, which the Padres desperately needed at the time. The position's been his ever since.

With Hernandez out, Leyritz traded, and Nevin moved to third base, rookie Ben Davis took over catching duties in 1999. The switch-hitter was the Padres' first-round draft pick in 1995, selected just behind Darin Erstad and ahead of Jose Cruz, Jr.

Davis didn't make an immediate impact—he hit just .244 with five home runs on the season—but he gained valuable major league experience. After Caminiti's departure, Davis was heir apparent as the team's heartthrob. He took some needling from teammates for a promotional ad, which showed throngs of screaming women chasing him on the beach.

Besides Arias, the Padres had another bust on their hands. Ruben Rivera inherited everyday centerfield duties from Finley, but he also failed to live up to his much-hyped potential. His average (.195) was below the 'Mendoza line', and he finished fifth in the league in strikeouts. Rivera showed occasional pop with 23 homers and he provided consistently outstanding defense. The Padres waited patiently, hoping he'd realize his potential with time. Scouts likened his all-around abilities to Winfield's, but it simply never materialized.

The 1999 Padres weren't as powerful as their predecessors, but they did have more speed. Four Padres—Owens, Veras, Sanders, and Jackson—swiped 30 or more bases that season.

Slowed by injuries once more, Gwynn led the team with a .338 average. Joyner underwent shoulder surgery during the season and his average dipped to .248. It was becoming clear that, although he'd signed a contract during the off-season, Joyner didn't fit into the long-term plans of the ballclub.

Despite his opening-day shelling in Monterrey, Ashby put together a solid season, logging over 200 innings for the third straight year. Back problems hindered his performance in the second half, but he still finished with a record of 14-10 with a 3.80 ERA. Hitchcock, Williams, and Clement all reached double figures in wins. Spencer (0-7) was a bust.

Hoffman was his usual outstanding self. His 40 saves represented 54 percent of the team's victories.

The Padres rode the previous season's momentum to a club-record in attendance, topping 2.5 million for the second straight year. But despite the 14-game winning streak, the Padres finished just 74-88, a full 26 games behind free-spending Arizona—a team they practically owned the previous year. Only the last-place Rockies spared San Diego another drop from first-to-worst.

**Ryan Klesko** With ballpark construction still gummed up in court, the Padres could not afford to raise payroll for the 2000 season. Seeking to shed salaries and add more power, additional changes were in store.

Shortly after the season, Ashby, who was entering the final year of his contract, was traded to the Philadelphia Phillies. In exchange, San Diego obtained three young pitchers: Carlton Loewer, Steve Montgomery, and Adam Eaton.

Though Ashby was a key figure in two division-championships and was held in high esteem by his teammates, the trade seemed to benefit the Padres, and from more than just a cost-cutting perspective. Ashby won just four of 11 decisions for the Phillies before he was traded to Atlanta during the '00 season. He went on to sign a three-year, $22.5 million contract with the Dodgers in 2001, but he missed most of the year with a torn muscle in his elbow.

The key figure in the trade was Eaton, who went 7-4 for the Padres as a rookie in 2000. He is regarded as one of the team's future stars.

Dan Miceli was also traded after the 1999 season in another cost-cutting / youth-building move. The Padres setup man was dealt to Florida for pitcher Brian Meadows (who in turn was traded for pitcher Jay Witasick, who was then swapped for shortstop D'Angelo Jimenez, one of the Yankees' top prospects).

The biggest off-season deal took place on December 22, 1999, when the Padres traded Joyner, Veras, and Sanders to the Braves for second baseman Bret Boone and first baseman Ryan Klesko.

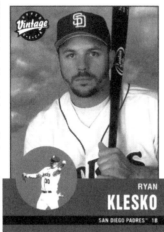

"I just talked to Bret and we're both excited about getting back to southern California," said Klesko, who was exuberant about the trade. "San Diego is where I would love to play."[117]

The move brought much-needed power to the Padres lineup. From their standpoint, the Braves wanted Joyner as a backup to Andres Galarraga, who was returning to the lineup after missing the entire '99 season fighting cancer.

Finally given the chance to play everyday—against lefties as well as right-handers—Klesko had an immediate impact. He finished second on the

Ryan Klesko joined the Padres in a trade with the Atlanta Braves after the 1999 season. (Courtesy, Upper Deck)

Padres with 26 homers, 33 doubles, and 83 RBIs in 2000. Boone contributed 19 homers with 74 RBIs, despite missing the last seven weeks.

The trade didn't work as well for Atlanta. Veras missed most of the 2000 season with a torn ligament in his right knee, and he was released by the Braves soon after. Sanders and Joyner were relegated to part-time roles. Joyner returned to the Angels for the 2001 season, and he announced his retirement soon after. Sanders spent one season with Atlanta, where he hit just .232, and he was with the Arizona Diamondbacks by the next season, where his career rebounded. On balance, the trade was another steal for Towers and company.

**You may kiss your brides** One move that wasn't as successful was the trade of John Vander Wal and two minor league pitchers to the Pittsburgh Pirates for outfielder Al Martin. Martin was an All-Star in 1999, when he hit 24 home runs and stole 20 bases. The Padres were in need of a leadoff hitter after trading Veras, and they saw Martin's combination of speed and power as a perfect fit.

Vander Wal turned in a career year with Pittsburgh in 2001. Playing regularly for the first time, he responded with 24 homers in just 384 at bats.

By contrast, Martin's tenure with San Diego began on a bizarre note. Late in spring training, he was accused of exchanging blows with a woman who claimed to be his wife. Martin, who was already married, admitted attending a wedding with the woman in Las Vegas—but he claimed he didn't realize that it was a real ceremony.

The ensuing police investigation didn't seem to affect his game. Martin hit a career-high .306 in San Diego, though his power and speed numbers were down. He wouldn't remain a Padre for long, however. On July 31, 2000, still seeking to reduce payroll, the Padres shipped Martin to Seattle for outfielder John Mabry and pitcher Tom Davey.

**A salute**  On the fifth annual Military Opening Day, the Padres wore camouflage-patterned jerseys and olive-green caps as a tribute to the United States armed forces. The Padres are the only major league team that offers a military appreciation day. One of the jerseys was displayed at the Baseball Hall of Fame.

The Padres announced that they would provide lifetime passes for all former prisoners of war from World War II and the Korean War. The ballclub also participated in a fundraising campaign for the national World War II Memorial in Washington.

**Infirmary**  Injuries became an epidemic in 2000. Sterling Hitchcock was the opening day pitcher, but he made only 11 starts before undergoing "Tommy John" surgery in June. He wouldn't return for over a year.

Carlton Loewer, acquired in the Ashby deal and slated as the Padres' third or fourth starter, fell out of a tree while hunting during the winter and suffered a compound fracture in his leg. He had to apply a tourniquet to himself and crawl for help. Even after his leg healed, Loewer's bad luck continued: While in rehabilitation, he blew out his shoulder and required surgery on his rotator cuff. He wouldn't pitch for the Padres until mid-2001, and he was ineffective when he finally returned.

Boehringer and Steve Montgomery (also acquired in the Ashby deal) had season-ending surgery on the same day.

Gwynn was batting .323 in just 36 games when his knee gave out. Gwynn's left knee had given him trouble ever since he underwent surgery almost ten years earlier to clean the knee and smooth out cartilage. In June 2000, he underwent his sixth operation on the knee, which was constantly painful and swollen, and had to be drained several times. The season was the shortest of his career, and the future of the greatest Padre was uncertain.

Because he fell short of 502 plate appearances, Gwynn's $6 million contract for 2001 was no longer guaranteed. Pending the outcome of the surgery and rehabilitation, the Padres would have to decide whether to pick up a $6 million option for 2001, or buy him out for $2 million.

The clubhouse resembled an infirmary. Gomez, one of the few hold-overs from the '98 pennant winner, underwent season-ending knee surgery, and his career was also in doubt. It was his third knee operation in two years. Mike Darr, who was called up from the minors to fill in for Gwynn, hit .268 with nine stolen bases and seven outfield assists.

**Something more important**  Of the Padres who spent time on the disabled list in 2000, Woody Williams faced the most frightening story of all. An angiogram revealed he had a life-threatening aneurysm near his right armpit.

After his first start of the season, his wrist was swollen and red. "I didn't think anything of it," he said at the time. "The second start, my fingers were numb and cold."[118]

Doctors initially hoped it could be treated with blood thinners. But the condition was revealed to be far worse than believed, and Williams was scheduled for emergency surgery.

"I realized there's something more important to me—my family, and my family's ok," said the Padres ace.[118]

Williams underwent successful surgery on May 5, forcing him to miss the next two months of the season. In his absence, teammates hung his jersey in the dugout during a game against the Marlins. It was a highly emotional time: Woody also received a message on his answering machine from Carlos Hernandez which was so touching that he never erased it.

Williams returned in July, and posted a mark of 7-6 with a 3.32 ERA over his final 17 starts. He made a complete recovery, getting the call as the Padres' opening-day starter for the 2001 season.

**Back in the cellar again**  Towers picked the pockets of the Boston Red Sox on June 30. The Padres traded veteran utility man Ed Sprague to the Bosox for minor league phenom Dennis Tankersley. Tankersley struck out 57 in 35.2 innings in the Gulf Coast League, while posting a 0.76 ERA. Sprague was released by Boston before the end of the year. The Padres snatched him back up again, meaning that in essence, they'd obtained a dominant young pitcher for free.

Carlos Hernandez was back behind the plate in 2000, his ruptured tendon having fully healed. But youngsters Davis and Winkleman ('Wiki') Gonzalez were waiting in the wings, and with Hernandez in the midst of a fat contract, he didn't figure in the Padres' plans much longer. On July 31, Carlos was traded to the St. Louis Cardinals for reliever Heathcliff Slocumb.

For the second straight year, Nevin was named team MVP. He hit 31 round-trippers with 107 RBIs to go with a .303 average, emerging as one of the league's finest third basemen.

Matt Clement led the staff with 13 wins, but he lost 17 games (second in the league), and had an ERA over 5. His 125 bases on balls led the league and also set a team record. Williams (10-8) was the only other pitcher to reach double-figures in wins in '00.

Hoffman, who saved 43 games and once again posted an ERA under three, was the Padres' lone representative at the All-Star game at Turner Field. He pitched the top of the ninth and allowed three runs as the N.L. fell, 6-3. By season's end, Hoffman saved *57* percent of the Padres' victories.

The 2000 Padres finished with a record of 76-86, two games better than the previous season, but now in the cellar of the National League West. For the smallest payroll in the division, a finish just five games under .500 wasn't as catastrophic as many expected. But it certainly wasn't where the Padres wanted to be, especially with the sweet successes of '98 still fresh on everyone's mind.

After his second straight disappointing year, the Padres finally lost their patience with Ruben Rivera. The young man once pegged as a future superstar was given his release at the end of the 2000 season. Rivera possessed the skills to be a five-tool player, often putting on sensational hitting displays during batting practice, but he was repeatedly unable to translate those talents into game situations.

As a Padre, Rivera hit .204 and struck out once for every three at bats. The Reds picked him up for the 2001 season, where he filled a utility role.

As the '01 season dawned, with the future of the new ballpark still uncertain, the Padres had to trim payroll from $54 million to $37 million (a substantial portion of which was Myers' contract, which finally expired). The club also chose not to exercise its $4 million option on Boone, who signed as a free agent with Seattle, where he went on to have an MVP-caliber season.

The Padres' entire 2001 payroll was $30 million *less* than its nearest division rival, and less than the salary of the Dodgers' starting pitchers!

**Phil Collier**  On February 24, 2001, longtime sportswriter Phil Collier passed away. Collier began his career with the San Diego *Union* in 1953 and had covered the Padres since their inception. Collier, who was 75, is a member of the writers wing of the Baseball Hall of Fame.

**2001**

# A Grand Farewell

TOWERS ENGINEERED TWO excellent trades to kick off the 2001 campaign, and then pulled back from a third deal which could have been disastrous.

First, reliever Donne Wall was sent to the Mets for outfielder Bubba Trammell. Wall suffered through an abysmal, injury-plagued season with New York.

Thomas Bubba Trammell (yes, that's his given name) became a semi-regular in San Diego, providing needed pop for the Padres from the right side of the plate. He shared the third outfield spot with Darr, who hit for a higher average but lacked the power usually expected of a corner outfielder.

The second significant trade prior to the 2001 season came during the closing days of spring training. Eric Owens and Matt Clement were dealt to the Florida Marlins for outfielder Mark Kotsay and minor league infielder Cesar Crespo.

The trade was difficult for many fans to understand: With his hard-nosed, all-out approach, Owens became a true fan favorite in San Diego.

Kotsay possessed one of the best arms in the game, contributing 53 outfield assists over the past three seasons. The Padres likened Kotsay to a young Steve Finley, and consider him a future Gold Glove candidate.

After the initial shock, the trade looked like a winner for the Padres. Owens was relegated to the bench with Florida, and Clement's record hovered around .500. Meanwhile, Kotsay became the Padres' everyday centerfielder and made an immediate contribution, both at bat and in the field. The Padres were so impressed that they signed a two-year, $7.5 million contract with Kotsay, securing his services through 2003.

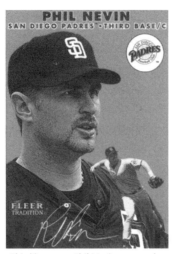

Third baseman Phil Nevin was a valuable part of the Padres' rebuilding.
Courtesy of Fleer/Skybox International LP.

With minor league third baseman Sean Burroughs waiting in the wings, Nevin's potent bat and low salary made him prime trade bait. At one point Nevin was nearly traded to the Brewers for outfielder Jeromy Bernitz.

The deal was all but done, but fortunately, Bernitz refused to take the "San Diego discount". When he demanded more money than the Padres were prepared to offer, the trade was nixed. The move, if executed, would have been devastating: Nevin made the All-Star team in 2001 and turned in a phenomenal season (.306, 41 HRs, 126 RBIs) en route to his third consecutive team MVP award. Bernitz's numbers weren't even close. In many ways, Nevin, along with his good friend Klesko, became the heart and soul of the post-Caminiti, post-Gwynn ballclub.

Nevin stated numerous times that he wanted to remain in San Diego, even for significantly less than he might fetch on the open market. But the trade rumors and contract negotiations became a distraction for the rest of the season.

**Twentieth season** As 2001 dawned, the question of the hour was whether Tony Gwynn, who turned 41 during the season, could stay healthy for at least one more year. Gwynn briefly tested the free-agent waters when the Padres declined their $6 million option for 2001. Rumors persisted that Gwynn might sign with an American League club, possibly Cleveland or Detroit, as a designated hitter.

Gwynn sincerely wanted to end his career with his hometown team, and to remain in the National League. It was difficult enough for Padres fans to watch so many of their other favorites change uniforms, but Tony Gwynn transcended that.

The two sides finally came together, and Tony signed an incentive-laden $2 million contract.

Coming off his sixth knee operation, Gwynn was told that he'd eventually require knee replacement surgery. Tony underwent months of rehabilitation to get himself in shape for the 2001 season, his twentieth as a San Diego Padre.

**Rickey gets on** A record crowd of 61,277 filled the Q for opening day, 2001. Despite all the changes, fans were still coming out in droves to support their Padres.

A familiar face, Rickey Henderson, signed a minor league contract during spring training. Henderson was cut loose by Seattle during the off-season, and no one else was willing to give him a look. The Padres offered the 42-year old a chance to for his 3,000[th] career hit (he needed just 86 more), and to set the all-time records for walks and runs scored.

On April 24, Henderson tied Babe Ruth's record of 2,062 career bases on balls. The following night, facing Phillies reliever Jose Mesa at Qualcomm Stadium, Rickey drew a walk in the ninth inning, officially breaking the 66-year old mark.

"The name comes to mind and you think about the greatest base-ball player that played the game, the guy that probably kept this game alive for so many years," Henderson said of the great Bambino. "Once you get in the category of a Babe Ruth, it means that you went out and you did the best job you can do.

"Babe Ruth is like the icon of this game," added Gwynn. "To be chasing one of his records, man, it's hard to put it in perspective."[119]

**Double no-no's** On May 12, the Padres were no-hit again, this time falling victim to one of the sloppiest no-hitters in history. Florida's A.J. Burnett surrendered no hits but allowed nine bases on balls, the most walks given up in a nine-inning no-hitter.

The Padres actually suffered the indignity of being no-hit twice in 2001. On September 3, before a large Labor Day crowd, the Cardinals' 21-year-old rookie Bud Smith also tossed a no-hitter. His was a bit ti-dier than Burnett's; Smith allowed just four free passes.

**Brenly's unwritten rule** After batting just 54 times the previous season, Chris Gomez was im-pressive enough during spring training that he was slated as the Pa-dres' opening-day shortstop in 2001. But after 40 games Gomey was hitting a scant .187, and he was released just two months into the sea-son. He was picked up by Tampa Bay, where he revitalized his career, batting .302 for the rest of the season. The Padres' seemingly endless quest for a top-notch shortstop would continue.

Adding to the Padres' misfortunes, Adam Eaton was diagnosed with a damaged elbow ligament in 2001, which ended his year and jeopardized his '02 season. He was the Padres' leading winner (8-5) at the time of the injury. Eaton's news came just days after teammate

Kevin Walker underwent "Tommy John" surgery and was also sidelined indefinitely.

Ben Davis made national headlines in May, when he laid down a bunt single to break up a perfect game by Arizona's Curt Schilling. Diamondbacks manager Bob Brenly was furious; he called the bunt "chicken-(bleep)". Brenly accused Davis of breaking the 'unwritten rule' that opposing players do not bunt to break up no-hitters after the sixth inning. But this was an unusual situation: The Padres and D'backs were locked in a tie for the N.L. West lead with identical 26-22 records, and Arizona's lead in the ballgame was a scant two runs. Davis said he was trying to get on base so that the Padres could climb back into the game.

Davis was San Diego's regular catcher for the better part of three seasons (1999-2001). His performance was solid but somewhat disappointing, given his much-hyped potential. After the '01 campaign, Davis was traded to Seattle for pitcher Bret Tomko and shortstop prospect Ramon Vazquez. The Padres opted to go with Wiki Gonzalez, who averaged a home run for every 20 at bats in limited playing time in 2001, as their catcher of the future.

**Exceeding expectations** From 1995-2000, the Padres reported annual losses of more than $10 million. By 2001, ownership finally demanded that the club cut its losses, which meant that another reduction in payroll was imminent.

With the Padres out of contention, Hitchcock was traded to the Yankees, his former team, on July 29 for two minor leaguers. A few days later, Williams was dealt to St. Louis for outfielder Ray Lankford.

Hitchcock struggled after joining the Yankees, splitting eight decisions with a 6.49 ERA. He returned to the World Series for the second time, and recorded a win in four scoreless innings against ex-teammate Steve Finley and the champion Diamondbacks.

Williams became the ace of the Cardinals staff for their stretch drive. His record with St. Louis was 7-1 with a sharp ERA of 2.28, earning him National League Pitcher of the Month honors for September. Williams won game two of the divisional series against Arizona.

At the beginning of the 2001 season, one sports magazine actually listed the Padres as the *worst* team in baseball. But by season's end, the low-budget Padres finished near .500 (79-83), well ahead of the last-place Rockies. Once again, the Padres exceeded everyone's expectations.

**Honoring Coleman and Bavasi** In spite of all the changes, one constant for the Padres has been their man in the broadcast booth, Jerry Coleman. Jerry and former team president Buddy Bavasi were inducted into the Padres Hall of Fame in August 2001.

"Buzzie's the one who hired me, some thirty years ago. Without him, I'd be out digging ditches," joked Coleman.

Added Jerry, "This whole thing is a treat for me. To be recognized for something I love to do is strange.

"This is not a job for me. I love it. I wouldn't know what I would do if I didn't have a baseball game to do every day. The worst part of the year for me is October to March. When the games start in March I'm back in business and I feel good.

Two Padre legends, Dave Winfield and Jerry Coleman (Courtesy, Hall of Champions)

"When we came back and won in 1984, that was the most exciting thing to ever happen to me in baseball," said Coleman of the league championship series, in which the Padres defeated the Cubs. "It was strange. I wasn't even playing. We went into Chicago and they popped us twice, but we came back to win three. I thought it was a great, great series."[12]

**Tony's farewell tour** Hoffman recorded his 300th career save on August 15, becoming the 14th pitcher to achieve the milestone. He was also the first pitcher in history to record seven straight seasons of 30 or more saves. Among pitchers with at least 150 career saves, Trevor's lifetime .882 save percentage is the best all-time. By the 2001 season, only Hoffman and Gwynn remained as holdovers from the Padres' pennant-winning campaign of just three years earlier.

And for Gwynn, the season was to be his last.

The eight-time batting champ was named as an honorary member of the 2001 All-Star team, joining teammates Nevin and Klesko for the trip to Seattle. During the game he and Cal Ripken Jr. received the Commissioner's Historic Achievement Award. (Ripken, whose career virtually paralleled Gwynn's, also announced his retirement at the end of the season.)

In an era of rampant free agency, arbitration, and salary dumps, it is extremely rare that a player spends his entire career with one team. But both Gwynn and Ripken committed to one organization for twenty seasons, an absolutely remarkable accomplishment in major league baseball today.

"I never would have imagined that twenty years ago I'd be standing here, 20 years later, talking about a career that's lasted this long," said Number 19. "I really surprised myself.

"It's a sad day, but then it's a happy day too, because I know I have more to offer than just playing baseball."

When SDSU head baseball coach Jim Dietz—Gwynn's former coach—announced his retirement plans, Gwynn expressed his interest in the position. "Everybody knows that I'm interested in the San Diego State job and if I'm fortunate enough to get it, I'll work just as hard at that as I did playing the game.

"I know the last home stand is going to be emotional for me…When you talk about saying goodbye, it's going to be difficult. It's really going to be tough, but you just have to find a way."

Said former GM Randy Smith: "He saved the franchise. If Tony had come up to me during the Fire Sale and said, 'I'm going to leave'—then you've got to close the doors. Instead, he came up to me and said, 'How are we going to get through this and make this club into a winner?' "

"Winning my first Gold Glove is still one of the highlights in my career," said Gwynn. "When I came into this game, I was a guy who could swing the bat and that was it. I had to work really hard at the other facets of the game."[120]

**Another one for the books** That last home stand was memorable indeed, but not only because of Gwynn's emotional farewell. Henderson also achieved two of his personal milestones during the final week of the 2001 season.

The Padres were scheduled to finish the season on the road, but the terrorist attacks of September 11 forced the postponement of several games until the first week of October. Because of the rescheduling, the Padres season ended at home, which thus allowed three memorable events to take place at Qualcomm Stadium, before the hometown faithful.

Having already established the all-time record for walks, Henderson set his sights on another seemingly invincible standard: Ty Cobb's record for runs scored in a career.

Of all baseball records, this may stand as the most significant. Everything that a batter does—hit, walk, hit for power, steal bases—has only one objective: to score runs for your team.

It was October 4, 2001 that Rickey made history once more. Facing the Dodgers' Luke Prokopec on a Thursday afternoon 'Businessman's

Special', Rickey homered off the top of the leftfield wall—the most improbable way for the greatest leadoff hitter of all time to score his record-breaking 2,247th run. Rickey kept his promise to slide across the plate.

After the game, Henderson acknowledged his teammates through the years who helped him achieve the record. During his 23-year major league career, Henderson played with some of the best sluggers in the game—Winfield, Mattingly, McGwire, Caminiti, and Nevin, to name a few—whose RBI stats were enhanced greatly by Henderson's presence at the top of the order.

Gwynn presented Henderson with a gold-plated home plate. Henderson later received the actual plate as well, which he helped to dig out of the ground himself.

The home run was also Rickey's 2,998th career base hit, leaving him two shy of the magic 3,000 mark.

Throughout his chase at these two incredible milestones, Henderson drew surprisingly little national attention. Barry Bonds was making a successful run at the single-season home run record and the playoff races were still in full swing, all of which overshadowed Rickey's remarkable accomplishments. *Sports Illustrated*, for one, devoted just a handful of lines to his record-breaking slide across the plate.

On Saturday, October 6, the next-to-last game of the season, Henderson doubled down the third base line for number 2,999. One game remained to be played, which, coincidentally, was to be Tony Gwynn's grand farewell. This presented a dilemma: Should Henderson play in that final game, possibly taking some of the spotlight from Tony, or should he sit it out, forcing him to wait until next season for his 3,000th hit?

Out of respect to Gwynn, Henderson asked not to play. But Gwynn urged him to go for it, and Bochy penciled Rickey into his familiar leadoff spot.

On the minds of the 60,103 fans in attendance was news that the United States commenced its military campaign in Afghanistan that morning. A patriotic theme enveloped Qualcomm Stadium throughout the day (after the terrorist attacks, "God Bless America" replaced "Take Me Out to the Ballgame" during the seventh-inning stretch). "Those men and women are out there so we can go to a baseball game on a beautiful Sunday," said one fan.

Henderson wasted no time delighting the capacity crowd. The opponent was the Colorado Rockies, and on the mound, thrown onto center stage, was young John Thomson. On the first pitch of his first at bat, Henderson looped a pitch inside the rightfield line, just out of reach of three Rockies fielders. The seeing-eye double made Rickey the 25th player to achieve the 3,000-hit milestone.

"Of all the things I wanted to have happen today, Rickey getting his 3,000[th] hit was at the top of the list," Gwynn said.

"It was a miracle to me," Henderson said. "As I'm running, I'm remembering that the hit I got for 3,000 is the same exact hit I got for my first hit."[121]

That first hit was on June 24, 1979. Henderson was a 20-year old rookie with the Oakland A's, facing John Henry Johnson of the Texas Rangers. In all, Rickey's career spanned four decades and the terms of five presidents.

As it turned out, Henderson's accomplishment took none of the luster off of Gwynn's farewell.

Said Gwynn during the postgame ceremonies: "Man, what a sight, Rickey cruising into second base and all his teammates running out there. That's what the game's all about. He's the all-time leader in steals, walks and runs scored, and today, he steps up to the plate and gets it done. I am so proud of you, Rickey, really happy for you. See, us old guys, we've still got a little something!"

When Henderson took his position in leftfield for the start of the second inning, Bochy sent Mike Colangelo out to replace him. This gave Rickey a chance to walk off the field to another standing ovation. Henderson was called on to coach third base in the bottom of the ninth, so he was on the field when Gwynn pinch-hit for his final appearance as a Padre.

**"Everyone was breaking down"** Governor Grey Davis, who threw out the first pitch, declared "Tony Gwynn Day" in California. "He's not only a great player, but he's a great role model to young people everywhere," said the Governor. Not an empty seat could be found as Gwynn strode to the plate for his final trip to the plate. Aiming for the 5.5 hole, he offered at the first pitch from reliever Jose Jimenez, grounding out sharply to shortstop. With that, Tony Gwynn walked off the field. His major league service was over.

Nursing his painful knee (which required surgery soon after the season), he received a thunderous ovation from the adoring crowd. Gwynn hugged each of his teammates when he reached the dugout and doffed his cap several times to acknowledge the fans. His last at bat was over quickly, but his legacy lives forever in the hearts of Padres fans.

Gwynn said that his two most memorable moments on the diamond had nothing to do with his own accomplishments. The first was witnessing Rose's record-breaking base hit sixteen years earlier. The other was the tribute to Ted Williams at the 1999 All-Star game in Boston.

(Courtesy, Hall of Champions)

Tony ranks eighteenth on the all-time list with 3,141 career base hits. His lifetime .338 average ranks twentieth—though every player ahead of him has been retired for at least 40 years. Among active players, his career average is thirteen points better than the runner-up (Piazza, .325). Gwynn hit .371 in two World Series appearances.

The Padres held a 90-minute ceremony to honor their hero after the game. Dave Winfield and a host of other dignitaries were on hand. Tony addressed the crowd for several minutes then circled the stadium, shaking hands and waving to fans.

"Emotionally, everyone was breaking down around me," said Gwynn. "You want to too, but the thing that kept me going today was that when it gets right down to it, I'm not giving up the game…I'm moving from the stadium to Tony Gwynn Stadium."[122]

Indeed, San Diego State announced three weeks earlier that Gwynn would become head baseball coach in the year 2002, giving him the opportunity to manage on the very field which was named in his honor.

During the postgame ceremonies, Padres players who were in the starting lineup for Gwynn's major league debut took the field. Gwynn's son, Anthony, a centerfielder with SDSU, took his father's spot in center. The team also announced that the new downtown ballpark will be located at No. 19 Tony Gwynn Drive.

# Epilogue

SO THEN, WHAT does the future hold for our San Diego Padres?

**The Henderson tax** On the same day that Tony Gwynn announced his retirement, the downtown ballpark project received a major boost. A judge upheld the legality of the San Diego City Council's action in early 2001 when it re-adopted ballpark contracts.

The delays, prompted by a string of lawsuits by anti-ballpark zealot Bruce Henderson, cost the city and the team more than $1 million *per month* in construction expenses, as the price of materials and labor increased over time. City attorney Casey Gwinn called the increased costs the "Henderson tax". Though Henderson and ballpark opponents lost every case they filed (a total of 16, at last count), they continued the expensive litigation for two and a half years. It is remarkable that under California law, the persistent efforts of just a few can thwart the will of so many. After construction was halted for over a year, the San Diego City Council approved a revised financing plan in November 2001 which got the ballpark back on track. The park is projected to be ready for opening day, 2004. Without question, the project is a win-win for the team *and* for the city as a whole; the redevelopment will revitalize the eyesore in East Village, stimulating even greater economic development and expanding San Diego's tax base.

**Small market, big hopes** The team will also enjoy a significant infusion of new revenue, which in turn will put the Padres on more equal footing with the rest of the division. The Padres play in a large city, but a small *market*, which is what is significant. San Diego is confined by the desert to the east, the ocean to the west, Mexico to the south, and the Dodgers to the north. The Padres enjoy a strong fan base and draw well (though attendance and revenue are projected to increase substantially at the new ballpark), but their market for television and radio remains comparatively limited.

The team has attempted to expand its presence into Mexico, the desert, and Orange County, all with moderate success. But the bottom line is that the Padres will never be able to compete with the Yankees, Dodgers, and other mega-market teams with bottomless pockets.

For better or worse, this is the reality of professional sports in the twenty-first century. Skyrocketing salaries paid by a handful of owners pose a serious threat to the viability of major league baseball, which should be of concern to all baseball fans. The Padres' payroll at the start of the 2001 season was $38,333,117 (an average of $1.4 million per player), which ranked 25th out of 30 teams.

The only hope for the survival and competitiveness of small-market clubs is for baseball to agree to additional revenue sharing. But that will be ardently opposed by Steinbrenner (baseball's leading spender) and other large-market owners, who seek to maintain a monopoly on the postseason.

Even the Players Association may oppose such an agreement, which may be the only way to keep the sport viable over the long-term. Baseball players have a special gift—as do teachers, police officers, engineers, and other middle-class workers, who can only shake their heads at the multi-million dollar contracts which are so casually thrown around in professional sports today.

**An unfortettable three decades**  Regardless of the outcome of this most recent labor dispute, this book was written to celebrate Padres history, not to nit-pick baseball's ailments. We can only look forward to more Baseball Nights in San Diego, Kids' Days, Businessman's Specials, and all that goes with the joy of being a Padres fan.

The Padres have a solid core of Ryan Klesko, Mark Kotsay, and Phil Nevin (who, after weeks or negotiations late in 2001, signed the largest contract in team history, a four-year $34 million deal) around whom to build, along with prospects such as Sean Burroughs, Dennis Tankersley, and Xavier Nady. San Diego boasts one of the best minor league organizations in baseball, which is a credit to our scouts and management.

We've had an unforgettable run for the past 33 years, even if we haven't captured a world championship—just yet.

Anyone who remembers the special days of 1998 *yearns* to see the Padres back in the postseason again.

A return to the World Series. If Padres fans keep the faith, it will happen, and sooner than we may think.

With Number 19 throwing out the first pitch.

# Trivia Answers

|                | Visiting team | Home team |
|----------------|---------------|-----------|

**Inning one**

*Visiting team*

1. McCovey, Fingers, Winfield, Perry, Smith
2. Jerry Mumphrey, Ozzie Smith, Gene Richards
3. Gaylord Perry, Randy Jones, Mark Davis
4. Preston Gomez
5. Ollie Brown
6. Eric Show, 100 victories
7. Jones, 92 victories
8. Whitson, 77 victories
9. Dick Selma
10. Caminiti, .540

*Home team*

11. Nate Colbert
12. Atlanta
13. McDonalds
14. Randy Jones, 1975—76, and Gaylord Perry, 1978
15. Kevin Mitchell
16. Gary Templeton
17. Winfield
18. Roger Craig
19. Frank Howard
20. Randy Myers

**Inning two**

*Visiting team*

21. Phillies
22. Colorado Rockies
23. Yankees and Mariners
24. Jack Clark (132 walks, 1989)
25. Ed Spiezio
26. Giants
27. Chris Gomez
28. Wiggins (70 steals, 1984)
29. Veras, Jackson, Sanders, Owens
30. Trevor Hoffman

*Home team*

31. Expos
32. Dan Smith
33. Andy Sheets
34. Angels
35. Carlos Hernandez
36. Andy Hawkins. (Hawkins allowed only one earned run in 15.2 innings of relief in the '84 post season.)
37. Vaughn, 50
38. Sterling Hitchcock
39. Houston
40. Joe Neikro and Al Santorini, with 8 wins each

| *Visiting team* | *Home team* |
|---|---|

**Inning three**

| Visiting team | Home team |
|---|---|
| 41. Dodgers | 51. Dodgers |
| 42. Fred Kendall, 1969-76 | 52. Caminiti, 1996 |
| 43. Kevin Brown, 257 K's, 1998 | 53. St. Louis Cardinals |
| 44. Honus Wagner. (Only Ty Cobb has more among all major leaguers) | 54. zero |
| 45. Fingers, 108 saves | 55. Bruce Bochy, 1996 |
| 46. Honolulu HI, at the Aloha Bowl | 56. Monterrey, Mexico |
| 47. Cardinals | 57. Graig Nettles |
| 48. Randy Jones | 58. Ken Caminiti |
| 49. Goose | 59. Matt Clement (125 BBs in 2000) |
| 50. Andy Benes, 1036 | 60. Show, 593 |

**Inning four**

| Visiting team | Home team |
|---|---|
| 61. Wally Joyner | 71. Caminiti (130 RBIs, 1996) |
| 62. Scott Brosius | 72. The Major League Players' strike |
| 63. Clay Kirby, against the Mets | 73. Ted Williams, 1941 |
| 64. Gaylord Perry | 74. Dave Roberts, 2.10, 1971 |
| 65. John Flaherty | 75. Rick Sutcliffe |
| 66. Randy Smith | 76. Rickey Henderson, 2001 |
| 67. None! | 77. Fred McGriff, 1992 |
| 68. N.Y. Mets | 78. Sheffield |
| 69. Jim Riggelman | 79. Bud Smith, 2001; A.J. Burnett, 2001; Kent Mercker (with relief from Mark Wohlers and Alejandro Peña), 1991; Milt Pappas, 1972; Phil Niekro, 1973; Dock Ellis, 1970 |
| 70. Bip Roberts | 80. Larry Bowa |

**Inning five**

| Visiting team | Home team |
|---|---|
| 81. Butch Metzger, 1976 (who tied), and Benito Santiago, 1987 | 91. Colbert, 866 |
| 82. Andy Ashby | 92. 1978 |
| 83. 4 wins, 6 losses | 93. Roger Craig |
| 84. Enzo Hernandez, .225 | 94. 1-8 |
| 85. Sandy Alomar Sr. | 95. Rollie Fingers, Dave Winfield |
| 86. LaMarr Hoyt, 1985 | 96. Greg Vaughn and Mark Sweeney |
| 87. Garth Brooks | 97. Kurt Bevacqua |
| 88. C. Arnholt Smith | 98. Eric Show |
| 89. Ozzie Smith—February 11, 1982 | 99. Dave Dravecky |
| 90. T. Gwynn | 100. Craig Lefferts |

|  | **Visiting team** | **Home team** |
|---|---|---|
| **Inning six** | 101. Ozzie Smith | 111. Mark Thurmond |
| | 102. Winfield | 112. It was a tribute to the Padres' late owner, Ray A. Kroc, whose initials were RAK |
| | 103. Nevin | |
| | 104. Donne Wall | |
| | 105. Gwynn | 113. Dick Williams, 1984 |
| | 106. McReynolds | 114. Marlins |
| | 107. Jimmy Jones | 115. Bruce Hurst, 55-38, .591 winning percentage |
| | 108. Fred McGriff and Tony Fernandez | |
| | 109. Hoffman, 2.70 | 116. Bill Greif, 29-61, .322 |
| | 110. Chris Gwynn | 117. Ted Leitner |
| | | 118. Terry Kennedy, 835 games |
| | | 119. Ozzie Guillen |
| | | 120. Tim Lollar |
| **Inning seven** | 121. Willie McCovey | 131. Benito Santiago |
| | 122. Colbert | 132. Kenny Rogers |
| | 123. Andy Ashby | 133. Vaughn, 1996 |
| | 124. Ryan Klesko, Bret Boone | 134. Buzzie Bavasi |
| | 125. Kennedy, 1982 | 135. Jay Witasick |
| | 126. Hoffman | 136. Dan Miceli |
| | 127. Finley | 137. Tom Werner |
| | 128. Ruben Rivera | 138. Randy Jones |
| | 129. Dave Winfield | 139. Gene Tenace |
| | 130. Dave Kingman | 140. Joyner |
| **Inning eight** | 141. Carmelo Martinez | 151. Roseanne |
| | 142. the hole between the shortstop and third baseman | 152. Sterling Hitchcock |
| | | 153. Woody Williams |
| | 143. Will Clark | 154. Bochy |
| | 144. Hamilton | 155. Mark Langston |
| | 145. George Arias | 156. Garvey |
| | 146. Gossage | 157. Gwynn, Winfield, Caminiti, O. Smith, Finley, Santiago |
| | 147. Washington D.C. | |
| | 148. Finley, 126 runs, 1996 | 158. Colbert, 773 K's |
| | 149. 7 wins, 7 losses | 159. Phil Plantier |
| | 150. Winfield | 160. Dave Winfield, Joe Carter, Steve Garvey, Ozzie Smith |

|  | *Visiting team* | *Home team* |
|---|---|---|

**Inning nine**

| Visiting team | Home team |
|---|---|
| 161. Finley, 655 at bats, 1996 | 171. Bob Shirley |
| 162. None! | 172. Carmelo Martinez |
| 163. Fred Kendall | 173. Houston Astros |
| 164. Andy Hawkins, 1985 | 174. Mark Sweeney |
| 165. Clay Kirby | 175. Gossage and Graig Nettles |
| 166. Luis Salazar, 704 | 176. Bret Boone |
| 167. Randy Jones, May 13, 1979 | 177. Mets |
| 168. Ashby, Brown, Vaughn, Gwynn, Hoffman | 178. Al Martin |
| | 179. Hamilton, 15 |
| 169. Houston Astros and New York Mets | 180. Carlos Hernandez, Jim Leyritz, Greg Myers |
| 170. Steve Arlin | |

**Inning ten**

| Visiting team | Home team |
|---|---|
| 181. Craig Lefferts, 83 games, 1986 | 191. Jack Murphy |
| 182. Fred Norman, 1972 | 192. Willie Montanez |
| 183. Bill Almon | 193. Roberto Alomar |
| 184. Henderson, with 2,063 walks | 194. Jack McKeon |
| 185. Chris Cannizzaro, catcher | 195. Steve Garvey, Rich Gossage, Tony Gwynn, LaMarr Hoyt, Terry Kennedy, Garry Templeton, Graig Nettles |
| 186. Rodney Myers | |
| 187. Expos, Royals, and Seattle Pilots (who would become the Milwaukee Brewers one year later) | 196. Gene Richards |
| | 197. Dave Stewart |
| 188. Derrel Thomas | 198. Tim Teufel |
| 189. Steve Garvey | 199. Greg Vaughn |
| 190. Lee Smith | 200. Nate Colbert, 38; Clarence Gaston, 29; Ollie Brown, 23 |